OECD and CCET *Economic Surveys* 1997 Electronic Books

The OECD *Economic Surveys*, both for the Member countries and for countries of Central and Eastern Europe covered by the Organisation's Centre for Co-operation with Economies in Transition, are also published as electronic books – incorporating the text, tables and figures of the printed version. The information will appear on screen in an identical format, including the use of colour in graphs.

The electronic book, which retains the quality and readability of the printed version throughout, will enable readers to take advantage of the new tools that the ACROBAT software (included with the diskette) provides by offering the following benefits:

- ❑ User-friendly and intuitive interface
- ❑ Comprehensive index for rapid text retrieval, including a table of contents, as well as a list of numbered tables and figures
- ❑ Rapid browse and search facilities
- ❑ Zoom facility for magnifying graphics or for increasing page size for easy readability
- ❑ Cut and paste capabilities
- ❑ Printing facility
- ❑ Reduced volume for easy filing/portability

Working environment: DOS, Windows or Macintosh

Subscription 97: FF 1 800   US$317   £230   DM 550

Complete 1995 series on CD-ROM:
FF 2 000   US$365   £255   DM 600

Complete 1996 series on CD-ROM (to be issued early 1997):
FF 2 000   US$365   £255   DM 600

Please send your order to OECD Publications 2, rue André-Pascal 75775 PARIS CEDEX 16 France or, preferably, to the Centre or bookshop with whom you placed your initial order for this Economic Survey.

OECD
ECONOMIC
SURVEYS

1996-1997

UNITED STATES

ORGANISATION FOR ECONOMIC CO-OPERATION AND DEVELOPMENT

ORGANISATION FOR ECONOMIC CO-OPERATION AND DEVELOPMENT

Pursuant to Article 1 of the Convention signed in Paris on 14th December 1960, and which came into force on 30th September 1961, the Organisation for Economic Co-operation and Development (OECD) shall promote policies designed:

- to achieve the highest sustainable economic growth and employment and a rising standard of living in Member countries, while maintaining financial stability, and thus to contribute to the development of the world economy;
- to contribute to sound economic expansion in Member as well as non-member countries in the process of economic development; and
- to contribute to the expansion of world trade on a multilateral, non-discriminatory basis in accordance with international obligations.

The original Member countries of the OECD are Austria, Belgium, Canada, Denmark, France, Germany, Greece, Iceland, Ireland, Italy, Luxembourg, the Netherlands, Norway, Portugal, Spain, Sweden, Switzerland, Turkey, the United Kingdom and the United States. The following countries became Members subsequently through accession at the dates indicated hereafter: Japan (28th April 1964), Finland (28th January 1969), Australia (7th June 1971), New Zealand (29th May 1973), Mexico (18th May 1994), the Czech Republic (21st December 1995), Hungary (7th May 1996), Poland (22nd November 1996) and the Republic of Korea (12th December 1996). The Commission of the European Communities takes part in the work of the OECD (Article 13 of the OECD Convention).

PER
HC
28.5
.46
074

Publié également en français.

Table of contents

Boxes

Tables

Text

Figures

BASIC STATISTICS OF THE UNITED STATES

THE LAND

Area (1000 sq. km)	9 373	Population of major cities, including their metropolitan areas, 1992:	
		New York	19 670 000
		Los Angeles-Anaheim-Riverside	15 048 000
		Chicago-Gary-Lake County	8 410 000

THE PEOPLE

Population, 1995	263 057 000	Civilian labour force, 1995	132 385 417
Number of inhabitants per sq. km	28.1	*of which:*	
Population, annual net natural increase		Employed in agriculture	3 456 000
(average 1988-93)	1 871 170	Unemployed	7 401 333
Annual net natural increase, per cent		Net immigration	
(1988-93)	1.06	(annual average 1988-93)	806 000

PRODUCTION

Gross domestic product in 1995		Origin of national income in 1995	
(billions of US$)	7 253.8	(per cent of national income[1]):	
GDP per head in 1995 (US$)	27 575	Agriculture, forestry and fishing	1.6
Gross fixed capital formation:		Manufacturing	17.6
Per cent of GDP in 1995	17.2	Construction and mining	5.3
Per head in 1995 (US$)	4 752.6	Government and government enterprises	14.1
		Other	61.4

THE GOVERNMENT

Government consumption 1995		Composition of the 104th Congress 1996:	
(per cent of GDP)	17.7		

	House of Representatives	Senate
Revenue of federal, state and local governments, 1995 (per cent of GDP) 31.3		
Democrats	198	47
Republicans	235	53
Federal government debt held by the public (per cent of GDP), FY 1995 51.4		
Independents	1	–
Vacancies	1	–
Total	435	100

FOREIGN TRADE

Exports:		Imports:	
Exports of goods and services		Imports of goods and services	
as per cent of GDP in 1995	11.1	as per cent of GDP in 1995	12.4
Main exports, 1995		Main imports, 1994	
(per cent of merchandise exports):		(per cent of merchandise imports):	
Food, feed, beverages	8.7	Food, feed, beverages	4.4
Industrial supplies	24.3	Industrial supplies	15.8
Capital goods (ex. automotive)	40.2	Capital goods (ex. automotive)	29.3
Automotive vehicles, parts	10.6	Automotive vehicles, parts	16.5
Consumer goods (ex. automotive)	11.1	Consumer goods (ex. automotive)	21.1

1. Without capital consumption adjustment.
Note: An international comparison of certain basic statistics is given in an annex table.

This Survey is based on the Secretariat's study prepared for the annual review of the United States by the Economic and Development Review Committee on 11th September 1997.

•

After revisions in the light of discussions during the review, final approval of the Survey for publication was given by the Committee on 8th October 1997.

•

The previous Survey of the United States was issued in November 1996.

Assessment and recommendations

Economic performance has been exceptionally good, with strong, well-balanced growth...

The United States has enjoyed a year of exceptionally good economic performance. Real GDP growth looks set to be around 3¾ per cent this year, the best among the largest seven Member countries of the OECD and the highest since 1988. This is all the more remarkable in this, the seventh year of the current economic expansion. Demand growth has also been extremely well balanced, with business investment leading the way. This has no doubt enhanced productivity and boosted capacity, which, in manufacturing for example, is now growing at over 4 per cent per year, the fastest pace in 28 years. Domestic demand growth has also been accompanied by robust exports, which have gained in market share despite the dollar's appreciation. Room for such persistent strength in private fixed investment and exports has been made by deficit-reducing moderation in government spending.

... combined with rapid increases in employment and falling joblessness

Such strength in demand has successfully called forth vigorous increases in supply: another 2½ million non-farm jobs were created in 1996 and nearly 2 million more thus far this year, bringing the cumulative total to over 14 million or 13 per cent since the recovery got under way. These cumulative employment gains are especially impressive in comparison with the losses suffered by the other OECD countries together. With such a buoyant labour market, participation has risen and labour

1

force growth has picked up. The overall unemployment rate has fallen to below 5 per cent, the lowest since 1973, and both joblessness among the disadvantaged and the numbers of those with only marginal attachment to the labour force, such as discouraged and involuntary part-time workers, have shrunk even more quickly.

Yet wage and price inflation have remained well behaved...

With such low unemployment and other signs of tightness in the labour market, price and wage outcomes have been surprisingly modest. While wage growth has edged up very slightly, especially for service occupations, other labour costs have been buffered by structural changes in the health care sector and employer vigilance regarding insurance premiums. Falling non-labour costs have also held overall cost pressures in check. As a result, a pickup in price inflation has not materialised, allowing households to realise healthy real income gains. Overall consumer prices have benefited from a reversal of last year's energy price upsurge and a near-stabilisation in food prices, but, more importantly, other prices have been quiescent, with even a slight easing in their year-on-year increase to $2^{1}/_{4}$ per cent of late, the lowest in over 30 years. Furthermore, there are no signs of incipient price pressures in any of the producer price indices. This inflation performance has been sufficiently impressive in the context of what have been seen to be taut markets that inflation expectations seem to have adjusted sharply lower as well. Without an inflation resurgence in sight to elicit higher interest rates, which could sap the economic expansion, investors have been willing to pay ever higher prices for equities whose indices have set numerous record highs over the past year.

... though the reason for this is unclear, possibly indicating a "new era", but more likely, at least in part, transitory favourable factors

The interpretation of this set of unparalleled outcomes is unclear. Some have argued that there have been fundamental structural improvements in the economy – that a "new era" has dawned in which capacity can be used more intensively than in the past without igniting a rebirth of inflation, owing, for example, to a plethora of computer-related technological changes over recent decades that are only now being fully exploited and to an intensification of competitive pressures as a result of domestic deregulation or of the ongoing opening of the US economy to trade and investment from abroad. However, even if some of these favourable developments have played a role, it would be premature to come to rely fully on them at this point. There are a number of possible alternative explanations for recent modest inflation outcomes, which are more temporary than structural in nature and whose implications are more sobering. The most important is the impact of the appreciation of the dollar, which has cut inflation considerably over the past year. The unusually ample availability of foreign supply and low world commodity prices, both due to asynchronous business cycles among OECD countries in the 1990s, have also probably contributed to price stability. As well, changes in the methodology of measuring inflation have provided some marginal benefit. For their part, labour costs have been held down by cost reductions in the health care industry that could prove to be one-off in nature and by productivity improvements that, despite much media attention, have not so far convincingly exceeded longer-run trends. And when considering the lower-than-expected acceleration in wages themselves, the fact that the unemployment rate did not drop below $5^{1}/_{2}$ per cent until June 1996 should be kept in mind; data are as yet available only for the ensuing twelve months, a period possibly too short for workers to have pressed their case for wage rises.

Monetary policy would best be tightened slightly to head off the risk of a reversal of inflation trends

The appropriate policy setting is therefore a function of which view of the situation is correct. If there is no excess demand at the moment and if capacity growth is greater than heretofore believed, then the Federal Reserve can afford to take a cautiously optimistic view about the prospects for inflation and to be relaxed about the need for any immediate increase in interest rates. But if, as seems at least equally likely, current rates of resource utilisation are too high to sustain the medium-term disinflation process, and in view of clear risks of additional capacity pressures in coming quarters, then some further monetary tightening would be well-advised, especially as the fiscal stance is becoming less restrictive, adding to the risk of overheating. Counselling such a course of action is like prescribing preventive medicine that should be taken before the illness – a pickup in inflation – is clearly visible, for by then the dose of medicine needed would be far stronger, with inevitable side effects. Should there be a "new era" of stronger potential growth and lower sustainable unemployment rates, then the cost of the recommended strategy would be fairly limited, as it would be unlikely to jeopardise the expansion, given the latter's undoubted vigour. But should the prevailing optimistic view in the financial markets prove wrong, if, for example, the nature of aggregate supply surprises turns unfavourable, then the virtuous circle of strong growth and low inflation could quickly turn vicious. And as an important factor holding down inflation seems to have been the rise in the dollar, any loss of confidence by exchange market participants – for example, were the monetary authorities to be perceived as tardy or indecisive in their policy response – could lead to a substantial reversal, with negative consequences for asset prices, the authorities' credibility and, ultimately, the economy.

If that is done, the outlook would be for some slowdown in output growth and only a limited pickup in inflation

The Secretariat's projection is that above-potential GDP growth will persist until the spring of next year, putting further pressure on capacity. With the customary assumption of unchanged exchange rates as from mid-September (with the dollar at 121 yen and 1.77 deutschemark), this would call for an increase in short- and long-term interest rates – put at around $3/4$ percentage point in the OECD projections – in order to curb some interest-sensitive demand. Business investment would slow to a more moderate pace, even if high-technology categories continue to grow rapidly in view of their persistent price declines. Housing investment and consumption of durables would slow rather more, especially as existing stocks now seem fully adequate to meet trend demographic needs. Stocks appear close to desired levels in most areas, but inventory adjustment should ultimately magnify the effect on production of the decline in final sales growth. Part of that decline will be reflected in imports, but export growth may also moderate as market share gains dissipate as a result of the dollar's recent prolonged uptrend. Overall, GDP growth could be around $3^{3}/4$ per cent this year and $2^{3}/4$ per cent in 1998, with the unemployment rate not moving far from its recent range around 5 per cent. Such a scenario is judged to be inconsistent with a stable rate of inflation. Both wages and prices would accelerate, although the lagged effects of the appreciation and lower inflation expectations would probably prevent the pickup from moving beyond $1/2$ percentage point from current rates. In that case, inflation, as measured by the consumer price deflator, would still reach only $2^{1}/2$ per cent in the second half of 1998 and possibly 3 per cent on a CPI basis, which would probably be nonetheless one of the higher rates in the OECD. The current account deficit might continue to rise, but at a slower rate than in most years of this

5

expansion due to the movement toward convergence in relative cyclical positions among OECD economies.

The recent agreement to target a budgetary surplus in 2002 is to be heartily welcomed...

With the economy at or beyond full employment and an opportune moment in the political cycle, the conditions were ripe for an agreement to confront the nation's longer-term fiscal problems. Indeed, an accord has been achieved to reach a budget surplus in the year 2002 following the impressive declines in the deficit achieved over the past five years. Cutting the deficit further and moving into budgetary surplus is desirable in order to reduce the federal government's debt ratio before it comes under strong upward pressure with the ageing of the baby-boom generation and the resulting demands on the Medicare and Social Security programmes. It should help to boost national savings, as past declines in the deficit have done, thereby making more room for fixed investment as a share of GDP to rise towards levels recorded by most other OECD Member nations without borrowing more from abroad. Increased US savings and a lower current account deficit would also stem the rise in net foreign liabilities in relation to the size of the economy, reduce pressure on interest rates world-wide and possibly help reduce trade tensions. As such, the agreement is without doubt a move in the right direction, as long advocated by this Committee.

... but there is no fiscal consolidation in the next year, and much depends on difficult future appropriations decisions, putting the plan's credibility into question

However, the Committee regrets that no more was done and is concerned about some of the ways chosen to improve the budgetary situation with no longer-term entitlement reform but with modest, up-front tax cuts. Despite the sizeable improvement in the starting point – the federal deficit is believed to have been about $1/2$ per cent of GDP in the fiscal year just ended, down from $4^3/4$ per cent in 1992 – it is unfortunate that negotiators did not take the opportunity to achieve a budget surplus earlier than 2002. For there is nothing extraordinary about a surplus: several OECD Member countries are already, or are projected soon to be, in budgetary surplus. Moving from a deficit of $1/2$ per cent to a surplus of $1/2$ per cent of GDP in five years is a modest amount of fiscal consolidation relative to what has already been accomplished in the past five years under previous deficit reduction accords. Indeed, only one-quarter of the deficit reduction is attributable directly to policy changes themselves, with the remainder due to revisions to the assumed baseline, the so-called ''fiscal dividend'' (the derived effects on revenues and outlays assumed to result from balancing the budget) and partially hypothetical one-off revenues from auctioning the electromagnetic spectrum (which constitute asset sales and do not change the fundamental fiscal position). Also, from a macroeconomic perspective, the plan calls for no deficit reduction in the next year when conjunctural conditions clearly warrant it. Indeed, nearly three-quarters of the deficit cuts resulting from the agreement are scheduled for the final two years, well above the 60 per cent which would result from a constant rate of deficit reduction. Furthermore, over half of all net savings in these two years are slated to be discretionary, that is, for future Administrations and Congress to implement. That is unfortunate, as monetary policy could be assisted in containing demand pressures by some restrictive fiscal changes in the short term when in fact the plan actually raises the deficit. This approach of promising future reduction in the deficit while allowing it to rise in the short term is a strategy which was proposed in 1993 and rejected for the same reason that it is unsatisfactory today: it lacks credibility, because governments, including US governments, have often not felt themselves bound by commitments made by their predecessors.

The tax cuts,
although modest,
add to complexity
and may be wasteful

While tax cuts are obviously attractive, the Committee is of the opinion that on balance the revenues thus sacrificed in the plan, even though modest, would have been better put to faster deficit reduction, in view of the need for demand restraint in the near term. Also, many of the proposed changes may not be optimal from a tax policy point of view. Most will make the tax code more complex, whereas tax simplification has long been a worthy goal. The targeted tax cuts have a number of drawbacks. Providing a child tax credit, even if politically appealing, does not reduce the distortions from a positive marginal income tax rate. Tax subsidies to increase access to post-secondary education are desirable from the perspectives of both equity and human capital development. But when the returns to post-secondary education are to an important extent private and at historically high levels, it is arguable that enhanced lending programmes might have been preferable, especially as the tax subsidies risk being partly absorbed in tuition increases and will probably go to some significant extent to those who would have gone to college anyway. The legislated cuts in capital gains taxation, even if they may have desirable positive effects on saving, add substantially to complexity and, by favouring that form of income, could encourage the fiscally astute to transform their income in that direction. Also, although capital gains tax cuts can reduce lock-in, the revenue loss on gains already accrued but not realised is a pure windfall and cannot change incentives. In sum, if tax cuts were to be made, a simple reduction in marginal rates on ordinary income would have been preferable.

Entitlement reform has been touched upon, but much remains to be done to confront the implications of an ageing population

The agreement fails to contain needed reforms to the entitlement spending programmes. Some of the changes to the Medicare health insurance programme for the elderly are only temporary fixes, designed to stave off bankruptcy for its hospital component. Other proposals which would have produced long-run structural benefits – such as boosting the eligibility age, means-testing benefits and ensuring that different kinds of plans are available – were ultimately dropped. Nevertheless, further attention will have to be paid to the implications of an ageing population for entitlements in the next century. The Committee is encouraged by the formation of a non-partisan commission charged with recommending a course of action to overhaul the Medicare programme to put it on a sound financial footing. Its remit could usefully be extended to confront the similar problems of the Social Security programme. But establishment of such commissions must be a prelude to legislative action, possibly, like the military base closures and trade agreements negotiated under ''fast-track authority'', in the form of a straight yes or no vote, not subject to amendment.

While commendable progress has been made in multilateral trade negotiations, some lingering tensions remain

There has been an impressive number of structural policy changes debated and enacted over the past year. Major progress has been achieved in several domains. On the trade and investment front, the United States was a leader in the successful completion of multilateral agreements to liberalise the telecommunications and information technology industries, each of which will allow substantial gains from trade. The Committee joins with the US government in hoping that the negotiations now underway in the financial services sector will equally lead to such a favourable outcome. The United States has also continued its strong advocacy for other new multilateral agreements which would boost trade and investment, such as the Multilateral Agreement on Investment being negotiated at the OECD. And it has strongly supported the World Trade Organisation and made heavy use of its dispute settlement procedures, rather than attempting to deal with trade frictions unilaterally. Nonetheless, US readiness to implement unilateral economic sanctions against nations with which it is on unfriendly terms – sometimes viewed by its trading partners as having extra-territorial application – has been a source of tensions. Further progress in trade liberalisation still awaits Congressional approval of "fast-track" authority. And tensions with trading partners are not far from the surface in some areas. In that regard, the Committee urges the early passage of the OECD Shipbuilding Agreement submitted by the Administration to the Congress. Though somewhat tangential to trade and investment issues, US delays in making specific commitments on greenhouse gas emissions have also caused frustration among other participants in climate change negotiation.

A series of regulatory and commercial reforms have been undertaken

Significant beneficial regulatory and commercial reform is proceeding in a variety of areas. Last year's new Telecommunications Act is gradually being implemented, with the first tangible benefits in the form of price declines for long-distance rates taking effect on 1 July. Retail competition in the electricity industry is set to be introduced in a number of states in the near future, and a number of federal bills would proceed in that direction nation-wide. Another push is underway to desegment the financial services sector, which might even go so far as to allow banks and non-financial firms to link up, while industry regulators are increasingly breaking down the walls between sub-sectors. Important new regulation is being implemented on emissions of fine particles and ozone; these are highly controversial because some contend that the costs outweigh the benefits, but the current legislation does not require any attention to costs in any case. Bankruptcy and patent laws are also being reassessed with a view to curbing abuse. Finally, a path-breaking initial agreement was reached in June between most states and the tobacco industry whereby cigarette prices would rise and manufacturers would pay as much as $368 billion over the next 25 years to settle outstanding lawsuits, with the money going to reimbursement of costs for smoking-related illness and, possibly, to providing health insurance for some of the nation's 10.5 million uninsured children (in addition to other similar efforts at the federal level as part of the budget agreement). However, the pact requires federal legislative approval, which remains uncertain. If implemented, it is hoped that it would produce significant health benefits by reducing smoking – especially by young people. In addition, it may allow the orderly resolution of a complex set of issues that involve great uncertainty and high costs (both public and private), including extensive litigation, but possibly at the cost of authorising the formation of an industry cartel.

Institutional characteristics allow entrepreneurship to flourish

The strong performance of the US economy is underpinned by a high level of entrepreneurial activity. In its broadest sense, this reflects the capacity of Americans to seize new opportunities which in turn lead to the most productive allocation of resources across the economy as a whole. This is often attributed to American drive and energy and attitudes towards risk-taking. It is impossible to establish whether Americans are inherently different in these respects or whether entrepreneurial spirit exists everywhere. However, it is clear that the institutional characteristics of the United States allow the entrepreneurial spirit to flourish. It is very easy to start a business in the United States and the cost of failure is remarkably low, which in turn encourages people to try. Financing rapid business expansion also seems to be relatively easy and private equity, especially venture and angel capital, is a major source of finance. Well-developed stock markets provide scope for realising the returns on private equity investments through initial public offerings and, by providing an easy exit route, play a role in encouraging such investment. The taxation burden is relatively light, especially with generous provisions for carry-forward/backward of losses. Nevertheless more attention could be paid to reducing the compliance burden. Finally, flexible labour markets and the ready availability of skilled labour have also facilitated the rapid response to changing needs, especially in rapidly growing companies.

Labour market performance has been excellent, but more attention needs to be paid to the weaknesses in the primary and secondary education systems

Many aspects of the nation's labour market performance have been exemplary. Not only is unemployment down to levels matched only rarely elsewhere, but real wages are improving and the income distribution has shown some signs of stabilising or possibly reversing some of the recent widening. The welfare rolls are also declining, as former recipients find work. Despite this favourable short-run context, it is appropriate for the authorities to focus on the longer-term problems that remain, the education system in particular. Besides the tax breaks described above, the Administration has proposed a number of other initiatives to ease the financial burden of post-secondary education, including incentives for employers to provide education and training subsidies. But, as was pointed out in the Chapter *Implementing the*

OECD Jobs Strategy in last year's Survey, the real weakness in the US system of human capital development lies in the primary and secondary stages, especially the latter. Standardised international tests show adequate performance by children at age nine but much less satisfactory outcomes at age 14. Empirical evidence is mounting that the public school system, especially in the inner cities, suffers from important administrative and pedagogical inefficiencies, but not enough is being done to deal with them. Continued progress in implementing national tests and standards is welcome despite recent strong opposition from the House of Representatives, as is expanded federal support for independently managed charter schools. However, in the constitutional framework of the United States, it is up to state and local governments to consider bolder steps to confront the endemic weaknesses in their systems.

Immigration is a contentious issue, with opposing ideologies involved

The United States remains easily the largest destination country for immigrants. In recent years immigration – the subject of this year's special chapter – has become a controversial subject, not only among professionals who study it but among politicians and the public at large. Many base their views on ideology and prejudice: its strongest proponents think people should be free to locate where they choose, while its most extreme critics fear environmental degradation due to overpopulation, point to greater welfare use and believe that the assimilation process cannot prevent social pressures from nearing intolerable levels. Between these extremes there is fortunately plenty of room for agreement once the available evidence is carefully examined and assessed.

It results in higher global output and incomes but may not always be beneficial to host countries

At the global level it is clear that people migrate for economic reasons only if their prospects in the destination country are substantially better than if they remain in their homelands. "Pull" or demand-related factors also play a role, as employers in the host country benefit from access to additional labour and consumers from the reduction in cost of the goods and services immigrants produce. Thus, there is a strong *prima facie* case that immigration leads to an increase in global output and incomes and that artificial barriers to immigration hinder the longer-term development of labour market complementarities. But this does not imply that there will be no losers, and there may well be externalities and rigidities involved: the country of origin gives up and the host country receives a resident who may contribute more or less than he or she consumes, through the tax/benefit system, for example. Domestic market prices of competing and complementary factors will adjust to the change in relative supply, but some unemployment problems may linger. In theory, natives may be permanently displaced from "prized" jobs by immigrants. Thus, it is perfectly feasible for some kinds of immigration at some points in time to be beneficial to some host countries, while others at different historical moments may prove harmful.

Immigration results in a small gain for the United States overall but has negative effects on the incomes of the unskilled

Immigrants provide a small surplus due to complementarities between immigrant labour and domestic factors of production. Perhaps somewhat surprisingly (although in a manner which parallels the effects of international trade), this surplus exists only if immigrants are not identical to US workers and is greater the more different are immigrants from native-born workers. The United States gains from the arrival of immigrant workers who have characteristics which are in relatively scarce supply in its domestic economy, thereby lowering the price of that kind of labour. That has traditionally been thought to be unskilled labour, demand for which plays an important role in determining the nature, quality and location of migrant workers. But with strong evidence of skill-biased technical change and complementarities between skilled labour and capital, it is possible that national gains would be maximised with a more skilled-labour focus to immigration. But whatever its nature, the distributional effects of immigration may swamp the favourable income effects. Much like the effects of international trade, recent US immigration is probably detrimental to the incomes of the least skilled in the US labour market. Many of those workers are earlier immigrants themselves. These workers are also suffering from a variety of other structural changes, including a serious effort to move welfare recipients into the workplace, a progressive opening of domestic markets to imports from low-wage countries, a parallel trend to greater outsourcing of production to such areas, declining unionisation and technological evolution which seems to favour workers who have high levels of human capital. There is therefore a strong case that if society decides that it will continue to allow these inflows of what is to a substantial extent unskilled labour, then the federal government should provide the affected states and localities with funding for them to develop programmes to boost the human capital of such workers, for example, through training subsidies.

Immigrants' impact on the budget is probably negative in the short run but beneficial in the longer term

Much of the public debate regarding the costs and benefits of immigration as well as policymakers' attention have been fixed on the impact that immigrants have on the budget. This Survey argues that such a focus is misplaced, for any losses to the government can, in principle, be made good out of the gains to the beneficiaries

15

of immigration. Nonetheless, for what it is worth, the evidence reviewed shows that immigrant welfare use has risen over time in line with the reduced human capital possessed by the average immigrant, and static analysis of their broader fiscal impact indicates a clear net cost, at least for those migrating from developing countries. The emerging evidence from forward-looking, dynamic analysis, however, shows net budgetary gains in present value terms from the average immigrant – despite a lengthy period of net costs – as immigration attenuates the budgetary impact of the ageing of the baby-boom generation. Dynamic analysis also shows that the 1996 welfare reform may have made only a small impact in present-value terms on the budget. Accordingly, the recent decision to restore previous immigrants' access to public transfers was both fair and sensible.

Whether to retain the current system based on family reunification is a difficult question

Perhaps the key global issue is whether to maintain the current system, which is so heavily based on the principle of family reunification and which has led to a phenomenon of ''chain migration'' (immigrants who follow others in their families) with migrants increasingly coming from Asia and Latin America, especially Mexico. This is a difficult question, for it is to a large extent a social and not an economic choice. The institution of a minimum sponsoring income level is perhaps the manifestation of a move away from the policies of recent decades. But advocates of the introduction of some sort of points-based system have not yet made a convincing case that this would succeed in changing the fundamental nature of the immigrants the United States receives. And it is less than clear that it is the government's role to pick individual immigrants, rather than just to establish the broad framework for their selection. Nevertheless, it can be said that there are obvious and substantial human-capital differences between immigrant groups, and Mexican immigrants in particular have a great deal of difficulty making headway in the US labour market. Their situation is intimately tied up with the problem of illegal immigration because of the porosity of the land border between the two nations and the enormous difference in standards of living. The labour-market assimilation of many recent immigrants looks set to continue to be difficult, and greater public efforts to offer English language training would probably prove well spent.

It is hard to enforce the immigration laws, but illegal immigration will be curtailed only by better economic prospects in source countries

The authorities have focused their other immigration-related concerns on some of the non-immigrant, temporary worker programmes and on illegal immigration. The former are indeed subject to abuse, and access to them could efficiently be limited to those who would use them in the way they were intended by the lawmakers. In particular, the maximum duration of visas (six years) is remarkably long. Enforcing the labour and immigration laws is proving to be a very difficult undertaking, especially with a notable lack of willingness to institute any verification scheme that might infringe on individual privacy or liberty. Some expansion of the number of wage and hour inspectors would be desirable to ensure that legal immigrants are not exploited and that employers conscious that they are hiring illegal immigrants pay an appropriate penalty. But there is no easy way of policing the nation's borders or preventing foreigners from overstaying their visas, and it will fall to other policies – freer trade in particular – to offer foreigners and their families additional opportunities to prosper in their native lands.

A wrap-up

To sum up, US macroeconomic outcomes continue to be extraordinary. Output growth has reached a new high for this cycle, the unemployment rate has fallen to a level not seen in a generation, and yet inflation shows no signs thus far of reacting to capacity pressures. Whether this is attributable to temporary favourable factors or it reflects more permanent changes is still unclear, but it would be unwise to embrace wholeheartedly the "new era" hypothesis until more evidence is available. Agreeing to achieve a budget surplus in 2002 is a worthy step forward, but it is far more important that entitlements be reformed in a thoroughgoing fashion and tax cuts be limited in the long-term so that the budget will stay as close to balance as possible thereafter. The structural policy agenda has been crowded, and much of value has been accomplished; what remains at the head of the list is to take a hard look at the basic services available to the poorer parts of the population – compulsory education and health care in particular – and to ensure that they are up to the high standards the nation has set for itself in so many other domains.

I.   Recent trends and prospects

Introduction

In 1995, policymakers seemed to have engineered a soft landing at a full-employment equilibrium as the economy expanded 2 per cent. Output averaged a little below its potential, and the unemployment rate remained between 5½ and 5¾ per cent, insignificantly different from most estimates of the non-accelerating inflation rate of unemployment (NAIRU). In the spring of 1996, however, economic activity took off again. Over the five quarters ending the second quarter of 1997, GDP grew nearly 4 per cent at an annual rate, much higher than the trend rate of growth, and the economy moved nearly a full percentage point above estimated potential. In the summer of 1997 the unemployment rate fell to 4.9 per cent, the lowest level since 1973. In spite of tight resource utilisation, the twelve-month change in consumer prices excluding food and energy edged down to below 2½ per cent, the lowest level in over 30 years.

Recent trends in aggregate demand

After stumbling at the beginning of 1996, when a second government shutdown and severe winter weather temporarily depressed output, economic activity picked up over the course of 1996, and GDP grew 2.8 per cent for the year in the revised national accounts (Box 1). In the first half of 1996, strong final domestic demand offset weakness in stockbuilding – in part due to a lengthy motor vehicle strike – and a sharp deterioration in the balance of trade. In the second half of the year, final domestic demand growth slipped a bit, but net trade improved, and inventory investment increased. In the first half of 1997, consumption and inventory accumulation accelerated further, while investment remained robust.

In July, the Bureau of Economic Analysis (BEA) released its annual revision of the National Income and Product Accounts, revising GDP, national income and their components back to 1993. Overall, the revision did not materially change the outlook for the economy. GDP was revised up slightly, continuing to show mediocre productivity performance over the cycle; much of the revision came from an increase in services consumption, parts of which BEA has to assume until it receives the annual benchmark data. Producers' durable equipment (PDE) spending and inventory accumulation were revised up substantially in 1996, while net exports shaved off a bit more of GDP growth last year after a like-sized upward revision in 1995. The growth rates of the GDP and private consumption (PCE) deflators were raised somewhat in 1996, but they still show a deceleration.

National income was also revised upward, with a sharp increase in the share of corporate profits. From 1993 to 1996, this share rose 2½ percentage points; much of this rise was at the expense of labour whose share fell 1½ percentage points. With consumption up more than personal disposable income, the saving rate was revised down in 1996 and now shows a decline of ½ percentage point between 1995 and 1996. The statistical discrepancy between GDP and gross domestic income (GDI) was narrowed in the first quarter of 1997 by about one-third to –$64.3 billion, still large in absolute value by historical standards. It is also unusual that the income-side measure of output is higher than the product-side measure. The statistical discrepancy has recently garnered a lot of attention, as some analysts argue that the faster growth in GDI more accurately reflects a stronger economy than is measured by GDP. The BEA, however, maintains that GDP is a more reliable measure of output than GDI because product-side data are more comprehensive and more timely than income-side data.[1]

1. For a fuller discussion of the difference between GDP and GDI source data see Parker and Seskin (1997). The Council of Economic Advisors (1997a) and Hensley and Burnham (1997) present arguments as to why one would have expected GDP to have been revised upward.

With healthy gains in disposable income, personal consumption (PCE) growth accelerated in the first half of 1997 (Figure 1). In the first quarter PCE surged; unit sales of light motor vehicles were a robust 15½ million units at an annual rate, and other consumer retail sales grew 9½ per cent. Analysts suspected that much of the first-quarter consumption binge was due to especially mild winter weather and predicted a second-quarter payback. Indeed, motor vehicle sales dropped, and PCE grew less than 1 per cent at an annual rate. Smoothing

Figure 1. **CONSUMPTION**

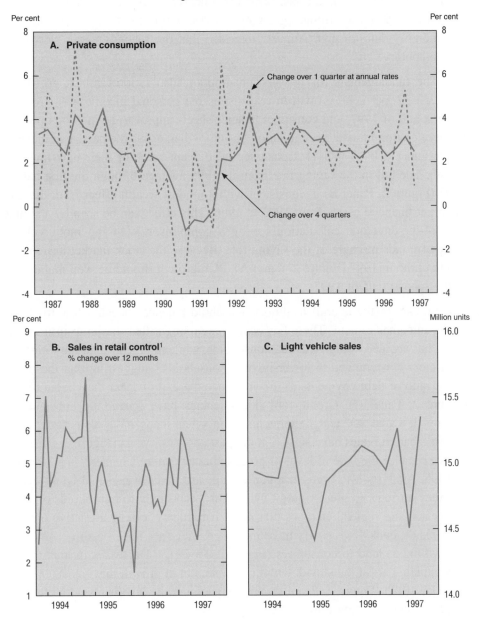

1. Retail trade excluding building materials and motor vehicle dealers.
Source: Bureau of Economic Analysis; Bureau of the Census.

21

through the quarterly gyrations, however, underlying consumer demand in the first part of 1997 was strong. PCE grew 3.7 per cent in the first half of the year, and monthly data through August suggested that the second-quarter slowdown was temporary.

The fundamentals for private consumption also support robust growth in 1997. At 3¼ per cent, growth in real disposable personal income was strong in the first half of 1997, and consumer balance sheets appear to be in good order, as the acceleration in asset accumulation has more than offset the persistent increase in consumer debt (Table 1). Consumers also spent some of their new financial wealth. The fall in the saving rate from its 1995 average through the first half of 1997 (Figure 2, Panel B) is consistent with a modest wealth effect from the run-up in net financial assets from 1995 to 1996. This effect can be seen by a simple back-of-the-envelope calculation[1] or by a comparison with the more volatile Flow-of-Funds measure of the saving rate. Because the stock market has continued to climb in 1997 (Figure 2, Panel A), PCE growth should be well maintained in the second half of 1997.

In spite of the overall health of household balance sheets, a few troubling credit outcomes remain. There has been some thought that the jump in financial assets has accrued to high-income households, while the increase in liabilities has been more concentrated in lower-income households,[2] suggesting that the runup in the ratio of debt payments to income since the end of 1993 may begin to bite (Figure 2, Panel C). Credit card delinquencies have moved up substantially (Figure 3, Panel A), and delinquencies on other loans have also risen. Non-business bankruptcies have surged in the past couple of years (Figure 3, Panel B), in part because the federal level of protected assets under Chapter 7 was doubled in 1995. Analysts also point to a general upward trend in personal bankruptcies that they attribute to greater credit availability, especially to households of modest means, and societal changes that make bankruptcy a more attractive option.[3] As a result, banks' write-offs have increased, and they have become somewhat less willing to lend to consumers (Figure 2, Panel C). Decreases in loan supply may explain part of the slowdown in consumer credit growth that has taken place since late 1995 (Figure 2, Panel D) and may temper the positive wealth effect on aggregate consumption a bit (McCarthy, 1997).

In late 1995 and early 1996 businesses invested little in inventories because stocks had moved up ahead of final sales and had to be pared back. Moreover, a

Table 1. **Household balance sheets**

$ billion, year end

	1991	1992	1993	1994	1995	1996	Average annual per cent change	
							1991-95	1995-96
Household tangible assets [1]	8 124	8 524	9 025	9 571	9 994	10 517	5.3	5.2
Motor vehicles	593	608	636	669	689	706	3.8	2.4
Household equipment	885	926	983	1 043	1 100	1 151	5.6	4.6
Other	457	471	491	522	550	575	4.7	4.7
Residential [2]	6 189	6 519	6 914	7 337	7 655	8 085	5.5	5.6
Financial assets [3]	16 448	17 356	18 482	19 146	21 625	23 889	7.1	10.5
Deposits	3 244	3 227	3 162	3 138	3 351	3 552	0.8	6.0
Credit market instruments	1 595	1 675	1 702	2 029	1 992	2 069	5.7	3.9
Mutual funds	587	728	991	1 047	1 248	1 583	20.8	26.8
Corporate equities	2 675	2 906	3 250	3 100	4 167	4 780	11.7	14.7
Life and pension reserves	4 284	4 653	5 134	5 377	6 148	6 852	9.5	11.5
Equity in non-corporate business	3 200	3 163	3 219	3 416	3 621	3 850	3.1	6.3
Other	863	1 004	1 024	1 039	1 099	1 204	6.2	9.6
Financial liabilities [3]	3 906	4 104	4 386	4 737	5 110	5 467	6.9	7.0
Mortgages	2 654	2 817	2 971	3 164	3 358	3 593	6.1	7.0
Consumer credit	797	801	863	988	1 129	1 215	9.1	7.6
Other	455	486	552	585	623	659	8.2	5.8
Net financial assets	12 542	13 252	14 096	14 409	16 515	18 422	7.1	11.5
Net worth	20 666	21 776	23 121	23 980	26 509	28 939	6.4	9.2
Memorandum:								
Ratios to disposable income:								
Assets	5.64	5.59	5.72	5.71	5.95	6.16		
Liabilities	0.90	0.89	0.91	0.94	0.96	0.98		
Net worth	4.74	4.71	4.81	4.77	4.98	5.18		

1. 1996 is an OECD estimate.
2. Private non-corporate residential capital.
3. Financial assets and liabilities include data for non-profit organisations as published in the Flow of Funds Accounts.
Source: Bureau of Economic Analysis; Board of Governors of the Federal Reserve System, *Flow of Funds Accounts*; and OECD.

first-quarter motor vehicle strike shaved $21½ billion at an annual rate off stockbuilding.[4] Thereafter inventory investment recovered steadily, reaching $71 billion in the first half of 1997 and contributing 0.9 percentage points to annualised real GDP growth. Although the rate of first-half stockbuilding was impressive, it was not immoderate compared to inventory accumulation in 1994,

Figure 2. **FAVOURABLE ASPECTS OF HOUSEHOLD FINANCES**

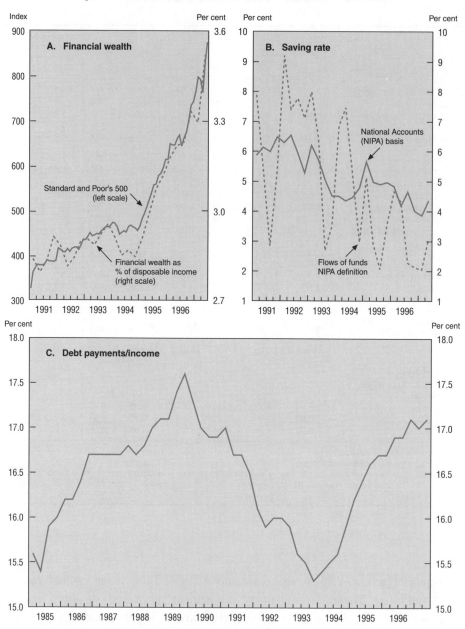

Source: Federal Reserve Board, Bureau of Economic Analysis and OECD.

Figure 3. **MORE TROUBLING FEATURES OF HOUSEHOLD FINANCES**

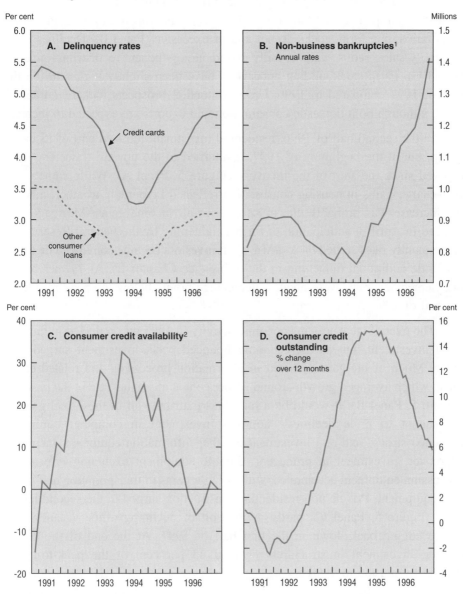

1. Based on annual data for 1991 to 1993.
2. Senior Loan Officers Survey: net percentage of banks indicating more willingness to make consumer installment loans.
Source: Federal Reserve Board, Bureau of Economic Analysis and OECD.

25

as measured as a percentage of potential GDP (Figure 4, Panel A). Moreover, final sales jumped around the turn of the year, and compared to trend inventory-sales ratios, non-farm stocks do not appear excessive (Panel B). Declines in the inventory-sales ratios were broadly based along the entire distribution chain (Panel C). Farm stockbuilding appears to have been slightly higher in the first half of 1997 compared to 1996. Crop production prospects look favourable in 1997, although both domestic consumption and exports are expected to increase.

In the second half of 1996, residential investment retraced part of its earlier runup, but at the beginning of 1997, it returned to the upward trajectory it has enjoyed since the start of the recovery (Figure 5, Panel A). While some of the first-quarter gains in housing construction reflected favourable weather, much of the increase was probably due to strong overall income gains. Mortgage rates jumped in April in anticipation of further tightening by the Federal Reserve, but subsequently rates settled back down when investors became convinced that there was little additional tightening in the offing (see Chapter II). At 7¼ per cent in late September, rates were about 2 percentage points below the peak reached at the end of 1994.

The overall weakness in economic activity in 1995 was reflected in business fixed investment, but as the economy bounced back, investment surged once again. Much of the gain occurred in information processing and related equipment, which averaged growth around 21 per cent at an annual rate in the past year (Figure 5, Panel B). It would be a mistake to attribute all of these real gains in investment to price declines;[5] nominal investment in computer equipment remained strong, and real investment in other information equipment increased. Moreover, investment in producers' durable equipment excluding information processing equipment accelerated, with volatile gains in transportation and industrial equipment. Private non-residential construction surged in the second half of 1996 (Figure 5, Panel C), partly as a result of declining office vacancy rates before edging back down in the first half of 1997. At the end of the second quarter, investment in structures regained 43 per cent of the peak-to-trough decline from 1985 to 1994.

Government spending on goods and services continued to grow more slowly than overall output in 1996 and looks poised to extend this five-year-old trend in 1997. In real terms defence expenditures on consumption and investment dropped in 1996, and federal non-defence outlays edged down. State and local

Figure 4. **STOCKS ARE LEAN**

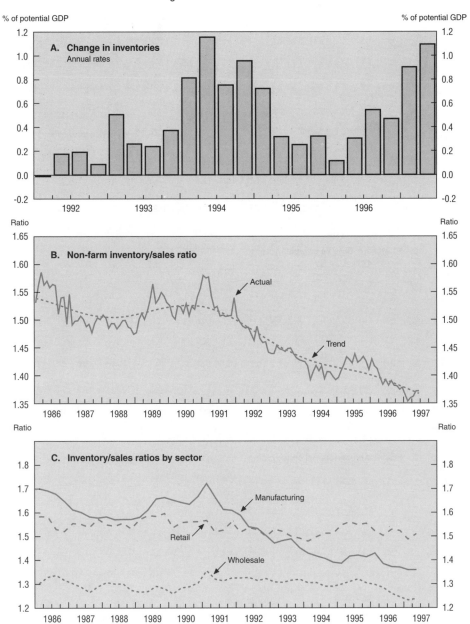

Source: Bureau of Economic Analysis.

27

Figure 5. **INVESTMENT**

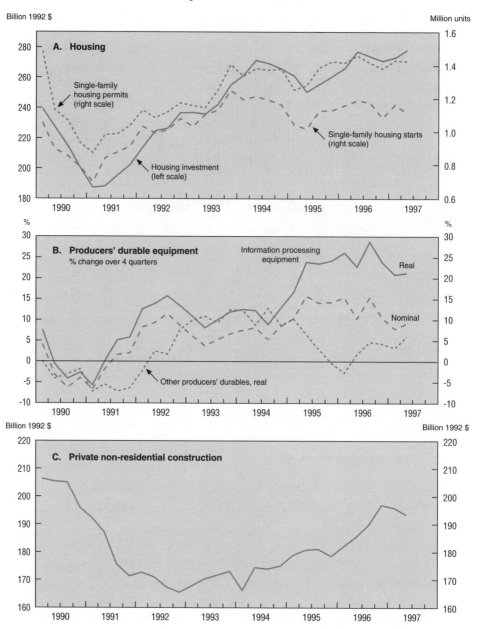

Source: Bureau of Economic Analysis; OECD.

consumption rose a bit less than GDP, while investment – mostly in structures – grew faster. Most government investment takes place at the state and local level, and in the past year the fastest growing components of public construction have been educational institutions, hospitals and other public buildings.

In 1996 real exports of goods and services grew only a bit less than imports, and the trade deficit widened by about 0.2 percentage point of GDP. With the recovery in the Mexican economy and a mild acceleration in Canadian demand, US real exports of goods rebounded in the three quarters ending in the second quarter of 1997, growing 17¾ per cent at an annual rate. Significant gains have been posted by exporters of computers, semiconductors and other high-technology goods, completed civilian aircraft and nondurable consumer goods. In spite of the relatively stronger US cyclical position, as well as the increase in the effective exchange rate that started in the spring of 1995, the overseas market share of US exporters has steadily risen. Imports accelerated throughout 1996 and into the first half of 1997, though the quarterly pattern was erratic because of problems with seasonal adjustment.

Largely as a result of the fall in the trade balance, the current account deficit widened by $17 billion in 1996 to a revised $148 billion or 2.0 per cent of GDP (Table 2). The balance of trade in goods fell by $18 billion but was partially

Table 2. **Current account**

$ billion, seasonally adjusted annual rates

	1995	1996	1996				1997	
			Q1	Q2	Q3	Q4	Q1	Q2
Current account balance	−129	−148	−132	−142	−171	−147	−160	−156
of which:								
Exports of goods, services and income	991	1 055	1 026	1 049	1 048	1 098	1 118	1 171
Imports of goods, services and income	1 087	1 163	1 115	1 157	1 183	1 198	1 243	1 291
Net unilateral transfers abroad	−34	−40	−42	−35	−36	−48	−35	−36
Balances:								
Goods	−174	−191	−172	−190	−210	−193	−199	−188
Non-factor services	72	80	74	79	80	88	82	82
Investment income	7	3	8	4	−4	5	−8	−14
Private transfers	−20	−21	−20	−21	−21	−22	−22	−23
Official transfers	−15	−19	−22	−14	−15	−26	−13	−14

Source: Bureau of Economic Analysis.

Box 2. The effect of exchange rates on prices

   Movements in the dollar can potentially affect prices in a number of ways: through their effect on import and export prices, through their effect on world commodities prices, and indirectly through changes in the competitive pressures domestic producers face and nominal wages. A sudden appreciation in the dollar has a large effect on non-oil import prices (Figure 6, Panel B), but its effect is spread over about eight quarters, with about half occurring in the current and the next quarters (Helkie and Hooper, 1988). Estimates of the long-run pass-through vary between a little over half (Hooper and Mann, 1989) to almost 90 per cent (Meade, 1991). The pass-through can be less than full if foreign exporters use US inputs, such as marketing or transportation services, or if aggregate supply curves are upward sloping.[1] Substantial empirical research using disag-gregated data, however, has shown that many exporters to the United States set prices as if they enjoy market power, keeping posted US prices more stable than their export prices in foreign currency terms (Goldberg and Knetter, 1996). Such pricing to market will occur if exporters to the United States want to preserve market share (Froot and Klemperer, 1989), or, more simply, if they wish to take advantage of the market power they enjoy in an environment of monopolistic competition (Krugman, 1986; Dornbusch, 1987). Research has also shown that US exporters price to market much less than exporters to the United States, which shows up in aggregate statistics as a much smaller exchange-rate effect on US export prices than on import prices.

   Import prices can also affect domestic prices. Price declines of imported inputs will lower prices of domestically produced final goods, although one would expect some rise in world commodity prices because US buyers are a large fraction of the market. A separate effect of exchange rates on the margins charged by US firms is more controversial. Feinberg (1989) finds that the effect of exchange rates on US producer prices varies across market structures, with the pass-through strongest among goods in highly competitive markets. Swagel (1995), however, separates out the effect of import prices on inputs and the mark-up charged by producers. While he finds a statistically significant effect of import prices on mark-ups in about half the industries considered, most of them are small.[2] Based on several older studies, Pigott and Reinhart (1985) add these various effects together and report a total effect of a 10 per cent dollar appreciation on the Consumer Price Index of 0.6 per cent in each of the next two years; while the trend increase in the ratio of imports to GDP would seem to suggest that this effect may have increased somewhat, other estimates of the impact of exchange rates on the CPI point to a slightly smaller impact.

---

1. Exchange rate pass-through can be zero if import restrictions are binding as may have been the case in the 1980s when Japan limited automobile sales to the United States (Goldberg, 1995).
2. Anecdotal evidence, however, suggests some impact in a few industries. In the case of steel, the producer price index for iron and steel blast furnaces has risen only 0.3 per cent in the past year, even though capacity utilisation remains at a high level. Import prices for iron and steel have fallen 10.8 per cent. US automakers have voiced concern about the dollar's appreciation; their market share has declined, and they have raised consumer incentives to attract buyers.

(continued ont next page)

(continued)

Figure 6. **FOREIGN SUPPLY**

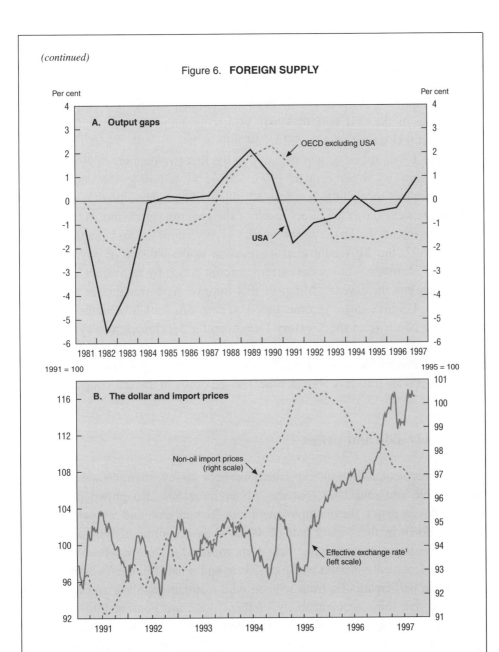

1.   Against 31 partner countries (1991 = 100).
Source: Bureau of Labor Statistics and OECD.

offset by an increase in net services exports. Roughly two-thirds of the widening in the merchandise trade deficit was due to a 20 per cent increase in oil prices. With the appreciation of the dollar (see Box 2), the terms of trade for goods other than oil improved 1½ per cent in 1996 and jumped another 1.9 per cent at an annual rate in the first half of 1997. With continuing net capital flows from abroad, net investment income fell by $4 billion, leaving only a small surplus on average in 1996; indeed, it was negative in the first two quarters of 1997. Private transfers grew by 6 per cent in 1996, adding $1 billion to the deficit, while official transfers rose a little less than $5 billion. About three-quarters of this last increase, however, was the direct result of the government shutdown that simply delayed payments due in the fourth quarter of 1995 until the first quarter of 1996. In June 1997, the BEA published its revision to the balance of payments data back to 1974, revising down the current account deficit by an average of $17 billion in the last three years. Much of this improvement was due to an upward revision to US investment income, based on new data on US holdings of foreign stocks and bonds from the Treasury Department's Benchmark Survey of Portfolio Investment Abroad, the first since 1943. Important upward revisions to net exports of non-factor services were also introduced using various source data, while net private transfers abroad were revised down in the last couple of years.

The supply side and prices

Employment, as measured by the household survey, strengthened considerably in 1996 and into 1997, but the labour force has also grown remarkably quickly.[6] As a result, the unemployment rate fluctuated around 5½ per cent until heading down in the second half of 1996 when economic activity accelerated further. Participation rates have picked up, mostly for women whose rates have increased 1 percentage point in the past year and a half (Figure 7). Some of this increase in participation is from women who maintain families, and it has been suggested that these women, many of them poor, are pouring into the labour market in response to recently enacted federal welfare legislation that limits the amount of benefits they can receive. It is difficult, however, to attribute much of this rise in labour force participation to federal welfare reform because participation rates for women who maintain families have been trending up for several years, perhaps in part due to welfare reforms and experiments by states. Looking

Figure 7. **PARTICIPATION RATES**

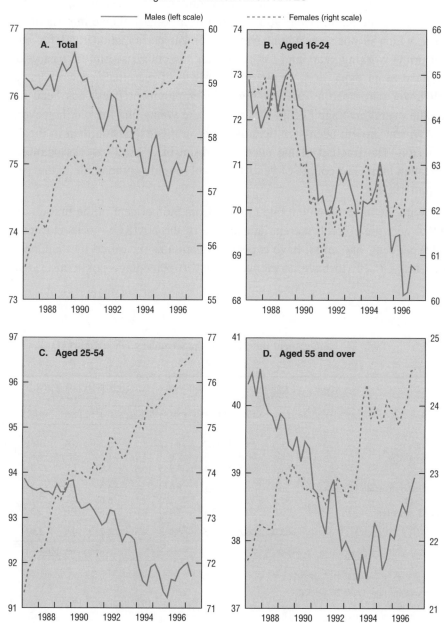

Males (left scale) ——————   Females (right scale) - - - - - - -

A. Total

B. Aged 16-24

C. Aged 25-54

D. Aged 55 and over

Source: Bureau of Labor Statistics.

33

across age groups, it is apparent that the overall weakness in participation rates of men since the beginning of 1996 is a result of the sharp plunge in rates of young males, which is not seen among young women; participation rates for men in their prime working years and for older men have increased in the past year. As is typical in an expansion, employment growth of marginalised workers (those with lower participation rates or higher unemployment rates) has been higher than the overall average (Table 3). Only for the young and the old, however, has employment growth been significantly better in this expansion than in the 1980s expansion. The fraction of the unemployed out of a job 27 weeks or more has also fallen in the last couple of years to a level roughly comparable to that seen in the mid-1980s.

With the unemployment rate moving from 5.6 per cent in the first-quarter of 1996 – near the current Secretariat estimate of the NAIRU – to its current level of 4.9 per cent, one might have expected inflation as measured by the Consumer Price Index (CPI) to have accelerated about $1/2$ percentage point; instead it has

Table 3. **Employment outcomes in the secondary labour market**

Per cent

	Participation rates		Unemployment rates		Employment growth Q4 over Q4				
	1988	1996	1988	1996	1984-88	1994	1995	1996	1997[1]
Black men	71.0	68.7	11.7	11.1	3.7	5.7	0.0	1.6	4.7
Black women	58.3	60.4	11.7	9.9	5.2	2.3	6.3	1.6	5.9
Hispanic	67.4	66.5	8.1	8.9	6.0	4.8	1.7	7.5	8.6
Women who maintain families	n.a.	n.a.	8.1	8.2	3.9	4.2	1.7	3.2	8.4
Aged 16-19	55.3	52.3	15.3	16.7	1.1	6.6	2.1	3.1	–1.3
Aged 55 and over	30.0	30.3	3.1	3.4	0.6	4.6	1.0	2.3	3.3
Total	65.9	66.8	5.5	5.4	2.5	1.7	0.6	2.0	2.1
					Average over period				
Memorandum:									
Unemployment rate: Over 26 weeks									
Share in total					15.0	20.3	17.2	17.4	15.8
Average duration: weeks					15.4	18.8	16.6	16.7	15.7

1. Growth rates for Q3 1997 over Q4 1996 at annual rates; average January-September for memorandum items.
Source: Bureau of Labor Statistics.

fallen (Figure 8). Inflation in food and energy prices increased around the middle of 1996, temporarily pushing the twelve-month change in the total CPI to 3.3 per cent in December, but both have subsequently fallen sharply. Crop prices received by farmers peaked in June 1996, while livestock prices have edged back from their September 1996 high. Oil prices have fallen $6 per barrel since the start of the year. The trend inflation rate in core consumer prices, the CPI excluding food and energy prices, has declined ½ percentage point in the past year and a half, and, at 2.3 per cent over twelve months, it is at its lowest rate since 1966. Several factors help explain the deviation of inflation from the implications of a simple Phillips curve model. Labour costs have not accelerated as quickly as one would have expected given the fall in the unemployment rate. Economic activity abroad has been weak, increasing available supplies. Capacity growth, especially among high-technology manufacturers, has accommodated the increase in production. Low levels of inflation in the past few years have also reduced inflation expectations – as seen in surveys and in bond yields – slowing the impetus to raise prices. Finally, there is a more mundane explanation for a

Figure 8. **INFLATION REMAINS TAME**

Per cent change over 12 months earlier

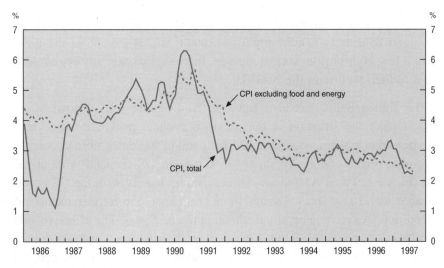

Source: Bureau of Labor Statistics.

small part of the good news on inflation: the Bureau of Labour Statistics has begun to reform the way in which it calculates the CPI, shaving over 0.1 percentage point off the change in the CPI inflation rate from the beginning of 1996 through the first half of 1997, with more reductions planned for the next couple of years (see Box 3).

Overall labour costs have not accelerated with the fall in the unemployment rate. Both wages and salaries and compensation more generally have remained flat in the Employment Cost Index (ECI), as the rate of growth in benefits has remained low (Figure 9). Employers have cut health care costs by trimming benefits paid to workers (see Chapter III) and have probably benefited from an overall decline in health care prices. Average hourly earnings decelerated over the summer, contrary to what one would expect given the current level of the unemployment rate. Some have suggested that workers are too afraid of losing their jobs to demand substantial raises. At first glance, it seems surprising that workers could be so anxious while consumers remain so confident – as measured by confidence indexes. New data from the displaced workers surveys, however, show that job losses because of layoffs, plant closings or similar reasons have not diminished, contrary to what would have been expected given the upturn in economic activity in the past few years (Farber, 1997a). Moreover, the probability of losing one's job has broadened into white collar professions. Survey data from 1992 to 1996 show a decline in perceived job security in the United States that is mirrored in other OECD countries (OECD, 1997b). In addition, strike activity is currently lower than it was at the end of the 1980s, in spite of a few high-profile work stoppages. Increased worker anxiety could show up as a further decline in the NAIRU.

The United States has also benefited from a few related positive supply shocks. Unlike the situation at the previous cyclical peak, the surge in GDP above potential has not been matched by parallel increases abroad, suggesting that foreign plants can easily supply increases in US demand without raising prices (Figure 6, Panel A) and are not competing heavily with the US producers for scarce world resources. Except for a couple of non-ferrous metals prices, commodity prices have generally declined in the past year. The effective value of the dollar has appreciated about 7 per cent in the past year, and non-oil import prices published by the Bureau of Labor Statistics (BLS) have plunged, falling $2^{1}/_{4}$ per cent in the past twelve months. At 12 per cent of domestic absorption, this

36

Box 3. **Bias in and changes to the consumer price index**

The Advisory Commission to Study the Consumer Price Index issued its final report in December 1996, arguing that the growth rate in the CPI is overstated by about 1.1 percentage points a year. The Bureau of Labor Statistics (1997) (BLS) strongly took issue with a number of estimates the Commission made, most importantly their estimate of the quality bias. The Advisory Commission identified three major sources of bias: imperfect adjustment for quality;[1] substitution bias, as consumers switch products based on relative price changes across broad categories (*e.g.* cars *versus* furniture) and within narrow categories (*e.g.* Golden *versus* Delicious apples); and outlet bias, as consumers switch to low-cost suppliers. Implicitly, the BLS counts the switch to discount outlets as a reduction in sales services and not as a reduction in prices.

Advisory Commission estimates of CPI bias

Imperfect quality adjustments and new products	.6
Substitution bias	.4
Upper level	.15
Lower level	.25
New/discount outlet bias	.1
Total	1.1
Range	0.8-1.6

The amount of a CPI bias is important because individual income tax brackets and cost-of-living adjustments for mandatory spending are indexed to the CPI, and even a small bias accumulates into large deficits over the 75-year projection fiscal authorities have to consider for Social Security and Medicare (see Chapter II).

Table 4. **Methodological reductions to the consumer price index[1]**

	Date	1995	1996	1997	1998	1999
1. Seasoning of food prices (formula bias)	1/95	.04	.04	.04	.04	.04
2. Modified imputation of homeowners' rent Replaced 1-month rent changes with 6-month chain	1/95	.07	.07	.07	.07	.07
3. Seasoning of other items (formula bias)	6-7/96	.00	.05	.10	.10	.10
4. Pricing delivered hospital services	1/97	.00	.00	.03	.03	.03
5. Updated basket (upper level substitution bias)	1/98	.00	.00	.00	.15	.13
6. Geometric weights for low level aggregation (lower level substitution bias)	1/99	.00	.00	.00	.00	.15
7. More frequent outlet sample rotation	1/99	.00	.00	.00	.00	.10
Total reductions to CPI		.11	.16	.24	.39	.62
Total reductions to CPI excluding food and energy[2]		.10	.16	.27	.44	.67

1. Estimated reductions in the growth rate of the consumer price index from technical changes.
2. OECD estimates.
Source: Bureau of Labor Statistics and OECD.

(continued on next page)

(continued)

Often ignored in this debate, however, are the methodological changes the BLS has already made to the index.[2] Table 4 presents rough estimates of the effects of recent modifications to the consumer price index, all of which have reduced its growth rate. As is evident from the table, they already have had an important effect on measured inflation, and more changes are set to be introduced. In 1998 the BLS will incorporate a new basket of goods for its Laspeyres-weighted series using expenditure data from 1993-95. In 1999 the BLS plans to aggregate some items within a substratum using a geometric mean formula. The effect of this revision can be seen in the Experimental CPI Using Geometric Means index that is released monthly one week after the regular CPI release. From December 1990 to February 1997, this index has risen one-third of a percentage point per year slower on average, but the various methodological changes instituted in 1995 and 1996 have narrowed this gap.

---

1. Besides Boskin *et al.* (1996), see Lebow, Roberts and Stockton (1994), Gordon and Griliches (1997), Shapiro and Wilcox (1996) and the Bureau of Labor Statistics (1997) for discussions of the issue of quality bias and bias in the CPI in general. The BLS does make some allowances for quality improvements; it estimates that the quality adjustments it made in 1995 shaved about 1.7 percentage points off the growth rate of the price index for commodities and services that excludes shelter and a few other minor services categories.

2. The Advisory Commission (1996) and Shapiro and Wilcox (1996) took account of some of these announced changes, such as the new seasoning procedures used to remove the formula bias. See also OECD (1996*a*), Greenlees and Mason (1996) and Jacobs (1997).

decline could have shaved up to 0.3 percentage point directly off of US prices. The fall in import prices may have also constrained price increases by competing domestic producers, but firm evidence on this effect is harder to find (see Box 2).

Overall, the abundant foreign supply of both finished goods and commodities may have kept a lid on producer prices and has meant that manufacturers could operate at levels of capacity utilisation that avoid bottlenecks. Producer prices for finished goods, excluding food and energy, have fallen on average in the past year (Figure 10). A hint of supply pressures may be in the offing, however. The factory operating rate has moved up smartly in the past few months, in spite of rapid capacity growth, and purchasing managers increasingly report vendor supplies have slowed. While neither measure is close to its 1994 peak, and price pressures have not emerged among core and intermediate goods producers, such trends bear close scrutiny.

Figure 9. **LABOUR MARKET PRESSURES**

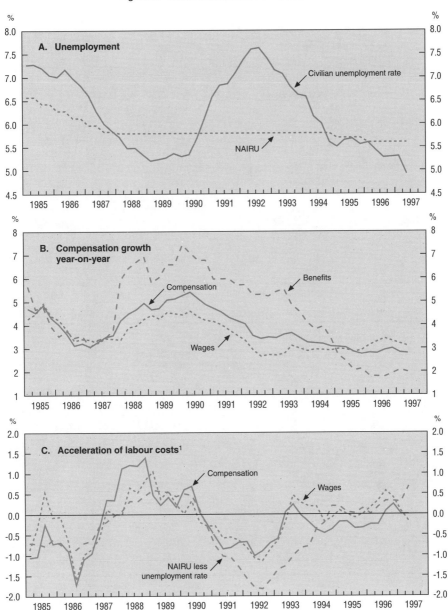

1. Twelve-month growth rate minus year earlier.
Source: Bureau of Labor Statistics and OECD.

Figure 10. **LITTLE EVIDENCE OF TIGHT GOODS SUPPLY**

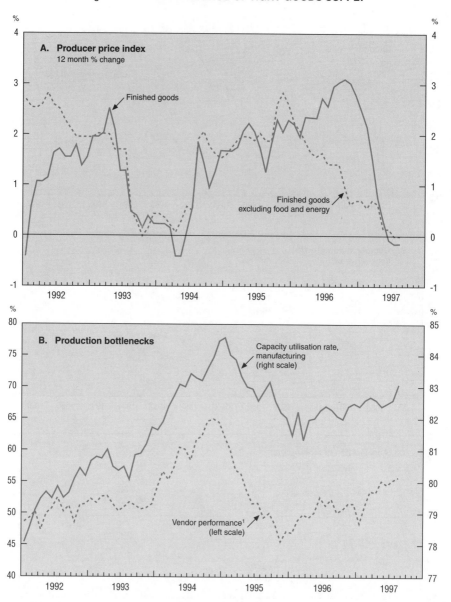

1. Index of purchasing managers' reports on whether deliveries of supplies are slowing. A value of 50 means no
    change, whereas a value of over 50 means deliveries are slowing.
    Source: National Association of Purchasing Management and Bureau of Labor Statistics.

Some have suggested that increased competition and productivity gains explain the benign inflation performance and that potential GDP could be growing 3 per cent or more per year compared with the 2¼ to 2½ per cent rate conventionally estimated. To be sure, measured over decades, structural improvements like the deregulation of some important sectors and a reduction in trade barriers have led to increased competition, but there is no sudden break one can identify to bolster the claim that the United States is in a "new era". Profit measures such as the ratio of corporate profits to national income, federal corporate tax receipts, and earnings per share of the S&P 500 seem too high to be consistent with a sudden increase in competitive pressures. Productivity growth as measured even by the income side of the national accounts has not been extraordinary. Measured productivity growth may be too low because of the CPI bias (see Box 3) and faulty implicit deflators for the non-corporate private business sector (Corrado and Slifman, 1996), but there is no evidence to suggest that this mismeasurement of productivity growth has worsened in the past few years. Moreover, if potential GDP is higher because of these measurement problems, then actual GDP is probably higher too, and the ratio – the output gap – remains unbiased.

Short-term economic prospects

The US economy is projected to grow well above trend in the second half of 1997 and the first half of 1998 before slowing under the impetus of higher interest rates and a strong dollar (Table 4). A slight pause in personal consumption in the second quarter of 1997 should prove to be temporary as economic fundamentals and monthly data point to further robust growth in the second half of 1997. With sizeable increases in equities prices, households have built up substantial wealth, and confidence has surged to record levels. Private investment levels should be well maintained, as long-term interest rates are low, and technological advances in the computer industry continue unabated. Credit supply is ample. Inventory stocks are not excessive compared with final sales, and exports have grown strongly in spite of price pressure from exchange rates. With output moving further above trend, it is assumed in the projections that monetary authorities will act around the turn of the year to rein in spending. In response to monetary tightening and rekindled fears of inflation, long-term interest rates should climb and begin to dampen aggregate demand in the second half of 1998. As the lagged effects of interest rate hikes move through the economy, the rate of stockbuilding should fall. All told, real GDP is projected to grow 3¾ per cent in 1997, slowing to 2¾ per cent in 1998.

Consumer price inflation is expected to increase over the projection horizon. With unemployment rates projected to remain well below the NAIRU, wage pressures should continue to mount, while employers may not be able to continue to avoid a turnaround in compensation growth. Domestic utilisation rates should tighten with above-trend output growth, while overseas slack is taken up as prospects improve in the rest of the world. The lagged effects of the appreciation in the dollar, as well as lower food and energy prices, could mute these inflationary pressures somewhat, and expectations of low inflation may be slow to undo. Altogether, consumer prices are expected to accelerate by roughly ¼ percentage point in 1998, with a similar increase in the growth rate of the GDP deflator.

In 1997, the deficit on goods and non-factor services is likely to edge up only a bit as robust import demand is mostly offset by the favourable swing in the terms of trade from the lagged effects of the appreciation of the dollar and the fall in oil prices, as well as surprisingly strong export growth in the first half of the year. In 1998, the balance may widen further as the improvement in the terms of trade dissipates and exports decelerate, leading to a current account deficit that could approach 2½ per cent of GDP. With the fall in the US net asset position, net investment income is expected to deteriorate, recording an annual deficit (on a revised basis) for the first time in 1997.

With resource utilisation apparently tightening at the same time as market participants appear satisfied with the inflation outlook, risks to the projection at this juncture are clear and may be described using two polar cases. On the one hand, output may slow on its own, as the surge in demand over the past year proves to be the result of temporary favourable surprises. With an easing of resource utilisation at just the right time, the monetary authorities might then not see any need for tightening. Furthermore, if the NAIRU has moved down to the 5 per cent range that some have claimed, unemployment could remain indefinitely lower, and output could grow at a sustainable pace just a bit below potential. In this scenario inflation would remain quiescent, validating the apparent faith financial markets have put in the "new era". On the other hand, aggregate demand could grow more quickly than expected, with consumers and

Table 5. **Near-term outlook**

Percentage change from previous period, seasonally adjusted at annual rates, volume (chain 1992 prices)

	1996	1997	1998	1996		1997		1998	
				I	II	I	II	I	II
Private consumption	2.6	3.1	3.3	2.9	2.0	3.7	3.2	3.7	2.8
Government consumption	0.0	1.0	0.5	−0.1	1.3	1.0	0.9	0.5	0.0
Gross fixed investment	7.5	7.3	7.6	10.1	8.1	4.8	11.6	7.6	3.9
of which:									
Private residential	5.9	2.6	2.5	10.7	0.7	2.3	5.4	3.0	−1.4
Private non-residential	9.2	10.8	10.8	10.3	12.9	7.3	16.0	10.6	6.4
Government	3.2	0.1	1.6	8.7	0.7	−1.6	3.0	1.5	0.3
Final domestic demand	3.0	3.6	3.7	3.7	2.9	3.5	4.3	3.9	2.6
Stockbuilding [1]	0.0	0.5	−0.3	−0.1	0.6	1.0	−0.6	−0.3	−0.2
Total domestic demand	3.0	4.1	3.3	3.5	3.5	4.5	3.7	3.6	2.4
Exports of goods and services	8.3	13.2	9.2	6.1	9.4	16.0	11.6	8.8	7.6
Imports of goods and services	9.1	14.3	12.1	10.6	11.7	15.6	14.5	12.8	8.4
Foreign balance [1]	−0.2	−0.4	−0.6	−0.7	−0.5	−0.2	−0.6	−0.8	−0.3
GDP at constant prices	2.8	3.8	2.8	2.9	3.1	4.4	3.2	3.0	2.2
Memorandum items									
GDP price deflator	2.3	2.1	2.3	2.4	2.2	2.1	2.1	2.3	2.4
Private consumption deflator	2.4	2.2	2.4	2.4	2.7	2.1	2.0	2.5	2.6
Unemployment rate	5.4	4.9	4.7	5.5	5.3	5.1	4.8	4.7	4.7
Three-month Treasury bill rate	5.0	5.1	5.9	5.0	5.0	5.1	5.2	5.8	6.0
Ten-year Treasury note rate	6.4	6.5	7.1	6.3	6.6	6.6	6.4	7.0	7.1
Net lending of general government									
$ billion	−82.0	−18.7	−22.6						
Per cent of GDP	−1.1	−0.2	−0.3						
Current account balance									
$ billion	−148	−167	−201						
Per cent of GDP	−1.9	−2.1	−2.4						

1. The yearly and half-yearly rates of change expressed as a percentage of GDP in the previous period.
Source: OECD estimates.

businesses spending more of their accumulated income and wealth, suggesting the second-quarter pause in consumption was anomalous. The central projection may have underestimated incipient price pressures that could manifest themselves in the very near term just as the positive effects from overseas slack began to wane. The monetary authorities would probably then feel the need to raise interest rates more forcefully. In this "boom and bust" scenario, the United

States could be faced with still rising inflation rates at the end of 1998 just as the economy appeared to be sliding towards a recession. The central projection chooses a middle ground between these two polar cases, built on the premise that, smoothing through the last several quarters, economic growth was robust, in part because the economy has benefited from several positive supply shocks that have held down inflation. Some of these positive shocks will probably begin to diminish in the next year and a half.

II. Macroeconomic policies

Fiscal policy

Overview

The federal budget deficit has narrowed significantly since 1992 through tax increases, structural spending reductions and a growing tax base. Indeed, the FY 1997 deficit is expected to be only $\frac{1}{2}$ per cent of GDP, the smallest share since 1974, while state and local governments continue to generate a surplus. This summer legislation was passed that could lead to a budget surplus in 2002, through further spending reductions, offset somewhat by modest net tax reductions. Longer-term budgetary problems associated with government health expenditures and the future increase in the number of retirees relative to the working-age population, however, remain unresolved.

Recent federal budgetary outcomes

In FY 1996, the federal budget deficit (budget basis) fell $57 billion to $107 billion or 1.4 per cent of GDP (Table 6). As had been the case in the several years preceding, this performance was much better than had been projected by the Administration and others. Led by a sharp rise in individual income taxes, revenue grew 7 per cent, faster than the $4\frac{1}{2}$ per cent growth in mandatory spending, excluding interest payments and deposit insurance receipts. Defence outlays were cut by $2\frac{3}{4}$ per cent from 1995 levels, and after a long battle between the President and Congress, which involved two government shutdowns, non-defence discretionary outlays fell 1.4 per cent.[7] Indeed, non-defence spending was much lower than the Administration had expected in February 1996.

Working to avoid a repeat of the 1995-96 "budgetary impasse", Congress produced appropriations for FY 1997 that were at about the level proposed by the President. As a result, non-defence discretionary spending in FY 1997 has proba-

Table 6. **Recent federal budget outcomes**

$ billion

	FY 1995 Actual	FY 1996			FY 1997		
		Feb. 95	Feb. 96	Actual	Feb. 96	Feb. 97	Sept. 97[1]
Receipts	1 355.2	1 346.4	1 426.8	1 453.1	1 495.2	1 505.4	1 577.7
Individual income taxes	590.2	588.5	630.9	656.4	645.1	672.7	
Corporate income taxes	157.0	150.9	167.1	171.8	185.0	176.2	
Social insurance taxes	484.5	484.4	507.5	509.4	536.2	535.8	
Excise taxes	57.5	57.6	53.9	54.0	59.6	57.2	
Estate and gift taxes	14.8	15.6	15.9	17.2	17.1	17.6	
Other	51.2	49.5	51.4	44.2	52.3	45.9	
Outlays	1 519.1	1 538.9	1 572.4	1 560.3	1 635.3	1 631.0	1 615.0
Discretionary	545.7	553.8	541.2	534.4	542.3	550.0	549.1
National defense	273.5	272.1	266.3	266.0	259.4	268.0	
Other	272.1	281.7	274.9	268.4	282.8	282.1	
Non-interest mandatory	741.3	750.9	790.2	784.9	854.5	833.6	820.3
Social security	333.3	333.7	348.1	347.1	364.8	364.2	
Medicare	156.9	154.4	174.9	171.3	187.4	191.6	
Medicaid	89.1	88.4	94.9	92.0	105.6	98.5	
Other means-tested[2]	92.5	96.1	96.8	95.3	103.9	103.8	
Deposit insurance	−17.9	−12.3	−13.5	−8.4	−4.3	−12.1	
Other mandatory	131.9	131.9	131.2	125.2	138.1	134.0	
Offsetting receipts[3]	−44.5	−41.4	−42.3	−37.6	−41.0	−46.5	
Net interest	232.2	234.2	241.1	241.1	238.5	247.4	245.7
Deficit, total	163.9	192.5	145.6	107.3	140.1	125.6	37.3
Excluding deposit insurance	181.8	204.8	159.1	115.7	144.4	137.7	

1. OMB estimate.
2. Mostly food stamps and nutritional programmes, earned income tax credit, supplemental security income and aid to families with dependent children.
3. Mostly federal employee retirement spending, unemployment compensation, veterans' benefits, student aid for higher education and agricultural subsidies.

Source: Budgets of the United States Government and *Mid-Session Review, FY 1998,* Office of Management and Budget.

bly been significantly higher than in the previous year, and defence spending edged up a bit. Tax rates were essentially unchanged; only a small package of business tax cuts were included in the bill that raised the minimum wage. The only reduction in entitlements Congress passed for FY 1997 was the welfare reform bill, which was expected to save a cumulative $54 billion over five years, though some of these cuts were subsequently restored.

In spite of the lack of any substantial changes in budget policy, the actual FY 1997 fiscal deficit improved further, largely because of a surge in revenue from strong economic growth and the effects of past legislation. Like most analysts, the Congressional Budget Office (CBO) had projected that the deficit would be over $110 billion, but in early May it revised its revenue projection upward by about $45 billion;[8] subsequent data point to even higher receipts. It is unclear whether this revenue surprise is the result of temporary or permanent factors. On the one hand, revenue may be temporarily higher as investors move to realise some of their stock market gains. On the other hand, average effective tax rates may have risen, as the income distribution could have shifted in favour of wealthier households that face higher rates, or the level of the tax base may be higher than currently estimated. Assuming these factors do not reverse, this higher level of revenue could be permanent. It will be a couple of years before enough data become available to judge the origin and permanence of the extra revenue. In its May revision to its previous baseline projection, CBO assumed about three-quarters of the surprise was permanent, with the temporary component slowly fading away in the medium term. With the lower 1997 deficit and higher revenue throughout the projection, as well as a slightly higher assumed rate of potential output growth, net interest payments were projected to be lower, offsetting the fall in the temporary component of the revenue surprise and producing roughly a constant $45 billion in lower baseline deficits.

Current deficit improvement continues the trend of fiscal consolidation that started after 1992 when federal net lending was –4.7 per cent of GDP[9] (Figure 11, Panel A). Since then, the deficit has shrunk every year and is projected to be 0.4 per cent of GDP in calendar 1997. Most of the improvement has been structural, through tax increases provided for in the 1993 Omnibus Budget Reconciliation Act (OBRA 1993), cuts in real discretionary spending and a slowing of mandatory spending growth; the cyclical recovery accounts for only about $1/2$ percentage point of GDP of the reduction in the deficit.

The improvement in the structural deficit has been important because it has increased national savings. Currently, the United States ranks towards the bottom of OECD countries in savings as a per cent of GDP because of its low rate of private savings, and it therefore needs to run a current account deficit and borrow from abroad to make up the shortfall between savings and investment. Federal structural deficit reduction, however, has probably raised national savings by about 1.9 percentage points of GDP in 1997 from where it otherwise would have been, had the structural deficit as a per cent of potential GDP remained at its

Figure 11. **BUDGET DEFICIT IMPROVEMENT**

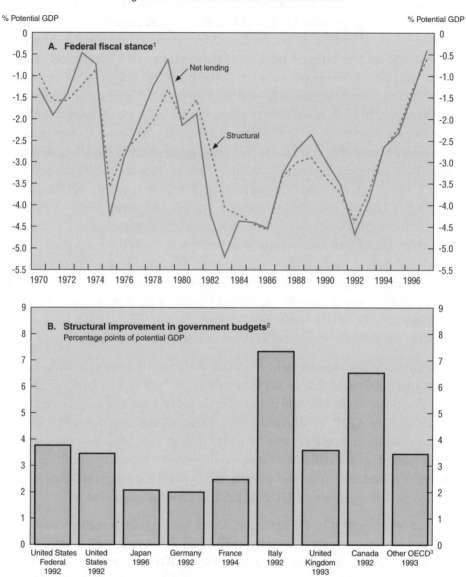

1. Federal government net lending on a national accounts basis by calendar years. 1997 is a projection based on data through the second quarter.
2. Improvement in general government structural budget deficit as a percentage of potential GDP from previous low since 1992 (as specified) to projected 1997 outcome.
3. Average of 13 other countries' deficit reductions weighted using 1996 potential GDP and exchange rates.
Source: OECD.

1992 level. The federal structural budget deficit as a per cent of potential GDP has fallen 2.9 percentage points, but regressions suggest that possibly one-third of this improvement has been offset by a decline in the private saving rate to this point.[10] Indeed, the saving rate did decline, as one would expect if households assume that higher government savings will lead to lower future tax liabilities. Some have argued that private savings should fully offset any changes to government savings, a proposition known as Ricardian equivalence, but there are sound theoretical reasons to suspect that the offset would be less than one-for-one. Empirical investigations generally reject the hypothesis (OECD, 1995a); for example, the CBO estimates the offset as somewhere between 20-40 per cent, consistent with the analysis above. Finally, another way of interpreting this increase in national savings would be to point out that if the structural budget deficit had not improved and if investment were not changed, the greater public dissavings would have had to be financed by additional foreign saving, and the US current account deficit would have been nearly double its projected size for 1997.

The 1997 projected federal structural deficit places the United States in the best-performing third of OECD countries. While recent US fiscal consolidation has been significant relative to past experience (top panel of Figure 11), it is not unusually large compared with recent budget outcomes in other OECD countries. The bottom panel of Figure 11 contrasts the improvement in the US structural deficit from its recent low point to the evolution of the structural deficits of other OECD countries as a percentage of GDP. As the figure shows, recent US fiscal consolidation falls near the middle for Major Seven countries, and it is only a bit better than the average for smaller OECD countries, some of whom like Greece, Sweden and New Zealand have had remarkable deficit reduction in the 1990s.

The 1997 legislation

With that part of the extra revenue that CBO estimates will continue from the 1997 windfall, reaching a balanced budget became much easier, and in May 1997 representatives of the Administration and Congress negotiated the outlines of a five-year budget plan that would eliminate the deficit in 2002. Congress quickly enshrined the agreement in a budget resolution for FY 1998 that controls aggregate spending levels. The added revenue meant that negotiators were able to include additional tax cuts and spending programmes and were able to avoid some more difficult measures such as legislated reductions in inflation allowances for tax bracket creep, Social Security payments and other expenditures, while still meeting the self-imposed target of a balanced budget in 2002. The deal also assumed substantial revenue generated from the auction of the electromagnetic spectrum, most of which occurs in 2002 for which the target of budget balance is set. In August, the President signed legislation implementing changes to taxes and mandatory spending programmes that are roughly the same as in the agreement (Table 7).

The "Taxpayer Relief Act of 1997" legislates the net tax cuts, which are a bit smaller than the original agreement and lead to a projected net revenue loss of $80 billion over five years and $242 billion through 2007 according to CBO. Gross tax cuts total $141 billion (1.8 per cent of 1996 GDP) over the five years. They include a $500 per child tax credit, tax credits for higher education, the reintroduction of interest deductibility on student loans, and additional pro- grammes designed to encourage private savings, each of which is phased out for high-income households.[11] In addition, the top tax rate on capital gains falls from 28 per cent to 20 per cent for assets held more than eighteen months, and in 2001 the rate will decline to 18 per cent for assets held more than five years. The Joint Committee on Taxation estimates that these capital gains tax cuts will raise revenue a bit in the first five years but lead to losses over ten years.[12] Finally, the exclusion on estate taxes is slowly raised over nine years from $600 000 to $1 million. The tax cuts are offset by other tax increases of $60 billion over five years, mainly an extension and modification of the airline ticket tax, increases in cigarette taxes and the extension of the Federal Unemployment Tax Act surtax.

The economic rationale for these tax cuts is not clear. The various tax credits do not reduce the distortions from a positive marginal tax rate, and in fact they boost the marginal tax rates on households whose incomes fall in the range where the credits are phased out. Much of the educational tax credits and interest payment deductions will go to students who would have gone to college in any case and will not boost their human capital investment. In addition, some of the tax incentives will be absorbed in the tuition charges of institutions for whom demand curves will shift out. The government should subsidise higher education only to the extent that there is too little human capital investment otherwise. Because a substantial portion of the returns are private, heavy subsidies could be justified only if imperfect credit markets prevent some from investing. Imperfect

Table 7. **FY 1998 CBO and OMB Budget projections**

$ billlion

	1997	1998	1999	2000	2001	2002	Total 1998-2002
CBO							
Revenue							
March baseline	1 507	1 566	1 633	1 705	1 781	1 860	
Economic revisions	23	41	45	47	50	57	240
Technical revisions	46	37	26	22	17	17	119
Policy changes	0	−9	−7	−23	−27	−15	−81
Current	1 578	1 635	1 698	1 751	1 821	1 920	
Outlays							
March baseline [1]	1 622	1 688	1 783	1 877	1 948	2 047	
Economic revisions	0	−2	−8	−19	−25	−31	−85
Technical revisions	−10	−7	−15	−16	−18	−19	−75
Policy changes	0	12	−10	−43	−48	−109	−198
Discretionary	0	11	−1	−14	−31	−53	−88
Mandatory	0	1	−10	−30	−16	−52	−107
Debt service	0	0	1	1	−1	−4	−3
Current	1 612	1 691	1 750	1 799	1 857	1 888	
Deficit							
March baseline	115	122	149	172	167	188	
Economic revisions	−23	−43	−52	−65	−75	−89	−324
Technical revisions	−56	−44	−41	−38	−34	−36	−193
Policy changes	−2	21	−3	−20	−21	−95	−118
September baseline	34	57	52	48	36	−32	
Memorandum items:							
Share of deficit reduction due to policy (%)		−31.8	3.1	16.3	16.2	43.2	18.6
Share of year's deficit reduction due to policy in total policy changes (%)		−17.8	2.5	16.9	17.8	80.5	
CBO projected deficit after May agreement	67	90	90	83	53	−1	
OMB							
September baseline deficit [2]	37.3	58.3	57.4	41.4	7.0	−63.1	
Revisions to deficit due to policy [2]	1.3	4.9	−28.8	−45.6	−65.3	−124.5	−259.3
Share of deficit reduction due to policy (%)		−8.0	34.8	52.9	64.4	76.0	52.3
Share of year's deficit reduction due to policy in total policy changes (%)		−1.9	11.1	17.6	25.2	48.0	

1. The CBO March baseline estimates include the 1998 discretionary caps. Afterwards spending grows with inflation, except for the effects of the 1998 caps on outlays and budget authority. Totals do not add because of rounding.
2. Includes "Other policy proposals".
Source: Congressional Budget Office and Office of Management and Budget.

credit markets, however, could be addressed more efficiently directly through the expansion of government student loan programmes; the new law does contain some extra money for such programmes. Moreover, state and local governments already subsidise higher education through public universities and community colleges.

Instead, many of these tax cuts are justified on equity grounds; they offset the regressive nature of the capital gains and estate tax cuts through income phase-outs.[13] The child tax credit can be used to offset some payroll taxes so that low-income taxpayers who qualify for the Earned Income Tax Credit can benefit at least partially from the tax credit. For those with low enough incomes the educational tax credits reduce tuition costs, dramatically so for those who attend public institutions.[14] Overall, including the estate tax exemptions omitted from the original work, research by the Department of the Treasury suggests that the Act will have little effect on the progressivitiy of the tax system.

On the spending side, the "Balanced Budget Act of 1997" reduces projected Medicare spending by $115 billion over the five years through payment cuts to service providers, increasing the growth rate of premiums and other reforms (see Box 4). The Act also shifts home health care expenditures, one of Medicare's fastest growing components, from Part A to Part B, helping to delay the expected insolvency of the Medicare trust fund until the year 2007.[15] It expands the choice of health care plans that Medicare provides, which is expected to reduce the future growth rate of costs, and it adds a few extra covered benefits such as annual mammograms and colorectal cancer screening. The Act also modifies other entitlement programmes. Medicaid expenditures are set to decline by $14 billion over five years from baseline levels by reducing disproportionate share payments made to teaching hospitals and other health providers that serve an unusually high number of Medicaid and Medicare patients and by giving states more flexibility to encourage savings. The Act restores some funds that were cut by the 1996 welfare bill, some of which will be used for training programmes, grants to high-poverty areas and work programmes for those who lose benefits. It creates a $3 billion fund to help States move the long-term unemployed into the work force. States can also exempt 15 per cent of food stamp recipients from the three-month limit on benefits, and legal immigrants in the country before August 1996 will have their benefits that were cut by last

Box 4. **Near-term Medicare savings strategies**

Several policies have been proposed to reduce Medicare spending in the near term. Collectively, they should be able to achieve the $115 billion savings assumed in the agreement. Most of the proposed savings come from lowering payments to health providers, a strategy that has worked well in the past (Congressional Budget Office, 1996). Some have pointed to the current slowdown of private health care costs, suggesting there are savings available to Medicare, while others argue that hospitals and physicians are already squeezed.[1] The top panel of Figure 12 plots the ratio of per capita Medicare outlays to per capita total private expenditures for home health care, nursing and hospice care, hospitals and physicians' services.[2] Medicare expenditures on home health care has exploded, and payments to nursing and hospice care providers have also increased. These are areas targeted for cost control. The ratio for physicians' services remained broadly flat, suggesting that there is not a lot of room for savings compared to the private sector. In his FY 1998 budget, the President proposed lowering payments to physicians by only $7 billion over five years, noting that there was not a lot of potential savings. The ratio for hospital expenditures has edged up only a bit since 1991 and remains below a peak reached in the 1980s. With the decline in utilisation rates at hospitals (Figure 12, Panel B), however, some cost reductions in expenditures could be realised. Occupancy rates in the United States have fallen and are far below rates in most large industrialised countries. Rates in Japan, Germany, France and Canada are all above 80 per cent, and while occupancy rates in Italy are closer to the United States, they have been moving up recently.

The specific proposals to reduce Medicare expenditure growth in the near term are listed in Annex I. Increasing the number of risk-based plans and keeping Part B premiums at 25 per cent of costs should lead to long-term savings, but most of the expenditure reductions do not successfully address the longer-term problems associated with rising health costs, demographic trends and the usual perverse incentive effects associated with insurance systems.

---

1. According to a study by the Urban Institute (Moon & Zuckerman, 1995), Medicare reimbursements were only 89 per cent of the costs of services in 1993, and the Twentieth Century Fund (1995) reports a poll of doctors who feel that the Medicare payments are inadequate and make it difficult to provide high-quality care.
2. Because the ratios are per capita expenditures and not expenditures per unit of service of care, they include both price changes and volume changes. The ratios are generally greater than unity because the population covered by Medicare is the elderly, who need more medical services.

(continued on next page)

year's reform restored. The agreement also includes about $24 billion to extend health coverage to uninsured children.

The "Balanced Budget Act" also renews two budgetary rules through 2002 that provide some discipline for Congress. The *discretionary spending caps* limit

(continued)

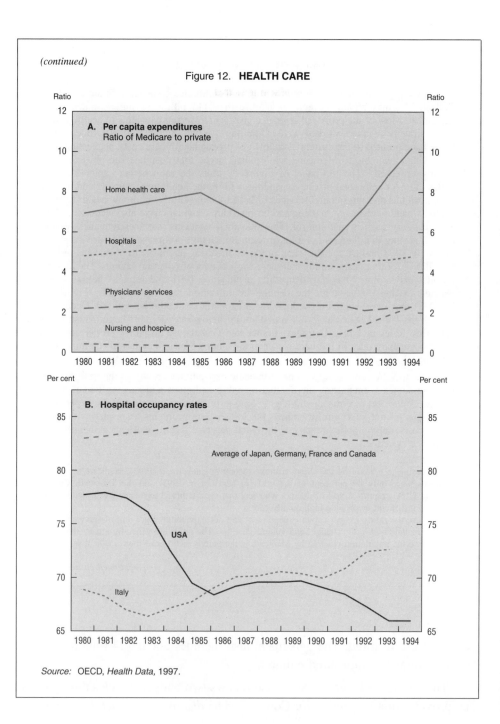

Figure 12. **HEALTH CARE**

Ratio

12

A. Per capita expenditures
Ratio of Medicare to private

10

8
Home health care

6
Hospitals

4

Physicians' services

2
Nursing and hospice

0
1980 1981 1982 1983 1984 1985 1986 1987 1988 1989 1990 1991 1992 1993 1994

Per cent

B. Hospital occupancy rates

85

Average of Japan, Germany, France and Canada

80

75
USA

70
Italy

65
1980 1981 1982 1983 1984 1985 1986 1987 1988 1989 1990 1991 1992 1993 1994

Source: OECD, *Health Data,* 1997.

the amount of outlays and budgetary authority Congress can set for discretionary spending. If these caps are exceeded, a "sequestration" rule is invoked, and expenditures are cut across the board. Separate caps apply to defence and non-defence spending in the first two years and then a total cap thereafter. The *PAYGO* provision requires that any changes to tax law or mandatory expenditures has to be accompanied by equal revenue increases or expenditure cuts elsewhere so as not to increase the projected deficit.

How successful the discretionary caps have been in limiting expenditures can be gleaned from Table 8, which lists the path of spending called for by previous budget agreements (OBRA 1990 and 1993) and the 1997 Budget Agreement. These caps have been adjusted over the years for several reasons allowed in previous legislation; these changes are spelled out every year by the Office of Management and Budget (OMB) in its annual sequestration report and are reviewed by the CBO in its report. Some of the adjustments are technical in nature, allowing for definitions of discretionary spending to change, providing a special allowance to bring OMB's caps in line with CBO's in the first few years of OBRA 1990 and allowing deviations of inflation from projected rates to show through to the caps. Other adjustments, however, introduce some flexibility, allowing the President and Congress to grant additional "emergency" spending.

Table 8. **Discretionary spending levels**

$ billion

	1991	1992	1993	1994	1995	1996	1997	1998
OBRA 1990/1993 caps	514.4	524.9	534.0	534.8	540.8	547.3	547.3	547.9
Adjustments for:								
Technical	2.9	4.4	5.9	6.7	6.6	0.7	−1.8	−2.6
Inflation allowance	0.0	−0.3	−2.5	−5.8	−8.8	1.8	2.3	0.9
Emergencies, including offsets	1.1	1.8	5.4	9.0	9.0	2.9	5.7	2.8
Gulf war	33.3	14.9	7.6	2.8	1.1	0.0	0.0	0.0
Adjusted caps	551.6	545.7	550.4	547.6	548.6	552.7	553.7	549.0
1997 Budget Act, incl. adjustments								555.9
Memorandum:								
Growth rate in real spending[1]	0.2	−3.9	−2.8	−4.9	−3.1	−3.5	−1.2	−1.7

1. Growth rate in federal consumption expenditures less consumption of fixed capital plus gross investment, in chained 1992 dollars (calendar years on a NIPA basis). 1997 and 1998 are OECD projections.
Source: *Mid-Session Review, FY 1998*, Office of Management and Budget, and OECD.

In the early 1990s the Gulf war temporarily boosted defence spending; since then, several small items such as natural and civil disaster payments and increased anti-terrorism spending raised the caps significantly. And again, in 1997, Congress added $8.6 billion in emergency spending for flood victims, Bosnian military operations and other smaller items (Table 8).

Two important points emerge from the table. First, the caps are not binding; there is room for fiscal authorities to boost spending through the emergency rule, though on average emergency spending has comprised less than 1 per cent of discretionary spending. Moreover, at any time Congress and the President can pass a new law setting new caps, as they have for FY 1998 when spending will be $7 billion higher than the effective OBRA 1993 cap. This brings into question how much of the FY 2002 nominal cut in discretionary spending will be realised. Only when that year's authorisation and spending bills are passed will authorities make the hard decisions of which programmes will be cut. That said, in spite of the elasticity of the caps, federal consumption and investment expenditures on a national accounts basis have fallen in real terms every year since 1991, so nominal expenditures have not grown rapidly during the time caps have remained in place. Even in 1998 real spending is projected to slip. Budget officials point to the discretionary caps as one reason why spending has remained muted, arguing that they make it difficult to increase spending substantially.

Overall, the two Acts raise the deficit slightly in FY 1998 and leave it little changed until the last two years of the budget window. While the bottom line is a significant improvement from the initial baseline estimates made one year ago, according to the CBO, most of the improvement in the outlook is the result of a revision to the baseline deficit from an improved economy and technical adjustments. As is shown in Table 7, according to the CBO, only 18.6 per cent of the five-year improvement in the deficit is due to policy changes. OMB scores the effects of the tax and Medicare spending cuts differently and assumes a higher baseline path for discretionary spending; as a result it estimates that over half of the reduction in borrowing is a result of policy. In addition, the plan to improve the budgetary situation is backloaded. In the first year, the budget worsens due to policy changes; the added deficit spending in 1998 means that the cyclically-adjusted budget deficit worsens a bit as a percentage of GDP. Moreover, most of the improvement is put off until the last two years. If the budget deficit were to be brought down in a straight line, 60 per cent of the total reduction in the deficit due to policy would occur in the final two years. According to CBO virtually all of it happens in the last two years, as the improvements in 1999 and 2000 simply unwind the deterioration in 1998. OMB calculations show that about three-quarters of the net improvement in the budget balance due to policy occurs in the last two years. That said, the negotiators persisted in achieving substantial savings in the last year of the plan even when it became clear that these cuts were more than sufficient to achieve balance, and the end result is that a sizeable surplus is projected in that year.

Longer-term outlook

Balancing the federal budget by 2002 helps address the long-term debt problems in the United States. As Table 9 shows, if the President and Congress keep the budget balanced between 2002 and 2007, the ratio of publicly held debt to GDP is not projected to return to its 1996 level until 2027. This is in contrast to what happens if the budget is not balanced and spending continues under

Table 9. **Long-term projection of the federal budget,[1] assuming balanced budget in 2002-07**

As a per cent of GDP

	1996	2000	2005	2010	2015	2020	2030	2040	2050
Receipts	21	20	20	20	20	20	20	20	21
Expenditures	22	21	20	20	21	23	27	33	55
Consumption and investment	6	5	4	4	4	4	4	4	4
Transfers, grants and subsidies									
Social security	5	5	5	5	5	6	7	7	7
Medicare	2	3	3	4	4	5	6	7	7
Medicaid	1	1	2	2	2	2	2	3	3
Other	5	5	4	4	4	4	4	4	4
Net interest	3	3	2	2	1	2	3	9	30
Deficit	2	1	0	0	1	3	7	12	34
Debt held by the public	50	46	38	31	29	34	64	126	283
Baseline assumptions without budget balance in 2002-07[2]									
Deficit	2	2	2	3	4	6	12	31	n.c.
Debt held by the public	50	48	48	50	56	68	121	266	n.c.

n.c. = non-computable (debt exceeds reasonable level).
1. Projections include deficit effects on interest rates and economic growth.
2. Assumes discretionary spending grows with inflation after 2007.
Source: Congressional Budget Office.

baseline assumptions. As the last line of the table shows, debt remains significantly higher and becomes unmanageable about ten years earlier than under the balanced-budget scenario. Without additional measures to deal with the long-term problems of Medicare, Medicaid and Social Security, however, the table shows that even if the budget is balanced for six years, the ratio of debt to GDP reaches 283 per cent in 2050. The budget agreement, for the most part, makes only temporary changes to the growth rate in Medicare and Medicaid spending, which has continued to increase faster than the economy in spite of past attempts to brake its growth. With the proposed changes, the Part A Medicare hospital fund is expected to go bankrupt in 2007, while Medicaid and Part B Medicare spending remains uncapped. The plan does nothing to solve the long-term problems associated with the Social Security system. Current projections using intermediate cost assumptions suggest that the Social Security trust fund will be depleted in 2029.[16]

Of the three large mandatory programmes, Social Security seems the easiest to modify. According to the Council of Economic Advisers (1997a), without changes to current law, revenue and existing funds should be able to pay for about 75 per cent of promised benefits in 2040. The 1994-96 Advisory Council on Social Security released its report in January 1997 presenting three plans, each of which would restore the system to balance (see Box 5). When considering the various proposals of the Council, policymakers will have to wrestle with several issues. Most important, they will have to consider the social insurance aspect of the system. The current system is a defined benefit plan that carries little risk for households, but the proposals that allow part of the fund to be placed in different investment vehicles at the discretion of households shifts some of the risk towards them. Such a shift represents a fundamental change in the philosophy of the system, rendering it inherently less solidaristic. Second, investment in equities raises a new set of issues. Massive increases of investment in equities could reduce the average equity premium investors have historically received. How much the premium would be reduced is not well understood, but it is important for formulating long-term budgets. Investment in equities would also introduce more risk into the system, and who ultimately bears that risk – retirees, current workers, or future generations – would have to be decided. In addition, safeguards to ensure that the government does not unduly interfere with the management of firms would have to be developed. Finally, in moving more towards a

Box 5. **Recommendations on Social Security reform**

In January 1997 the Quadrennial Advisory Council on Social Security released its final report. The members could not agree on one final plan, and instead, they issued three proposals, each of which would restore the system to balance. All three plans share some features: they would extend Social Security benefits and taxes to state and local government employees, assume BLS will make changes in the CPI to reduce the cost-of-living bias and include as taxable income benefits received in excess of employee contributions. Proposals I and III would redirect these proceeds to the Social Security trust fund, while Proposal II would not. The three plans differ on more substantive changes. The first proposal keeps the social-insurance aspects of the system in place, while the other two move more towards a defined-contribution system. The specifics of the three proposals apart from those enumerated above are:

I. Maintenance of benefits proposal

1) Invest part of the trust fund in equities.
2) Divert proceeds from the Hospital Trust Fund for Medicare Part A to the Social Security Trust Fund.
3) Extend the period on which benefits are computed from 35 to 38 years, reducing their level on average by 3 per cent, or raise payroll taxes on employers and employees contributions by 0.15 percentage points.
4) Increase the payroll tax rate by 1.6 percentage points in 2047.

II. Publicly-held individual accounts proposal

1) Create mandatory defined-contribution accounts funded by an increase in the payroll tax rate of 1.6 percentage points that would be managed by the government. At retirement these accounts would be paid out as an inflation-indexed annuity with the proceeds added to the regular benefits.
2) Slowly lower the conversion factors used to compute benefits for middle and high-wage workers and include benefits in excess of employee contributions in taxable income.
3) Extend the period on which benefits are computed from 35 to 38 years.
4) Increase the eligibility age to 67 more quickly and index to longevity thereafter.

III. Privately-held individual accounts proposal

1) Reallocate 5 percentage points of the employees' share of payroll taxes to a defined-contribution account managed by individuals.
2) Devote the rest of payroll taxes to a flat benefit that would have paid $410 per month in 1996 and index to inflation thereafter, with different benefits accruing to workers who are 25-54 in 1998.
3) Eliminate the earnings test.
4) Increase the eligibility age to 67 more quickly and index to longevity thereafter.

fully funded system from a pay-as-you-go system, the question of how much of the additional burden the current working generation will shoulder would have to be reopened.

The problems with Medicare and Medicaid are more serious and are harder to correct. First, except for some marginal changes, the federal government cannot reasonably control trends in health costs, which, until recently, had been growing rapidly. Second, as discussed by the Council of Economic Advisers (1997a), adverse selection and moral hazard present difficult challenges for policy makers. In the case of Medicare, most senior citizens have supplementary coverage that pays deductibles and co-payments, removing the incentives to shop for lower prices; for poor senior citizens, Medicaid makes up the shortfall from Medicare. Managed care providers are not a panacea, as they can "cherry-pick" the healthiest seniors to enrol. As the current experience with Medicare health maintenance organisations attests, it is hard to develop a cost-effective compensation scheme for private insurers, while encouraging them to enrol all seniors. A few suggestions have been made such as raising the age of eligibility, increasing cost sharing with seniors, and moving away from a defined benefit plan to a defined contribution plan, leaving health risks with the elderly. Others argue for a significant increase in the coverage by private insurers, along with regulations to require more broad-based enrolment. For instance, some members of Congress advocate the introduction of key features of the system that covers federal employees and retirees (the Federal Employees Health Benefits Program).[17] As with the reform of the Social Security system, the question of how much risk will be shifted from the government to individuals also needs to be addressed. The FY 1998 budget creates a bipartisan commission that will be charged with making specific recommendations to Congress on long-term Medicare reform; a report is expected in the winter of 1999.

The state and local sector

State and local government budget balances as a share of GDP have deteriorated in the national accounts somewhat since 1994 (Figure 13), but current saving is still more than enough to cover net investment, which remains strong. As with the federal government, expenditures on transfers, such as the state portion of Medicaid, have grown much more rapidly than the economy as a whole, more than offsetting substantial revenue growth from the economy and

Figure 13. **STATE AND LOCAL GOVERNMENT FINANCES**

Per cent of GDP

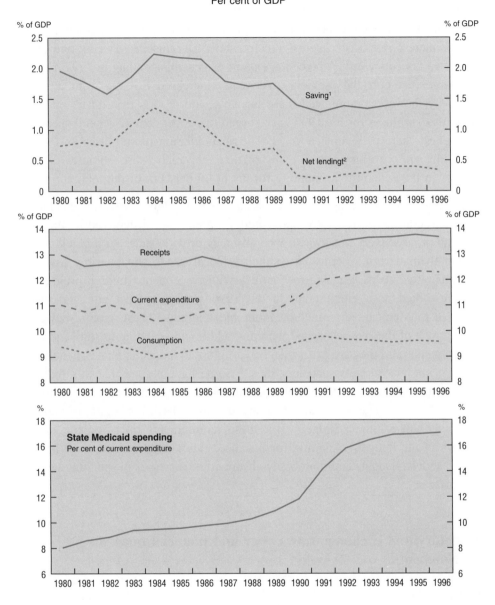

1. Saving = Receipts less current expenditure.
2. Net lending = Saving less gross investment net of consumption of fixed capital.
Source: Bureau of Economic Analysis.

moderate declines in consumption expenditures. While the growth rate of Medicaid expenditures has recently slowed, it remains one of the fastest growing components of current expenditures. With the relative decline in net lending and lower interest rates, net interest receipts have diminished. Twenty-one states approved tax cuts worth ¾ percentage point of general spending in 1997, following larger tax cuts the previous two years. Increased revenue from a strong economy, however, dominated these tax cuts, and reports from state treasuries show that surpluses for FY 1997 have surged to 7.3 per cent of general spending, its highest share in seventeen years. The accumulation of surpluses was somewhat uneven, with nine states, many of them especially susceptible to cyclical swings in the economy, accounting for about 60 per cent of the total surpluses.

Looking forward, the biggest uncertainty state and local governments face is the restructuring of federally sponsored programmes. Federal authorities are moving progressively to a system whereby they provide states with block grants, letting them design systems best suited to local needs and possibly lowering administrative costs. The Aid to Families with Dependent Children programme was reworked as a block grant in the 1996 welfare reform bill, and recent changes to Medicaid also include more block grants. These grants, however, leave much of the risk associated with any additional spending to state and local governments, and they are often used by Congress to reduce federal expenditures, shifting burdens to states and localities.[18] Some have argued that this move to more fiscal federalism will limit spending and increase general government savings because state and local government usually have constitutional requirements to balance their budgets. But these requirements often include only a portion of the budget, excluding for instance, capital requirements, and as Figure 13 shows, budgets could probably absorb some increases in spending without any offsets.

Monetary and exchange-rate policy and financial market developments

Introduction

The Federal Reserve has spent most of the past year evaluating how to react to an economy that continues to grow at a pace that is unsustainable over the medium term when there is no clear sign of a pickup in inflation either in product or labour markets and when some observers, especially in the equities markets, have begun to proclaim the dawning of a new age. The momentum of demand and output has been such as to lead to a much lower unemployment rate than most members of the Federal Open Market Committee (FOMC) had expected[19] and below most previous estimates of the rate that could be sustained without leading to an acceleration in wages and prices. The Chairman of the Federal Reserve indicated in remarks in May before the Stern School of Business at New York University that he shares the view that "conventional notions of capacity are becoming increasingly outmoded and ... domestic resources can be used much more intensively than in the past without added price pressures''. But others may argue that, while wages have accelerated only modestly thus far, cost growth has been held down by persistent moderation in non-wage costs (which cannot be counted on to last indefinitely) and cyclical improvement in productivity performance, and pricing power has been limited more by the temporarily ample availability of supply abroad and the unusual strength of the dollar than by a variety of structural changes which have boosted competition at home (see Chapters I and III). Thus, the issue facing policymakers has been whether monetary policy is sufficiently restrictive to prevent credit creation from becoming excessive and undermining the sustainability of this lengthy expansion.

Recent interest rate developments

After the FOMC decided to cut the federal funds rate twice to 5¹/₄ per cent in late 1995 and early 1996 in order to help ensure a resumption of moderate growth following the 1995 slowdown and the accompanying decline in actual and expected inflation, that rate began a long period of stability. The ensuing pickup was, however, more rapid than foreseen, and the yield curve steepened (Figure 14). By July 1996, market rates had risen about 1.4 percentage points at the long end of the maturity spectrum, and the futures market indicated that markets expected a further increase in the funds rate of around ³/₄ percentage point over the next six months. The FOMC too began to think it more likely that their next move would be to increase restraint in reserve provision, having lost hope that the combination of higher market rates and an appreciating currency (see below) would be sufficient to curb the resurgence in activity.[20] Rates showed little trend over the summer of 1996, but signs of the hoped-for slowdown began to manifest

Figure 14. **INTEREST RATES**

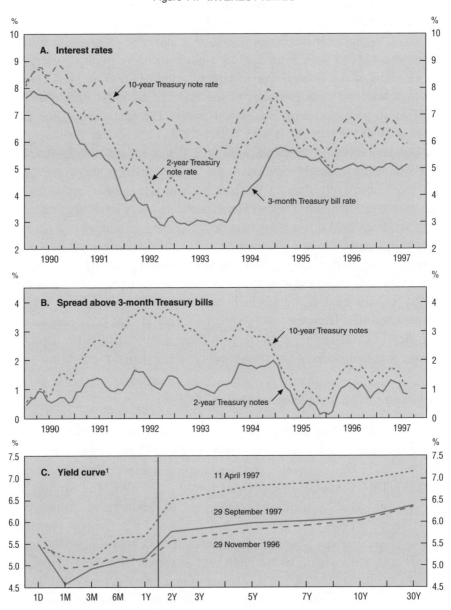

1. One-day rates are for Federal funds; one month to 1 year are Treasury bills; two-year to 30-year rates are redemption yields for benchmark bonds.
Source: Datastream and Federal Reserve Board.

themselves quite clearly as from September, most notably in a series of monthly labour market reports of more moderate job creation. The autumn therefore marked a period of generally falling market rates, with more than half of the first-half runup being reversed.

But with the renewed vigour of the real economy in the fourth quarter of 1996 and the first quarter of 1997, markets once more shifted course, and the yield curve steepened anew. Even though there were still few signs of imminent inflation increases, the FOMC too decided that the risks of overheating out-weighed those of excessive weakening in demand and finally put an end to the 14-month period of stability in policy-controlled rates when it raised the target funds rate by $1/4$ percentage point on 25 March 1997. Market participants expected further funds rate rises in the future and continued to boost market rates for a few weeks thereafter, effectively undoing the easing in market rates, espe-cially at the long end, which had taken place in the autumn. By April, 30-year rates were once again above 7 per cent. However, with the economy operating at a lower unemployment rate than in 1994 and with similar momentum, it is noteworthy that long rates at the April peak were about a percentage point lower, probably due to lower inflation expectations[21] and, to a lesser extent, to lower budget deficits. Since April, markets have again reacted to incoming data, which initially seemed to show a moderation in activity and have throughout reflected surprisingly good inflation news; encouraged by the FOMC's decision to leave the funds rate untouched, long-term rates have dropped three-quarters of a per-centage point. Short-term market rates have also fallen quite sharply, and an unusually large gap between short-term Treasury bill rates and the funds rate has opened up. As a result, all of the restrictive effect of the March tightening has since been undone in the interim.

Over the past few years the Federal Reserve has been assisted by the financial markets, the bond market in particular, in regulating aggregate demand. Medium- and longer-term interest rates have reflected the state of spending and activity (Figure 15, Panel A), but they also served to slow the economy down when economic slack was eliminated at the end of 1994, began to boost activity in the spring of 1996 (Figure 15, Panel B). But fundamental changes may be afoot in 1997, as the equities market has been serving to stimulate private demand and the bond market may have been restraining spending only sporadi-cally this year. Thus, it has been mainly the foreign exchange market that, by

Figure 15. **THE RELATIONSHIP BETWEEN LONG-TERM INTEREST RATES AND REAL GROWTH**

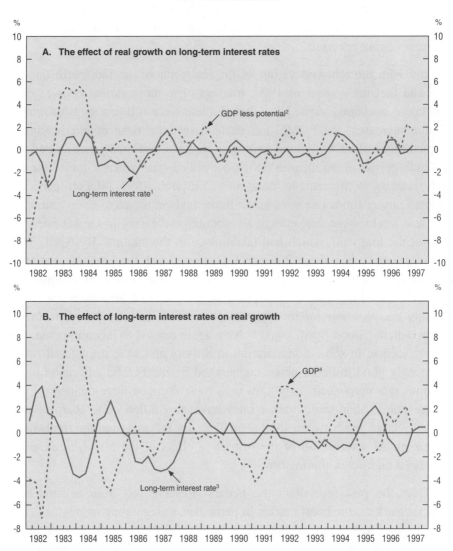

1. Change over two quarters.
2. The two-quarter per cent change in real GDP at annual rates less the two-quarter per cent change in potential GDP at annual rates.
3. Change over four quarters lagged four quarters.
4. The four-quarter per cent change in real GDP less the year earlier four-quarter change at annual rates.
Source: OECD.

raising the value of the dollar (see below), has helped to buffer excess demand for US goods and services.

An increased appetite for risk?

One interesting aspect of the evaluation of the appropriate level of interest rates is whether or not there is evidence of an increased appetite for risk on the part of investors and financial institutions. Such evidence, if it existed, would be relevant to policymakers concerned about "irrational exuberance" (as the Chairman of the Federal Reserve put it[22]), especially in the context of a domestic equities market that has arguably enjoyed the greatest bull run in history and is currently at very high levels. Current stock market valuations are justified if one expects further substantial earnings growth and is willing to attach a lower level of risk to a downturn in those earnings, due to the fact that there have been only eight months of recession in the past 15 years. Nonetheless, it must be remembered that the Dow Jones Industrial Average has risen by a factor of 10 in the past 15 years, a compound annual rate of $16\frac{1}{2}$ per cent. The only other periods in this century of such extended strength were 30 October 1923 to 3 September 1929 (compound annual growth of 29 per cent) and 28 April 1942 to 18 January 1966 (10.5 per cent per year). Of course, such buoyant equities prices lower the cost of equity capital and encourage greater business investment spending.[23] This increases supply and helps to hold down inflation, but it probably also stimulates consumer spending and may, in principle, sow the seeds of a bubble – poorly directed capital spending with unfavourable risk/return characteristics – such as occurred in Japan in the late 1980s, for example. Fortunately, few other asset prices have thus far manifested signs of excess. Most commodity prices have fallen; however, commercial real estate prices, which rose only slightly in real terms in 1996, have begun to move up more substantially this year in some areas, although residential real estate is rising only moderately in price.

Fixed income yield spreads provide another clue to the possibility of a decline in risk aversion. The differential between emerging market bonds and corresponding US Treasurys did indeed shrink to a record low by February 1997, but there has been something of a reversal since then. The gap between US corporate BAA or even junk bonds and Treasurys provides a similar domestic measure. It fell noticeably from the beginning of 1996 until early this year and has been fairly stable since then (Figure 16), but it has a definite cyclical

Figure 16. **YIELD SPREAD ON BONDS OVER THE BUSINESS CYCLE**

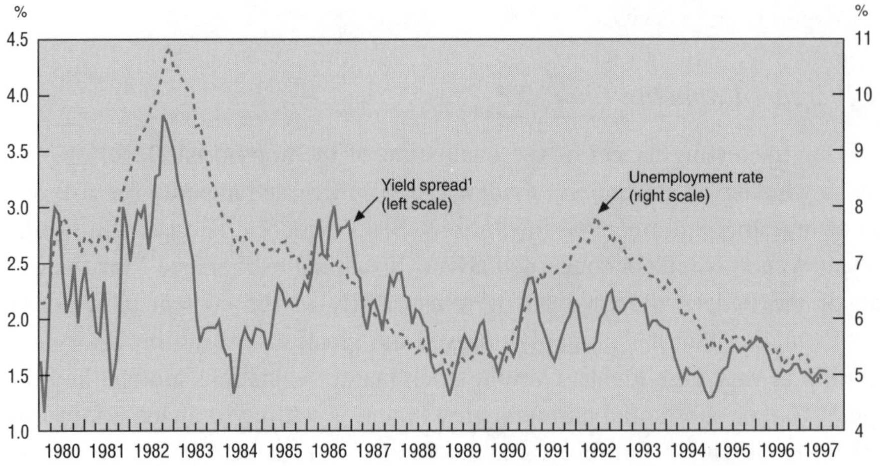

1. Spread between Moody's seasoned BAA corporate bond rate and 10-year Treasury note rate.
Source: OECD.

component that would seem to account fairly completely for its recent evolution.[24] In terms of structural change, there are some signs of greater willingness to bear risk: with $48 billion in new issues in the first half of 1997, junk bond issuance looks likely to set a new record this year. These bonds are becoming a vital form of corporate financing, especially in the booming high-technology sectors. The supply of 100-year corporate bonds – with their combination of tax deductibility and quasi-equity characteristics – grew strongly as well. In December 1996, the Comptroller of the Currency also warned of excessively risky syndicated loans. Finally, the expansion of what is called the ''subprime'' market for institutional lending to higher-risk customers or on terms entailing unusually high loan-to-value ratios – up to around 130 per cent for home-equity loans – might also be taken as a sign of some change in risk aversion – and there have indeed been some supplier problems in this area. These lenders may previously have been making loans that were totally unsecured, so their risk may have declined, but households' willingness to risk their homes may have increased. Overall, however, there would seem to be little of additional serious concern to policymakers, as the reduction in risk aversion would appear to be no greater than what is normal for this point in the business cycle. Nevertheless, past experience shows that even an increased cyclical willingness to bear risk is a hallmark of an expansion nearing its end.

Developments in money, credit and banking

Most money and credit aggregates have shown little change in their growth rates for most of the past year compared with earlier trends. However, a noticeable break occurred over the summer, with signs of accelerating money growth. Prior to recent renewed growth, narrow money (M1) was falling at a steady pace of around 5 per cent per year because of the persistent expansion in arrangements which "sweep" excess balances out of reservable retail transactions accounts into non-reservable non-transactions accounts, normally savings accounts. These arrangements started in January 1994 for retail customers and began to spread in earnest in May 1995. Initial amounts swept have since cumulated to around $200 billion, of which $116 billion occurred in 1996. Without that decline, M1 growth would have been over 5 per cent, both in 1996 and over the past year. Besides restraining narrow money growth, the sizeable resulting decline in required reserves has not brought about any major problems for the implementation of monetary policy, as depositories must still hold clearing balances to pay for Federal Reserve-provided services such as cheque-clearing. The predictable rise in the volatility of the federal funds rate has fortunately been modest (Bennett and Hilton, 1997). But the reduction in reserve balances must be matched by lower Federal Reserve holdings of Treasury securities and therefore ultimately less interest income to the Treasury.

The Federal Reserve still fixes benchmark ranges for the broader monetary aggregates consistent with price stability (assuming velocity is in line with historical norms), even though they do not target them in any short-run policy sense. These aggregates have behaved in expected fashion over the past year. M2 growth seems to have returned to a path which is predictable using income growth and opportunity cost factors as from the third quarter of 1994 after a three-year hiatus of instability during which its velocity shifted by nearly 20 per cent. Since then it has grown at an average annual rate of around 5 per cent (the top of its monitoring range), with some acceleration in evidence from last October until April and, more substantially, as from August, bringing it above the upper limit of its monitoring range. M3 has been growing for some time above its monitoring range (2 to 6 per cent per year), at almost 9 per cent since the Q4 1996 base period, again with some sign of an autumn 1996 acceleration, consistent with the pickup in real activity, and another in the summer of 1997. M3 growth has been faster than that in M2 because more buoyant market conditions in the United States have led to strong loan growth at US branches and agencies of foreign banks who are not permitted to finance their lending by using retail deposits (which are in M2).

Overall credit conditions continue to be accommodative for the large part, even though total real private non-financial debt has continued to grow by only around 4 per cent per year, which is low by historical standards in the expansionary phase of the business cycle.[25] Lenders have, however, tried to shift their focus to some extent away from lending to households and towards business, and 1996 saw the first decline in the household share of total loans in at least a decade. As mentioned in Chapter I, terms and conditions have been tightened for credit cards and, to a lesser extent, consumer instalment loans, due to rising delinquencies, bankruptcies and write-offs. As well, credit card solicitations fell from 2.7 billion in 1995 to 2.4 billion in 1996 and are expected to plunge to around 2 billion this year. As a result, consumer credit growth has slowed from year-on-year rates of around 15 per cent in the first half of 1995 to 5 per cent over the year ending in August. Residential mortgage lending growth has also slowed, but there has been little change in bank lending standards for this kind of credit, and, as discussed above, finance company loan availability has improved. On the other hand, the impact on the business sector of the higher interest rates on longer-term funds in 1996 and early 1997 has been offset to some extent by the easing of banks' terms and conditions, as well as by the aforementioned narrowing in the margin of corporate over Treasury bond rates and the lower cost of equity capital as measured by the earnings/price ratio. Commercial and industrial loan growth doubled from a range of 6 to 7 per cent year on year last summer to more than 10 per cent since then. Commercial real estate loan increases have also picked up steadily since the 1992 trough, with expansion around 7 per cent of late. Overall bank credit and loans and leases accelerated around the summer of 1996 from around 5 per cent to over 7 per cent, but the share of credit supplied by depository institutions, banks in particular, fell in 1996 as an increasing share of loans was securitised. While the securitisation of consumer credit slowed, albeit to a still rapid pace, mortgage-backed securities enjoyed even faster growth.

Thus, the share of the increase in non-federal debt which ended up on the books of depositories fell from 44 per cent in 1994 and 1995 to 38 per cent in 1996.

Bank profitability remained at historically high levels in 1996 for the fourth consecutive year, and early indications for 1997 point to a continuation of this trend. Recently around 99 per cent of all bank assets have been on the books of banks which are officially classified as well capitalised, up from 97 per cent at the end of 1995 and 30 per cent at the end of 1990. These favourable developments are ascribable to a persistent fall in non-interest expenses relative to assets, expansion of off-balance-sheet activities and revenues such as fee income from the sale of mutual funds, strong loan growth, continued low provisioning for loan losses as a result of good asset quality, and, above all, the maintenance of high interest margins.[26] The main negative factor in the short term is the continued heavy credit-card losses, while over the medium term banks are facing growing competition from other financial firms, such as brokerages, leading to political efforts to desegment the industry (see Chapter III). Thrift institutions' underlying profitability has also improved, but in 1996 they were hurt by a one-time assessment for the recapitalisation of the industry's deposit insurance fund. Despite such sustained profitability, the number of commercial banking organisations continues its inexorable decline, reaching some 7 500 in 1996, down from around 11 000 a decade earlier.[27] This ongoing consolidation in the sector is also reflected in a steady rise in the share of bank assets held by the top 50 bank holding companies: 64 per cent in 1996, up from 57 per cent in 1986.

Exchange rate developments

Over the past few years, the official position of the US authorities has steadfastly been that a strong dollar is in US interests; accordingly, there has been no official intervention in the exchange market since 15 August 1995. But that view has been coming under somewhat greater public pressure, and markets have interpreted officials' statements regarding the prospects for a renewed rise in external imbalances, especially the Japanese external surplus, as implying some possible softening in that position. By the end of April 1997, the trade-weighted value of the dollar had reached its highest level in 11 years against 31 partner countries; that represented a cumulative gain since its spring 1995 trough of 23 per cent, but the dollar was still 16 per cent below its 1985 peak (Figure 17). A moderate correction ensued, but it has since been reversed.

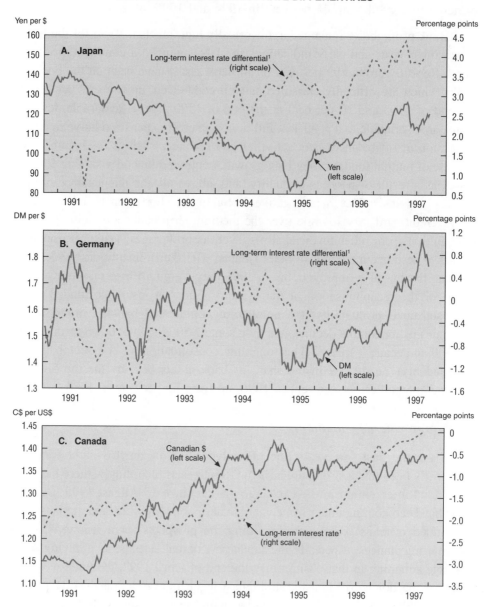

Figure 17. **BILATERAL EXCHANGE RATES
AND LONG-TERM INTEREST-RATE DIFFERENTIALS**

Yen per $ Percentage points

A. Japan

Long-term interest rate differential[1]
(right scale)

Yen
(left scale)

1991   1992   1993   1994   1995   1996   1997

DM per $ Percentage points

B. Germany

Long-term interest rate differential[1]
(right scale)

DM
(left scale)

1991   1992   1993   1994   1995   1996   1997

C$ per US$ Percentage points

C. Canada

Canadian $
(left scale)

Long-term interest rate[1]
(right scale)

1991   1992   1993   1994   1995   1996   1997

1.   US long-term rate less partner country long-term rate.
Source: OECD.

72

The dollar's strength is related to its relative cyclical position and, to a lesser extent, to interest-rate differentials. The output gap remains large in major OECD trading partner economies, but few would argue there is any slack left in the US economy (Figure 5). It can be seen that the dollar's course against the Deutschemark (and other European currencies) has followed quite closely the long-term interest-rate differential, as German yields dropped below their US counterparts in the spring of 1996, as they had in 1994, and then diverged further to as much as 100 basis points in 1997. But no such medium-term relationship has existed for the yen/dollar rate, which fell almost monotonically in the four years up to the spring of 1995 and rose virtually without interruption in the following two years, while the long-term interest-rate differential moved progressively in the United States' favour because of different cyclical developments. The bilateral exchange rate with Canada has also tended to move independently of long-term differentials in recent years. The Canadian dollar fell steadily from late-1991 to early 1995, as short-term interest rates were maintained at low levels, thereby keeping the long-term differential in the range of 1 to 2 percentage points in their favour. But the exchange rate has been fairly stable since then, despite the gradual elimination of the interest-rate differential across all maturities. While this is no doubt partly attributable to less favourable cyclical developments in Canada, there is some modest evidence of a more structural portfolio shift, perhaps in recognition of the even more substantial improvement in the fiscal situation and in the inflation outlook in Canada.[28]

International capital flows

Recorded net capital inflows in 1996 increased by more than $50 billion and, as in 1995, more than covered the current account deficit (Table 10). The flow of US assets abroad rose by around 15 per cent, but this was dwarfed by an even larger increase in foreign assets in the United States. Private-sector net inflows edged up from $44 to $67 billion (and jumped to $163 billion at an annual rate in the first half of 1997). The deficit on direct investment account continues to shrink, as inflows (especially from Germany, France and Japan) have now easily eclipsed the peak recorded in the late-1980s; indeed, in the first half of this year there was a surplus, something which has not been sustained for a full year since 1990. Private foreign purchases of US securities surged to a new

Table 10. **Balance of payments**

$ billion

	1995	1996	1997 S1 (annual rates)
Current balance	−129.1	−148.2	−158.0
Per cent of GDP	1.8	2.0	2.0
Change in US assets abroad	307.2	352.4	446.9
US official reserve assets, net	9.7	−6.7	− 8.5
Other US government assets, net	0.5	0.7	0.5
US private assets, net	296.9	358.4	454.9
of which:			
Direct investment	86.7	87.8	111.0
Foreign securities	100.1	108.2	71.7
Other claims reported by:			
US non-banking concerns	35.0	64.2	88.9
US banks	75.1	98.2	183.3
Change in foreign assets in the United States	451.2	547.6	667.8
Foreign official assets	110.7	122.4	50.3
of which:			
US government securities	72.7	115.6	32.3
Other US government liabilities	0.7	0.7	2.5
US liabilities reported by US banks	34.0	4.7	20.1
Other foreign official assets	3.3	1.3	− 4.6
Other foreign assets	340.5	425.2	617.4
of which:			
Direct investment	67.5	77.0	119.0
US Treasury securities and US currency flows	111.8	172.9	204.2
Other US securities	96.4	133.8	180.7
Other liabilities reported by:			
US non-banking concerns	34.6	31.8	24.4
US banks	30.2	9.8	89.1
Statistical discrepancy	−14.9	−46.9	−62.8

Source: Bureau of Economic Analysis.

record once again, reaching more than $300 billion ($385 billion in the first half of 1997 at annual rates); most of these took the form of Treasury securities and US currency.[29] Indeed, foreigners bought far more securities in 1996 than the Treasury issued and raised their share of Treasury debt outstanding to nearly one-third, double the share a decade ago. US purchases of foreign securities edged up in 1996 but then fell fairly sharply in the first half of this year. US official assets fell back in 1996 and so far in 1997, mainly due to the repayment by Mexico of its loans from the US Treasury and the Federal Reserve.[30] Foreign official holdings of US assets also reached a new record in 1996, despite a sharp fall in holdings of bank deposits. Part of this is a result of exchange market intervention by G10 central banks, which seems to have helped push up the value of the dollar, but more than half of the increase was in official holdings of other countries.

III. An overview of structural policy developments

Introduction

Once again a wide range of structural policy changes are being debated and legislated in the United States. The incentives for their adoption vary, but they generally include a variety of mostly efficiency-enhancing motives – such as a desire to expose previously protected parts of the economy to the disciplines of competition, the fall-out of technological and other structural change on existing regulation and the search for cost reductions in public-sector activities – as well as equity concerns that arise in the course of economic development and a need to comply with international agreements. The need for new legislation to be approved by both houses of Congress and the President may imply a healthy dispersion of power, but it also means that at times reforms are less coherent than they might be in alternative systems.

Trade and investment policy

The recent past has been notable for significant progress on the trade policy front: major multilateral agreements have been reached; many bilateral disputes have been resolved; and the US use of the anti-dumping and countervailing duty instrument has diminished.[31] But important debates and decisions are imminent, and advocates of freer trade have been on the defensive recently, while restrictionist forces seem to be gaining ground. These forces often resort to mercantilist arguments that exports are good and imports bad and focus their attention mistakenly on bilateral imbalances between the United States and various trading partners, in particular Japan and, increasingly, China.

The United States helped achieve worldwide trade liberalisation through the completion of two major WTO agreements concluded thus far in 1997. First, in February 69 countries agreed to open their *telecommunications* markets for domestic and international telephony, fax and data transmission, private leased circuits, satellite communications, mobile telephony and paging services. Talks had been going on for some three years under the aegis of the General Agreement on Trade in Services (GATS)[32] without success. A 1996 deadline had passed without an agreement, as the United States had found the offers then on the table inadequate because they covered only around 60 per cent of global trade in these services. In contrast, the accord reached in February covers about 95 per cent of the market, whereas US firms, for example, then had access to only around 17 per cent. The agreement must be ratified by 30 November. Liberalisation is to begin in 1998 for the main developed countries, with others following over the next few years. The agreement covers not only trade in services but also opens up domestic markets to foreign ownership and includes commitments on pro-competitive regulatory principles, with disputes to be handled by the WTO's Dispute Settlement Body (DSB). Estimates by the Institute for International Economics of the global income gains from the greater competition amount to as much as a cumulative one trillion dollars over the next decade (0.4 per cent of GDP per year), with telephone rates falling as much as 80 per cent.

The second major international accord came in *information technology* (IT) products. The scene was set for a global agreement when the world's four major trading areas decided in December 1996 to seek to eliminate tariffs on most IT trade (valued at $500 billion per year) by the year 2000. For the agreement to come into effect, other countries had to agree such that a total of at least 90 per cent of the world market was covered; in the event, by March 40 countries representing 92 per cent had agreed to terms. In most cases the tariff reductions occur in four equal steps beginning 1 July 1997. This accord has been estimated to result in global income gains of $50 billion per year when implementation is complete.

Determined to maintain the momentum of removing trade barriers and distortions, the United States continues to pursue trade liberalisation regionally and bilaterally as well. It and most observers believe that this multi-pronged strategy promotes increased overall trade, but a small number claim that these regional agreements threaten to impede progress toward freer trade by diverting policymakers' attention away from global negotiations and by artificially stimulating within-area trade to the detriment of non-members. The *North American Free Trade Area* agreement (NAFTA) is up for a three-year review this year; the Administration issued a report to Congress in July that stated NAFTA has had a small but positive effect on jobs and incomes. In some quarters the view is that NAFTA has been a failure, since the bilateral trade deficit with Canada and Mexico together has moved sharply higher since it was implemented and some manufacturing capacity has been shifted to Mexico.[33] But there is no necessary causality in this sequence of events because other factors besides NAFTA have played an important role, the 1994-95 Mexican peso crisis in particular. What is clear is that the existence of the agreement helped Mexico to make two-thirds of the necessary balance of payments adjustment to overcome the crisis through increased exports rather than import compression, compared to only one-third following the 1981-82 crisis. Thus, in the wake of the crisis, the United States enjoyed a greater advantage from NAFTA, as Mexico raised its tariffs to levels bound in the Uruguay Round for non-NAFTA countries. As a result, the volume of trade has increased between the two countries.

The US Administration would like to have Chile join the NAFTA – Chile has already negotiated separate deals with Canada and Mexico – and to bring about hemispheric free trade through a *Free Trade Area of the Americas* (FTAA) by 2005. For both it needs to get approval from the Congress to provide the Administration with so-called "fast-track" authority under which negotiated agreements would be subject to a straight vote without amendments in Congress. The Administration made such a request to Congress in September, but differences of view over the role of labour and environmental issues remain. The Administration would like to begin detailed FTAA negotiations in 1998 on tariffs and other trade issues and then ultimately to broaden the agreement to deal with other hemispheric issues such as security, drugs, the environment and labour. Other potential FTAA participants would prefer to deal with trade issues in a more phased manner and are not presently prepared to contemplate any broadening of the agenda.

The United States has also been working to make trade and investment freer and fairer in a number of other fora. It has recently been a strong advocate of multilateral moves in the OECD in particular to limit *bribery* and other corrupt practices related to foreign business transactions. This would not only level the playing field for US firms who, since 1977, have been constrained by the terms of the Foreign Corrupt Practices Act and cannot deduct bribes paid to foreign officials from taxable income, but it would also help countries currently suffering from such practices at home to attract more inward direct investment (Wei, 1997). OECD Member countries have agreed to remove the tax deductibility of bribes paid to foreign officials and to criminalise such actions. The US Administration has also called for the creation of a "global free-trade zone" on the *Internet*. There seems to be agreement that no new trade barriers or taxes should be imposed on electronic commerce and that government regulation in this area should be kept to a minimum, but there is no consensus as to whether taxes that apply to other trade, such as VAT, should apply equally to Internet-based transactions. In addition, legislation to implement two UN World Intellectual Property Organisation treaties regarding *copyright laws* are to be sent to the Congress soon. A *Mutual Recognition Agreement* between the European Union (EU), the United States and Canada was successfully negotiated in June 1997 after four years of discussions. It provides for the mutual acceptance of testing, inspection and certification of products such as telecommunications and electrical equipment, medical devices, veterinary products, recreational craft and pharmaceuticals. This covers some $47 billion in trade and should save producers an estimated $172 million in annual export-related regulatory costs. The Administration also supports the *African Growth and Opportunity Act*, legislation that would shift the emphasis in US policy toward sub-Saharan Africa from aid to trade and investment. It would eliminate quotas on textiles and clothing from Kenya and Mauritius once safeguards against transhipment are in place, establish funds for equity and infrastructure investment with Overseas Private Investment Corporation backing, boost lending by the Export Import Bank and extend the Generalised System of Preferences to more products for countries pursuing pro-growth policies.

The United States has shown strong support for the *World Trade Organisation* (WTO) and favours expanding its membership to include China,[34] Russia, Saudi Arabia and Taiwan. It has made extensive use of its dispute settlement procedures; indeed, it has brought more cases before the WTO than any other nation, and it has had a fairly good record so far in winning cases it has brought and in implementing changes when its policies are ruled in contravention of world trade law. Among others, over the past year WTO procedures have helped resolve disputes:

- with a number of countries over US textile and clothing quotas imposed under safeguard clauses;
- with Japan over its differential taxation of imported distilled spirits;
- with Canada over preferences given to Canadian magazines;
- and with the EU over its banana regime, its grain import duty system, hormones used in the production of meat[35] and rules of origin for certain textile and apparel products.

WTO procedures have also been initiated in a number of other areas involving the United States as plaintiff (for example, the honouring of intellectual property rights commitments by Denmark, Sweden, Ireland and Ecuador; Hungarian export subsidies; Argentinean duties on textiles, clothing and footwear; Turkish taxation of box office receipts from foreign films; and EU reclassification of certain equipment) and defendant (such as shrimp imports from a number of countries).

The United States has also come to a number of *agreements with Japan*. Japan agreed in December 1996 to open up its primary non-life insurance market so that foreign firms can compete on price and policy innovations by the end of 1998. In June 1997 the two nations announced an enhanced initiative on deregulation to improve market access and enhance consumer benefits in a number of sectors. Also, in April 1997, under the threat of severe fines on Japanese vessels entering US ports, Japan agreed to modify certain restrictive port practices, with the details of its promised significant reform measures to be announced by the end of July. However, this deadline was not met, and those fines began to be imposed in September, the first such sanctions implemented since 1987. Bilateral conflicts are also still outstanding in: the photographic film case; supercomputers, where the Commerce Department has made a preliminary ruling that dumping has occurred; US farm exports, where consultations are underway over the allegedly excessive use of quarantine treatment; and air passenger services, where "open-skies" talks are ongoing.

Yet there remain some areas of multilateral concern where progress has stalled or where frictions are at best in abeyance. The *shipbuilding agreement* negotiated at the OECD has still not been approved by the Congress (although there is reason to hope movement is imminent), and signs are that other partners to the agreement are being drawn towards renewed subsidisation: for example, the European Union has agreed to provide over $2 billion in aid to yards in Germany, Spain and Greece. The United States also continues to implement *unilateral sanctions* against nations with which it has fundamental differences in views, most recently against Burma in April 1997. State and local governments have also begun to impose similar procurement constraints, giving rise to WTO consultations requested by the European Communities and Japan. A recent study by the National Association of Manufacturers cited 61 laws and executive actions over the past four years which have been aimed at getting 35 countries to change their policies. Without multilateral support, such policies may well simply divert trade away from the United States, costing it economic activity and jobs. The Libertad (Helms-Burton) Act is another case where frictions exist with trading partners, even though under an understanding reached in April 1997 the European Union agreed to suspend its WTO challenge and to work with the United States toward developing binding disciplines which would protect property rights worldwide and require ''prompt, adequate and effective'' compensation in the event of expropriation. For its part, the US Administration promised, *inter alia*, to seek to obtain from Congress a waiver of Title IV of the Act, whereby corporate executives and their families who are accused of dealing in expropriated Cuban assets can be barred from entering the United States. The two sides set a deadline of 15 October so that the envisaged disciplines can be introduced into the OECD negotiations over a Multilateral Agreement on Investment. A further possible unilateral action may occur in the area of ''accounting rates'' in international telephony: in December the Federal Communications Commission (FCC) announced that it would cut these rates between the United States and the rest of the world in line with falling costs, despite a lack of an agreement among members of the International Telecommunication Union. Several foreign firms who benefit from some of the estimated $5.4 billion in net settlement payments by US firms have indicated they will mount legal challenges to these actions. Finally, the issue of the *extra-territorial application of antitrust policy* came to the fore once again in the context of the Boeing merger with McDonnell Douglas. The US Federal Trade Commission expressed some concerns over the use of exclusive provider agreements but ultimately approved the merger. But the European Commission claimed jurisdiction and, before dropping its opposition to the merger, successfully sought the elimination of existing and future exclusive provider agreements, the separation of the two firms' accounts on commercial operations and the provision of regular reports showing that defence and commercial finances are not being mixed. Bilateral co-operation arrangements between competition policy authorities may not prove sufficient over the long term to deal with such frictions, and a broader co-ordinated regime may be required.

Financial markets

In 1996 several *financial services reform measures* were passed. A rider was attached to the FY 1997 Omnibus Appropriations bill that overhauled the Savings Association Insurance Fund (SAIF) by charging thrifts a one-time assessment of 0.66 per cent of insured deposits and that mandated that banks pay most of the interest payments on outstanding bonds that financed the cleanup of the thrift industry. Also attached was a bill that provided modest regulatory relief by easing disclosure requirements, overhauling credit reporting, streamlining application processes and clarifying the safe-harbour provisions in environmental acts for lenders who foreclose on contaminated property. A securities bill was also signed into law that clarifies state and federal jurisdiction over securities regulation and eases investment in hedge funds.

Attempts at major financial services reform died in the Congress in 1996, but momentum for consideration of the repeal of the Glass-Steagall Act (which limits the financial activities of banks and prohibits commerce and bank associations) has been rekindled in 1997. In May, the Treasury Department issued its reform plan. It contains five components:

- *a)* It would permit banks, securities firms and insurance companies to affiliate.
- *b)* It offers two choices for the banking-commerce clause of the Glass-Steagall Act:
  - Under plan A, "the basket approach", bank holding companies could receive some fraction of their revenue from non-financial activities. It would prohibit any affiliation between a bank holding company and a non-financial firm with assets greater than some threshold, such as the size of the 1 000th largest non-financial company by assets. Under this

plan, the federal thrift charter would be eliminated, and the Bank Insurance Fund and the SAIF would be merged.

– Under plan B, "the financial-only approach", bank holding companies would continue to be prohibited from engaging in non-financial activities (as preferred by the Federal Reserve); the existing thrift charter would be preserved, and the two insurance funds would remain separate.

c) It would allow firms to choose how to organise their financial activities and therefore by which institution they would be regulated.

d) It would create a new type of organisation, called wholesale financial institutions (WFIs), that would accept wholesale uninsured deposits and would be regulated by the Office of the Comptroller of the Currency (OCC) or the Federal Reserve Board.

e) All social regulation like the Community Reinvestment Act and consumer protection clauses would continue and be extended to the WFIs. A National Council on Financial Services would be created to co-ordinate regulation and resolve jurisdictional issues.

Since then, similar legislation has been reported out of a Committee of the House of Representatives; it would limit the revenues from non-financial activities that companies owning banks may earn to 15 per cent of the total and not require them to guarantee the banks will remain well-capitalised, but it would retain some constraints on banks' ability to enter insurance markets.

The impetus for major banking reform has also been boosted by regulators. In late November 1996 the OCC issued regulations that permit subsidiaries of national banks to engage in other financial activities like securities and insurance underwriting on an application-by-application basis. In December, the Federal Reserve Board raised the limit on revenue a subsidiary of a bank holding company may derive from underwriting certain securities from 10 per cent to 25 per cent.[36] In addition, it recently eliminated most of the firewalls between these subsidiaries and the bank holding company. The private sector has begun to take advantage of the new regulatory environment. Bankers Trust, the seventh largest US banking company has proposed and has had Board approval for a merger with Alex. Brown, Inc., a major regional brokerage house. Several other top ten commercial banks have followed suit. The trend to financial conglomeration has continued, with the proposed merger of Travelers (which is both a major insurance company and brokerage house) and Salomon (an investment bank). These new regulations, which are more favourable to banks, have led firms engaged in other financial services, who once were opposed to major banking reform, now to push for new legislation that would allow them to move into other financial markets. In the process of writing a bill, legislators need to resolve three remaining controversies: whether to remove the "banking-commerce" clause; whether to consolidate the banking and thrift industries; and which agency will have regulatory jurisdiction. The current House bill calls for the Federal Reserve Board to serve as an umbrella regulator of each holding company, while other banking and securities regulators would continue their activities. Separate legislation that clarifies state jurisdiction on branch banking across state lines has also been passed.

Congress and regulators are also considering significant *securities markets* reform. A bill currently in committee would ease federal regulations of US commodity exchanges, placing the burden on regulators to show why a new product should not be traded and speeding the regulatory review process. The bill would also exempt the over-the-counter derivatives market from the US Commodity Exchange Act, which regulates the US futures markets, clarifying a Supreme Court ruling in favour of deregulation. In order to be able to compete with the over-the-counter market, the exchanges would be allowed to set up unregulated markets for "professional traders". Backers of the bill argue that reform is needed because the United States is losing market share in the global futures market. Congress also threatened to mandate that stocks be priced in cents rather than eighths of a dollar; the industry ultimately agreed to make this change on its own. Its supporters suggest that a one-cent reduction in transactions costs would save investors at least $1 billion a year. In the wake of some high-profile derivatives losses, the Securities and Exchange Commission (SEC) and the Financial Accounting Standards Board (FASB) have issued separate proposals that require more disclosure of derivatives holdings; FASB would require that all companies book derivatives they own at "fair market" prices as from 1999, a proposal that some have argued would be too costly for firms to implement and would dissuade them from using derivatives to hedge risk. The SEC is also considering sweeping reform that would encourage the formation of Internet stock exchanges and reduce the regulatory burden on smaller exchanges.

Other regulatory reform

Two industries have been the focus of regulatory reform efforts over the past year. The first is *telecommunications* where the process of implementing last year's Telecommunications Act is ongoing. In so doing, the Federal Communications Commission (FCC) has initiated a number of proceedings and adopted rules intended to facilitate robust competition. For example, it adopted rules governing the duties of incumbent local telephone companies to open their markets to competitors, especially long-distance telephone companies in August 1996. These rules called for only small cuts in the $20 billion in access charges paid yearly by the long-distance firms to the local telephone companies to complete their calls (45 per cent of the cost) so as not to force too much rate "rebalancing", *i.e.* raising local rates towards cost by diminishing the cross-subsidy from long-distance, variously estimated at $6 to $15 billion per year. Then, in October, some local telephone firms succeeded in convincing a federal court to block implementation, arguing that forced discounts are confiscatory. The court ruled that the FCC could not impose national pricing rules for what is essentially a local service and that it should be left to the state regulatory commissions to adopt interconnection rules. However, non-pricing aspects of the FCC's August 1996 order remain in effect.

The 1996 reform also sought to spur competition in the long-distance market by allowing local telephone companies to offer long-distance service once the FCC is satisfied that their local market is open to competition.[37] Most recently, the FCC managed to come to an agreement with the largest long-distance carrier, AT&T, in May under which a universal service fund of $3 to $4 billion per year would be created by raising charges on additional residential lines and new levies on wireless telephone and paging services in order to ensure Internet connection for all schools, libraries and rural healthcare providers as well as to continue to subsidise poor, disabled and other rural customers. At the same time, the FCC adopted a plan to reform carrier access charges for the origination and termination of interstate long-distance calls. First, $4 billion in such charges were shifted from per minute to monthly rates to the benefit of heavy users. Second, it lowered access charges by $1.7 billion in the first year and a total of $18.5 billion over five years. Basic residential rates will remain unchanged, but long-distance rates were reduced by an average of around 8 per cent on 1 July 1997. Access charges can be reduced to cost levels only if cross-subsidies are also cut, and while some claim that this would impinge on the guarantee of universal service, lower aggregate welfare and hurt the poor (Wolak, 1997), competition from new technologies should make it possible to eliminate cross-subsidies without raising prices for local service.

Deregulation of the *electricity* industry is also proceeding apace due to changes in technology and the costs of efficient generators relative to regulated prices (White, 1997). The Federal Energy Regulatory Commission has already opened up the transmission grid to inter-producer competition at the wholesale level. Five states have also passed laws opening their retail markets to provider competition,[38] most prominently California, which decided to scrap a four-year phase-in period in favour of immediate customer choice starting next January. Utilities in that state have agreed to cut tariffs by only 10 per cent at that time, which should allow so-called "stranded costs" (the costs of assets which are uneconomical to operate at current prices but which are protected by regulatory mechanisms – nuclear plants in most cases – an estimated $150 to $200 billion in book value terms) to be covered until the year 2002. New Hampshire, on the other hand, has proposed to cut tariffs 19 per cent in January which would allow only 60 per cent of stranded costs to be covered; this has been challenged in the courts. A flurry of bills has been introduced in Congress to proceed nationally with retail deregulation as from anywhere between 1999 and 2003; one would not allow for any recovery of stranded costs at all. Since these assets were acquired with regulatory approval, this would seem to impose an unfair burden on the relevant shareholders. In any event, the deregulatory trend in the industry is expected to lead to a fall in retail prices of some 20 per cent (worth roughly $42 billion to users) over the next five years as cheaper producers move into the market in higher-price regions. Excess capacity will be cut back, as producers will no longer be guaranteed a regulated return on assets. Marketing will gain in importance, and specialist retailers, whose revenues rose eight-fold in 1996, will compete with producers to an increasing extent. In this regard a new electronic market for electricity opened in January. Also, greater industry consolidation is a likely outcome,[39] as scale economies are believed to be substantial. Last, there will be important implications for greenhouse gas emissions of the expected shift from nuclear to lower-cost fossil-based power. Also, to the extent that cost savings result in lower prices, demand will rise, leading to more pollution, even if the composition of production remains the same.

Environmental matters

A number of important environmental policy questions are currently being debated. By far the most important on the domestic front are the new rules proposed by the Environmental Protection Agency (EPA) in November 1996 under the Clean Air Act and approved by the President in June 1997 with a lengthy phase-in period. The first set of rules will for the first time limit the *emissions of fine particles* of 2.5 microns or more. The Act requires that no attention be paid to the costs, but the EPA estimates that its standards will save up to 17 000 lives per year. It values these benefits at $20 to $110 billion per year using the rule of thumb that any life saved is worth up to $4.8 million, depending on age or health status. EPA estimated costs at $37 billion. However, industry officials point out benefits are probably at the low end of the range, as those dying prematurely are likely to be elderly and frail and therefore unable to benefit as fully from lower pollution levels. The debate has centred on whether the epidemiological evidence is sufficiently clear – is it the size of particles or their chemical composition that matters? – to justify such a high standard in this one dimension when there is not even a monitoring system yet in place. The second set concerns *ozone*: the limit is to be fixed at 0.08 parts per million over an eight-hour period rather than the current 0.12 parts over one hour. Costs are estimated at $9.6 billion, with benefits evaluated at $1.5 to $8.5 billion. EPA admits that its cost estimates, like its benefits are uncertain. For example, experience with sulphur emissions trading has shown that market prices have settled at a small fraction of prior estimates ($120 per ton rather than anywhere from $300 to $800).[40] This tradeable permits approach has succeeded in reducing emissions by around half at a cost between one-third and one-half of what would have been incurred under a traditional command-and-control approach. The sulphur emissions scheme will be extended in the year 2000 from the 110 heaviest polluters to 700 more fossil-fuel-burning firms.

The other still outstanding domestic issue is the amendment and reauthorisation of the *Superfund* toxic waste cleanup bill. The Senate Republican bill introduced in January no longer calls for the repeal of the current law's provision of retroactive responsibility for waste dumped legally before the original legislation was enacted in 1980 but would exempt up to 75 per cent of such businesses (including all small businesses) in order to speed cleanups, boost cost effectiveness and reduce litigation, albeit at a substantial cost to the taxpayer. The House bill would, however, allow the EPA to recover costs if additional contamination is found after the property is certified as clean and would try to unblock the current situation (in which little cleanup is taking place) by providing some seed money to get business and local governments to clean up sites with only minor contamination. In May the Administration released principles for reforming the programme, arguing that existing liability standards must be maintained, although it has reached legal settlements with 14 000 businesses that pollute in small quantities to remove their liability. Negotiations are likely to continue into the autumn. In April the Administration had expanded its Toxics Release Inventory programme under which firms are required to make public reports on the levels of their emissions. The new rules would call on the 7 000 existing reporters to provide more details and cover 6 100 additional sites (a 30 per cent increase) in seven new sectors. As well, the EPA endorsed the cheaper of two options for the paper industry to cut its emissions of *dioxins*, but it will still cost about $1.4 billion to eliminate around 90 per cent of the discharges of this carcinogen.

On *climate change*, the United States issued a position paper in December 1996 in which it said it favours a "realistic, verifiable and binding medium-term emissions target" for greenhouse gases. It supports an international system of tradeable permits for carbon emissions for the OECD and the former Soviet Union with multi- rather than single-year targets and an eventual set of targets for all participants. It admits that compliance and monitoring of an international system of tradable permits would be more difficult than for a purely domestic system, but the cost of reducing carbon emissions could be cut substantially. In June, at the Denver summit, it did not endorse a proposal to target a 15 per cent reduction in emissions from 1990 levels by the year 2010, as a policy position on targets and timetables for reductions has not been formulated yet.

Labour market policies and developments

The US labour market continues to surprise observers by recording exemplary performance (see Chapter I). The unemployment rate has maintained its downward trend to levels which nearly all experts believe to be inconsistent with stable wage and price inflation, but no clear signs of any pickup of those are yet evident. Real wages are finally growing on a sustained basis for the first time in several decades, and even the latest income distribution indicators point to some improvement,[41] as the low unemployment rate boosts wages at the low end more than at the high end of the distribution (Blank and Card, 1993), the legal minimum wage is raised,[42] the number of workers employed part-time for economic reasons (involuntarily) has fallen and even the marginalised have been able to find jobs. Nevertheless, the job cuts are still proceeding at a rate of nearly half a million per year, a rate more characteristic of a period of weak labour markets; and 22 per cent of the 8.3 million independent contractors in February 1995 were previously working for their current employer in a traditional working arrangement, nearly one quarter of which had changed status involuntarily, 411 000 workers in all (Polivka, 1996, Table 12). Perhaps as a result, job insecurity is still unusually high for an economy at full employment (see Chapter I), even though there is no evidence that long-term employment relationships are in serious decline (Farber, 1997b). However, evidence is accumulating that simple downsizing has some obvious costs which might offset the expected benefits: according to the American Management Association, disability claims rise, wrongful termination suits become more prevalent and morale worsens, so that overall there is little, if any, positive impact on company earnings or stock prices. Productivity and profits improve in less than half of all cases, with the evolution of the firm's training budget over the period of downsizing a key determinant of the direction of the outcome.[43] Accordingly, in February 1997 the National Association of Manufacturers called on US firms to commit 3 per cent of their payroll to education and training activities, as well as to broadening incentive compensation such as stock ownership programmes.[44]

There are substantial reform efforts underway to improve the nation's *human capital development* system. The Administration has made education one of the cornerstones of its second term in office. The tax breaks for post-secondary education, which are part of the budget deal and have been described in Chapter II, may, however, in large measure go to those who would pursue such studies in any case, as the share of those aged 18-24 in college has been on a rising trend (35 per cent in 1994, up from 26 per cent in 1980), bringing the college wage premium down from 79 per cent in 1990 to 73 per cent in 1994. The Administration had originally proposed to increase the maximum value of Pell grants (for the poor) by 10 per cent to $3 000 per year and broaden their coverage to include those over the age of 24. Interest rates on student loans would have been shaved by 2 points to 2 per cent for need-based loans and by 1 point for others. But these were not part of the final budget agreement, even though the latter included a tax deduction for student loan interest of $1 000 rising to $2 500 by 2001. Exclusion from taxable income of employer-provided educational assistance will be extended.

However, increasing college attendance is arguably not as important as improving the performance of the primary and secondary systems ("K-12"). International comparisons show that US pupils perform well in reading, mathematics and science at age 9, but by age 14 they have lost much of their lead in reading and science and fallen toward the bottom of the pack in mathematics. The Administration is continuing to encourage states to adopt national curriculum standards and standardised tests of reading at the Grade 4 level and mathematics at the Grade 8 level, but thus far only seven states have complied. The Congress, however, has taken the position that such standards are intrusive and is threatening to cut funding for their implementation. But the Administration's position has recently been supported by research showing that pupils in countries (and provinces) which have standardised mandatory exams significantly outperform others where they are lacking (Bishop, 1997). Many observers claim the problem lies in the impact of teachers' unions[45] and in the quality of teaching and administration. The National Commission on Teaching and America's Future called the status of teaching a "national shame", pointing out that one-quarter of high school teachers are not even qualified to teach their primary subjects (56 per cent in science) and that new teachers are usually allocated the toughest assignments, leading to a 30 per cent early-career quit rate. Providing some school choice figures most prominently among reform efforts.[46] Proponents point to increasing evidence that Catholic schools are more cost effective, in part because teacher salaries are much lower, and achieve higher pupil performance, at least for urban schools (Neal, 1997). Charter schools paid for out of public money but managed independently now number nearly 500 and are growing quickly, with attendance in 1996 reaching 105 000, but they are prohibited in 25 states. They face a formidable challenge, as they must fund their own capital and maintenance outlays, and they are not permitted to select by ability. But their results have been so impressive that the Administration, despite teachers' union opposition, requested $100 million in support in the FY 1998 budget (double this year's expenditure and up from $5 million in FY 1995), targeting the establishment of another 3 000 charter schools by the end of the decade.

The Administration's FY 1998 budget also had a number of other K-12 initiatives. It called for a one-time appropriation of $5 billion to aid in the modernisation and repair of school buildings; the establishment of a reading assistance programme; and the expansion of a number of other existing programmes, such as the Goals 2000 programme of education standards, the technology literacy fund and bilingual education. It remains unclear which of these changes will be approved by the Congress.

A number of small, separate legislative changes affecting the labour market are moving through or have been considered by the Congress. Consolidation of some 60 job training and literacy programmes into three block grants was approved by the House of Representatives in May 1997, but the Senate has not acted on this question thus far. More controversial was a bill that would have allowed employers to give workers the option to have overtime pay or compensatory time off in the event of overtime hours worked. Despite the apparent enhancement in flexibility, unions feared that employers will use coercion to avoid paying overtime premiums, and the bill did not become law. Finally, a Presidential veto threat is also hanging over so-called "TEAM" legislation; it would allow firms to set up groups of workers and managers to address such issues as productivity, quality control and workplace safety, all things that would be handled by unions, where they exist. Not surprisingly therefore, unions are opposed to this bill, as is the Administration which vetoed a similar bill last year.

Several of these reforms address the recommendations made in the chapter *Implementing the OECD Jobs Strategy* in last year's Survey (OECD, 1996a) while other recommendations have yet to be implemented in any meaningful way (Table 11). In particular, the Committee recommended that the United States reduce work disincentives for the poor and the disabled and improve access to training, child care and health insurance. The 1996 welfare reform bill improved work incentives by limiting the benefits able-bodied adults could collect, while it increased funding by $4 billion over seven years for child care. It also contained penalties for states who fail to move enough welfare recipients into "work activities"; how much flexibility states should have in defining what constitutes work, in particular how to classify those participating in educational activities, is expected soon to be decided by the federal authorities. The 1998 budget looks set to contain additional money for training and for health insurance for poor children. While the child care funding increase may be inadequate to meet the

Table 11. **Implementing the OECD Jobs Strategy – an overview of progress**

Proposal	Action	Assessment/recommendation
I. Reform unemployment and related benefit systems		
• Reduce work disincentives for the poor	1996 welfare bill limits time able-bodied adults can collect benefits. Some changes in 1997 give states flexibility.	Balance between legitimate education and training and work avoidance efforts needs to be struck.
• Increase access to training for the poor	Federal training programmes grouped into three large state block grants. Additional training funds in FY 1998 budget.	Training programmes and government jobs may not be enough to provide work for those currently on welfare, especially if the economy turns down.
• Increase access to child care for the poor	Additional child care funds in 1998 budget agreement.	The demand for child care by those affected by welfare reform may increase even more than the added funds.
• Increase access to health insurance for the poor	Money available for health care for poor children in federal budget and modest Medicaid reform.	Additional coverage for poor children helps, but improved access help for poor adults is needed. Long-term Medicaid reform is also needed.
• Reduce work disincentives for the disabled	None.	Workers' compensation and social security for the disabled should be consistent with the Americans with Disabilities Act.
• Expand the Earned Income Tax Credit, rather than raise the minimum wage	Law passed in 1996 to raise minimum wage. EITC recipients can claim at least some of the child tax credit.	Minimum wage hike will not have large effects, but improved EITC would have been preferred.
• Increase eligibility for unemployment benefits	None.	The work experience requirement is too restrictive; all those with substantial labour market attachment should have access to such benefits.
II. Improve labour force skills and competencies		
• Promote curriculum or output standards for primary and secondary schools	Goals 2000 initiative, which includes national standards, funded in FY 1997 but may be cut in 1998. States have set up information clearinghouse to measure relative performance.	Improved performance by students, especially in secondary schools is needed.

Table 11. **Implementing the OECD Jobs Strategy – an overview of progress** *(cont.)*

Proposal	Action	Assessment/recommendation
• Provide more equitable financing of school districts	A few states plan to reformulate their educational funding systems. Systems have been declared unconstitutional in 14 states with 8 more law-suits pending.	State governments need to take an active role to make financing more equitable instead of fighting lawsuits. Federal government needs to make financing across states more equitable.
• Improve urban school systems	Some small state-run experiments in cities funding alternative schools and paying for private education are being run. Additional federal funding for charter schools may be budgeted.	The limited programmes and experiments need to be evaluated and expanded. The expansion of charter schools is a good step.
• Increase information about the quality of programmes provided by community colleges and technical institutes	None.	Performance and quality of community colleges and technical schools need to be made more widely known.

Source: OECD.

increased demand for child care resulting from the mandated decrease in welfare caseloads, states would seem to have enough savings from reduced caseloads to have already implemented a number of innovative programmes. In 1990, Congress and the President passed the Americans with Disabilities Act (ADA) that prohibited employer discrimination against the handicapped, but other programmes to help the disabled such as workers' compensation and Social Security have not been reformulated to be consistent with the new Act. Under current law it is possible to collect Social Security benefits for a permanent disability yet still sue an employer under the ADA.

With respect to education, the Committee recommended that the United States promote curriculum standards for primary and secondary schools, improve urban school systems and provide more equitable financing of school districts. As discussed above, the federal government has created programmes like the Goals 2000 initiative to promote national educational standards, while states have set up an information clearinghouse to measure relative performance. Additional money for charter schools has been included in the FY 1998 budget, while a few programmes to increase urban education alternatives, like the Milwaukee voucher experiment, have proceeded.[47] Reform of the tax system that pays for primary and secondary education has not moved forward much, as state governments seem more intent on fighting lawsuits aimed at encouraging a more equitable distribution of resources than developing their own plans. Since 1989, systems in 13 states have been declared unconstitutional, and eight more cases are pending. Despite court action, the proportion of public school spending funded by the state, as opposed to local governments, fell between 1987 and 1995, with only fourteen states showing an increase.

Health care reform

While the prospects for comprehensive health care reform remain bleak, the system is nevertheless undergoing substantial evolutionary change. An estimated 74 per cent of the insured population was in some sort of managed care programme in 1996 (33 per cent in health maintenance organisations or HMOs), up from only 29 per cent in 1988. Over the past year the number of people covered by HMOs has risen by 14 per cent. There is some question as to the amount of employer savings attributable to the spread of managed care as well as whether these economies represent merely one-time reductions. Employer cost decreases may be more a result of a declining fraction of workers covered and a large but similar decrease in premiums for both managed care and fee-for-service plans[48] (Table 12). Furthermore, most of the savings have been at the expense of providers who are increasingly compensated on a per-episode basis. Some have expressed the fear that the period of cost restraint may be coming to an end as doctors are now banding together to increase their bargaining power and because in 1995 the courts determined that HMOs and other such institutions could be sued for malpractice, ending the so-called "ERISA shield". Even though average health insurance costs per worker have risen only marginally in the last few years, the reputation for the quality of treatment provided by HMOs has suffered; for example, law makers' perceptions were that HMOs and employers have been narrowing coverage to such an extent that legislation was passed to guarantee 48 hours post-natal hospital care and patients' rights to seek emergency room treatment, forbidding so-called "drive-through mastectomies" and preventing "gag clauses" which stop physicians from discussing treatment not covered by the patient's insurance. Indeed, in September 1997 three large HMOs joined with two consumer groups to propose the imposition of 18 new federal standards on the industry in order to protect consumers.[49] Employers have also been offering steadily less choice in plans to their workers: by 1996 the share of employers offering only a single plan rose to 47 per cent from 41 per cent in 1995, and only 57 per cent offered any fee-for-service plans, down from 63 per cent the previous year. In addition, even if the decline in employer-provided health insurance has now largely ended, according to the General Accounting Office (1997a), 18 million employees had no such coverage available whatsoever and a further 5 million were offered insurance only for themselves and not for their families.

The result is that the key issue this past year (other than achieving budgetary savings on Medicare, described in the previous chapter) has been how to cover the rising number of uninsured children.[50] The Congressional Budget Office estimates that around 10.5 million children are uninsured at any one time, about 1 million more than in 1989, despite the fact that Medicaid has picked up about 6 million extra children, as the number covered by private insurance has decreased.[51] Medicaid now covers more than one in four children, and a further 3 million uninsured are eligible for Medicaid coverage but do not enrol because of the stigma attached to the programme, parental ignorance of their eligibility or

Table 12. **Trends in employer-provided health insurance costs, premiums and coverage**

	1981	1987	1991	1992	1993	1994	1995	1996
A. Private industry costs								
Employment cost index (second quarter, year on year) percentage change								
Total compensation			4.4	3.7	3.6	3.4	2.8	2.9
Health insurance			11.1	9.6	7.0	5.0	0.6	0.1
Level of employer costs per hour worked for health insurance (dollars)			1.01	1.02	1.10	1.14	1.06	1.04
As a per cent of total compensation			6.5	6.3	6.4	6.7	6.2	5.9
B. Health insurance premiums (dollars)								
Single person: fee for service			n.a.	1 701	1 846	1 940	1 992	n.a.
HMO			n.a.	1 677	1 816	1 912	1 920	n.a.
Family: fee for service			n.a.	4 437	4 814	5 059	5 196	n.a.
HMO			n.a.	4 433	4 801	5 056	5 076	n.a.
C. Coverage								
Current Population Survey data for per cent of civilian wage and salary workers with own employer-provided health insurance	62.0	56.6	55.5	54.2	57.6	58.5	n.a.	n.a
Employee Benefits Survey data for per cent of full-time workers in private industry participating in health insurance								
Small establishments	n.a.	n.a.	70	71	69	66	n.a.	n.a.
Medium and large establishments	97	93	83	83	82	82	n.a.	n.a.
Total	n.a.	n.a.	76	76	75	73	n.a.	n.a.
Per cent in fee-for-service plans								
Small establishments	n.a.	n.a.	71	69	62	62	n.a.	n.a.
Medium and large establishments	n.a.	79	67	59	50	50	n.a.	n.a.
Total	n.a.	n.a.	69	63	56	53	n.a.	n.a.

Source: Krueger and Levy (1997).

a belief that they can enrol at short notice if treatment is required. A Senate bill would have covered all uninsured children by providing states with a block grant worth $20 billion over five years, paid for by an increase in the federal excise tax on cigarettes from 24 to 67 cents per pack. But it was defeated and has, in any case, been superseded by part of the recent budget agreement that established a new block grant to states aiming to cover approximately 3.4 million children (about 2 million of which were previously uninsured) at a cost of $20 billion over five years, financed, in part, by a 15 cent-per-pack rise in cigarette taxes. The initiative allows states considerable flexibility: for example, coverage may be provided by expanding Medicaid or enrolling children in private plans.

Miscellaneous structural policy changes

There are a number of other areas where noteworthy policy change is underway. First, the 1996 *welfare reform* has begun to take effect[52] just as big declines in the number of recipients continue. Since the beginning of the Clinton Administration, the number of recipients has fallen by some 22 per cent (3.1 million people) to 4 per cent of the population, the lowest share since 1970. Much of the reduction may be merely the result of declining unemployment: 44 per cent of the decline according to the Administration (Council of Economic Advisers, 1997*b*). But states' experiments with welfare reforms, allowed under federal waivers, have also been shown to have made a large contribution (31 per cent) to reducing the rate of welfare receipt. Other factors that may have worked to shorten the welfare rolls are the expansions of the Earned Income Tax Credit and a rise in public spending on child care. It will take time to see how individuals and states respond to the incentives in the new law, in particular whether any states have diverted resources to other, more popular, uses. The Administration's goal is to move a million more people from welfare to work by the year 2000.

In June 1997 states' attorneys-general and representatives of US *tobacco* firms reached an agreement to end 40 state lawsuits and 17 class-action lawsuits against the industry. Tobacco companies agreed to pay up to $368 billion over the next 25 years (the amount would fall the greater the decline in cigarette consumption), to limit advertising and distribution of cigarettes with specific measures to discourage youth smoking, and to allow the Food and Drug Administration to regulate nicotine as a drug, with the ability to ban it after 2009. Of the average annual $15 billion payment, $5 billion would reimburse states for smoking-related Medicaid expenses, and $2 billion would fund health insurance for uninsured children. The rest would pay individual claims and fund anti-smoking initiatives. In exchange, tobacco companies would not face any class-action lawsuits and would not have to pay punitive damages for past industry misconduct. The Congress needs to enact the agreement into legislation for the President to sign. Congress has begun to consider the matter, but the Administration has demanded certain changes be made. Congress will have to decide the mechanics of the compensation scheme, especially important because it will help to determine the degree to which the tobacco companies – who will ask Congress to give them relief from anti-trust regulation – will decide to raise their prices. In order to fully offset the $15 billion annual cost, cigarette prices would have to increase as much as 40 per cent, or 75 cents a pack. In that event, the consumer price index would experience a one-time rise of 0.64 per cent.[53] But it would still leave US retail cigarette prices below those in many other OECD countries, as the current tax share is among the lowest in the zone.

Federal *housing policy* is also under review, as the United States Housing Act of 1937 is being rewritten. The main change would be to unlink rents in public housing from income in order to reduce disincentives to work.[54] The proposed bill would also require the unemployed to perform eight hours of community service per month or, in most cases, risk eviction. The main bone of contention is over the appropriate degree of ''targeting'', that is the share of units made available to those earning 30 per cent or less of the median income in the area: the current figure of 75 per cent is endorsed by the Administration, but Republicans favour a figure no higher than 50 per cent.

In the commercial area increasing attention is being paid to *personal bankruptcy law*. The number of filings has soared in recent years (see Chapter I), and write-offs reached $10.4 billion in 1995, up over 40 per cent in the year. A National Bankruptcy Review Commission was established in 1994 and is due to report by the end of the year. The key issue is whether the incentives to repay debts are too meagre, especially under Chapter 7 under which 70 per cent of all bankruptcies are now filed. Creditors feel that this procedure, which liquidates all debts, should be available only after a court determines that the debtor cannot repay his obligations. Otherwise, it seems reasonable that the debtor should be required to file under Chapter 13 under which a three- to five-year repayment plan is worked out. The Commission is also expected to recommend that refiling be barred for two years to curb abuse.

Another commercial law which is under review is the *patent law*. Legislation which has passed both House and Senate Committees would turn the Patent and Trademark Office into a semi-autonomous public corporation linked to the Commerce Department. Heavily debated is a clause which would require that patents be published 18 months after filing (as in the EU and Japan), rather than when granted; another contentious issue is whether anyone should be allowed to challenge a patent. Small businesses and independent inventors fear early publication could open their ideas to potential theft, which they would be in a weak position to pursue in the courts for lack of resources. Another attempt is also being made to pass new *product liability* legislation. A bill that is quite similar to last year's vetoed version is moving through Congress. It would cap punitive damages at $250 000 or double the sum of economic and non-economic damages: for large firms the cap would be the greater of the two, for small firms the lesser. The Administration wishes to avoid undermining the ability to get compensation in legitimate suits.

As previously announced, the US Treasury began to issue *indexed bonds* (Treasury Inflation-Protection Securities or TIPS) in January 1997 with an initial offering of $7 billion of 10-year maturity. Bids were received for more than 5 times the amount offered, and the clearing yield was 3.45 per cent. The issue was then reopened in April for a further $8 billion, but with a more normal coverage ratio of $2\frac{1}{4}$. The yield rose to 3.65 per cent, and it has remained near that figure since then. The July issue was for a five-year note, and a 30-year bond is planned for 1998. The Treasury expects total issuance eventually to reach $70 billion per year. But secondary market trading in this new instrument has been very limited because of their tax features[55] which make them most attractive to tax-deferred retirement plans and pension funds that hold them to maturity. The thin secondary market means they will provide little information on inflation expectations to policymakers except when there are simultaneous auctions of conventional and indexed bonds of identical maturities. Nevertheless, the Chicago Board of Trade has indicated that it wishes to trade futures and options on TIPS.

Finally, the *line item* veto, which was legislated in 1996 and would give the President the power to strike individual items from spending bills, was challenged before the courts by a number of legislators this year. It was to have taken effect at the beginning of this year and expire eight years later. In April a federal judge ruled it unconstitutional, but the Supreme Court decided that these legislators lack standing and that a legal challenge must await its exercise.

IV.   The economics of US immigration policy[56]

"Give me your tired, your poor, your huddled masses
yearning to breathe free..."

Introduction

So reads the famous inscription on the Statue of Liberty in the harbour of
New York City. While not alone, the United States has long been the principal
destination and the country of settlement for the world's emigrants. Migrants
have arrived in waves, and their arrival has always brought mixed feelings right
back to the days of original European settlement. But in time all these waves
have been successfully integrated into US society, as the "melting pot" has
worked its ways. Institutions of all kinds – economic, political and social – have
been set up in such a way as to allow new arrivals all the opportunity to succeed
or to fail according to their individual capabilities and efforts. Thus, if any
country can "handle" immigration and can benefit from it, it is surely the United
States.

Another wave of immigration has been underway now for some time without having shown clear signs of cresting, and it too has brought private and
public-policy reactions arising out of many of the same concerns as its
predecessors:[57] in particular, will these recent and expected immigrants manage
to find their way, to assimilate and to make a positive contribution to their new
homeland? Or will they cause social problems by working in illegal sweat shops
and in low-wage jobs more generally, displacing native-born workers and lowering their wages, thereby contributing to income inequality? Is the nation already
or at risk of becoming overcrowded, placing an unsustainable burden on the
environment? While many of the factors that will determine the answer to these

questions are the same as they have been historically, others are arguably different and unique. This chapter will examine to what extent there have been changes in the nature of the flow of immigrants and the conditions in which they struggle to make a new life for themselves and their families.

A brief description of the policy environment under which immigration has been governed in the United States will be provided at the outset. Following that, the basic character of the current stock of the foreign-born will be described, and the situation will be contrasted with those in other OECD Member countries. The importance of the changing source country distribution of US immigration for the average "quality" of immigrants and for their labour market outcomes will be emphasised. A third section will present some simple theoretical expectations for the effects of immigration on the domestic economy and subsequently review the empirical evidence on the labour market and distributional impacts, assimilation effects, price effects and influences on the public finances. A brief discussion of the demographic impacts of immigration follows. Thereafter some social aspects of immigration are covered, the possible relationship with crime in particular. The 1995-97 policy debate is then described, and the chapter finishes with the enumeration of some options for policy reform.

The current policy environment

The basic framework of US immigration policy remains the same today as it has been since the system became one based on family reunification in 1965 (Box 6). However, landmark legislation passed in 1986 (the Immigration Reform and Control Act or IRCA) provided for the legalisation of aliens in the country in an unlawful status since prior to 1982 as well as certain "Special Agricultural Workers" who had been in the labour force during the three years prior to application, ultimately 2.7 million people in all, mostly in 1989-91. It also authorised for the first time the use of employer sanctions for knowingly hiring, recruiting or referring illegal aliens for a fee.[58] At a time of expected future labour shortages in high-skilled occupations, the Immigration Act of 1990 modified the system to allow for more skills- or employment-based immigrants (a quota of 140 000 per year in five preference classes), more source-country diversity (*via* a special quota of "diversity immigrants" per year)[59] and, once family-sponsored immigrants are included, a flexible overall cap (in the sense that the number of

Box 6.   A brief history of US immigration

The absolute number of immigrants to the United States began to rise appreciably as from the end of the Napoleonic wars in Europe and the war of 1812-15 in North America. Cheaper and surer transport, deteriorating economic conditions in several source countries and rising US real wages owing to the industrial revolution were the main factors drawing immigrants. A *laissez faire* attitude on the part of the authorities,[1] given the nation's underpopulated condition, provided a sufficiently attractive environment for there to be no need for overt encouragement in the form of subsidies, in contrast with some other destination countries. This first wave reached a crescendo just after the turn of the century when nearly a million immigrants arrived every year, an annual rate of around 1 per cent of the population (Figure 18). The First and Second World Wars, as well as the Great Depression, limited the possibilities for such migratory flows to continue unabated, and policy had already turned increasingly restrictive.[2] Then Congress "closed the floodgates" by passing first the Quota Law of 1921 (the first comprehensive quantitative limits on immigration) and then the follow-up Immigration Act of 1924 which established the national origin quota system which operated for nearly half a century. It allocated visas in proportion to the national origins of the US population recorded in the 1890 Census, based on the view that certain races were superior and that the ethnic balance of the nation needed to be preserved. The result of the new system was that legal immigration levels dropped by nearly 40 per cent. But, in addition, its tightness led to a rise in illegal immigration, as Europeans migrated to Canada and Mexico, which were not subject to quotas, and then entered illegally. This led to the establishment and expansion of the Border Patrol. In 1940 the Immigration and Naturalization Service (INS) became part of the Justice Department, whereas previously immigration matters had been the responsibility of the Department of Labor.[3]

In 1952 the Immigration and Nationality Act eliminated race as a bar to immigration, modified the quota formula and introduced for the first time a special category for the family of US citizens and legal permanent residents. This presaged the Immigration and Nationality Act Amendments of 1965 (passed in an era when the focus on civil rights and economic freedoms was acute) that abolished the national origin quota system – which had in any case been steadily abandoned by means of special exemptions – and grounded the US system in family reunification. In a seven-category preference system for numerically restricted immigrants, "relative preferences" were given priority over "occupational preferences" and refugees, and immediate relatives of adult US citizens were exempted from quota limitations altogether. Since then, unforeseen by the policymakers of the time, immigration has steadily rebounded, averaging about double the level of 1821 to 1920 and more than triple that observed in the intervening national origin quota period, and culminating in more than a million immigrants a year thus far in the 1990s. But, given the much enlarged population base, recent immigration flows represent a significantly smaller share of the population – about 0.3 per cent per year.

(continued ont next page)

(continued)

Figure 18. **US IMMIGRATION LEVELS AND RATES**

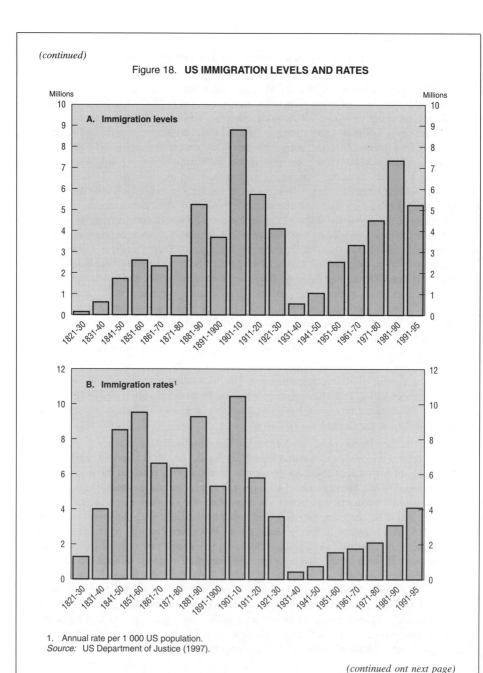

1. Annual rate per 1 000 US population.
Source: US Department of Justice (1997).

(continued ont next page)

104

(continued)

Nevertheless, in stock terms, the foreign-born population reached 20 million in 1990, double the level it had been for most of the century up to 1970.

---

1. Immigrants of almost all types were welcomed for much of the Nineteenth Century, with one noteworthy exception: those from China were barred as from 1882. Along with other destination countries such as Argentina, Australia, Brazil and Canada, the United States began to impose restrictions with increasing frequency thereafter, as the frontier closed and pressures on existing relative economic positions of different groups were felt (Timmer and Williamson, 1996). Late in the century the share of immigrants from northern and western Europe fell, replaced by those from eastern and southern Europe. The stage was set for the first official recognition of a potential problem with the establishment by the Congress of the Joint Commission on Immigration (the "Dillingham Commission") in 1907. It recommended the institution of a literacy requirement and the continuation of the ban on Asian immigrants.

2. Various pieces of legislation added to the list of inadmissible immigrants, introduced a head tax, codified the grounds for deportation and ultimately instituted a ban on all Asian immigrants and an immigrant literacy test in 1917. For more details on the history of US legislation dealing with immigration and naturalisation, see US Department of Justice (1997).

3. The Federation for American Immigration Reform (1992) is critical of this arrangement, arguing that oversight by Congressional Judiciary Committees composed almost exclusively of lawyers, has led to a lack of interest in the economic consequences of immigration. At the end of its term, the US Commission on Immigration Reform (1997) recommended that the INS be dismantled, with its various functions allocated to the Justice, State and Labor Departments.

immediate relatives, assumed to be 254 000 per year, remains unlimited) of 675 000 per year (excluding refugees and asylees) as from FY 1995[60] (Table 13). Under the terms of the Refugee Act of 1980 refugees are those who are unable or unwilling to remain in or return to their country of nationality because of persecution or the well-founded fear of persecution and apply for admission while still outside the United States (US Department of Justice, 1997). They enter as non-immigrants but may adjust their status after a year's continuous residence in the United States to lawful permanent resident. Their numbers are controlled at the global level by annual ceilings negotiated between the Administration and the Congress. The situation of asylees is essentially the same, except that they are already in the country; the number of their adjustments (legal acquisition of that status) is now limited to 10 000 per year, with a backlog of pending applications in June 1997 of 421 000, down from a peak of nearly half a million in March 1996. Since January 1995 asylum applicants have been ineligible for work

Table 13. **Immigration by category: quotas and outcomes for FY 1996**

Categories	Quotas	FY 1996	Shares of legal immigration
Family based, total	Unlimited	596 000	69.4
of which:	Unlimited	302 000	33.1
1st preference: Unmarried adult children of US citizens	23 400	21 000	2.3
2nd preference: Spouses and unmarried adult children of legal immigrants	114 200	183 000	20.1
3rd preference: Married adult children of US citizens	23 400	25 000	2.7
4th preference: Siblings of US citizens	65 000	65 000	7.1
Employment based, total	140 000	118 000	12.9
of which:	40 040	28 000	3.1
1st preference: Priority workers	40 040	18 000	2.0
2nd preference: Professionally exceptional	40 040	63 000	6.9
3rd preference: Skilled workers and professionals	9 940	8 000	0.9
4th preference: Special immigrants	9 940	1 000	0.1
5th preference: Investors			
Lottery/Diversity	55 000	58 000	6.4
Refugees and asylees	100 000	140 000	15.4
Legal immigrants, total		912 000	100.0
Illegal alien settlers (estimate)		300 000	–
Total immigration, 1996		**1 212 000**	–

Source: The Federation for American Immigration Reform and the Center for Immigration Studies.

permits until their applications are granted or unless they remain unresolved for more than 180 days.

The actual inflow of recent legal immigrants by entry class is shown in Figure 19. The longer-term rise in immediate family admissions (which have risen steadily from 33 000 in 1965 to 302 000 in 1996) may be giving rise to a phenomenon of "chain migration" whereby admission of one immigrant leads to eligibility and admission of others. IRCA legalisations have caused the only major volatility since 1980, although worker preferences have grown thanks to the changes made in the 1990 legislation. Currently, however, all categories of family-based immigration quotas are oversubscribed, although most employment-based categories are undersubscribed.[61] Refugee and asylee adjustments have averaged just over 100 000 per year for the past two decades, slightly more in the early 1990s and then substantially less in 1995 and 1996. Their share of total immigrant inflows has fallen from an average of around one-quarter over the period 1945-90 to less than half that in the last two years; refugee approval rates have fallen from over 90 per cent in the early 1980s to 71 per cent in 1995, and asylee rates have been only around 20 per cent of late.

The United States also admits around 600 000 non-immigrants per year who have the right to remain and work in general for up to six years.[62] This category has grown rapidly since 1981 – an average annual rate of around 11 per cent. While they may form only a small share of all non-immigrant entries into the country (including tourists, for example), they are about five times as numerous as those admitted as immigrants under employment preferences. They may have similar labour market impacts,[63] especially as they often eventually become permanent residents and as over 80 per cent are skilled workers, a higher share than in other OECD countries (OECD, 1997a, Table I.1). Legal and illegal immigrants and non-immigrants together comprise the foreign-born population, also referred to as the immigrant population in the context of labour market studies based on Census data and in the remainder of this chapter.[64]

Illegal immigrants are those who either enter without inspection (estimated to be about 60 per cent of the total) or overstay the expiration date of the visa under which they legally entered (the remaining 40 per cent). Recent estimates by officials of the Immigration and Naturalization Service (Warren, 1997) put the estimated number of illegal aliens in October 1996 at around 5 million (over a fifth of the total foreign born), at least as many as before the 1986 legalisation

Figure 19. **RECENT INFLOWS OF PERMANENT SETTLERS BY ENTRY CLASS**

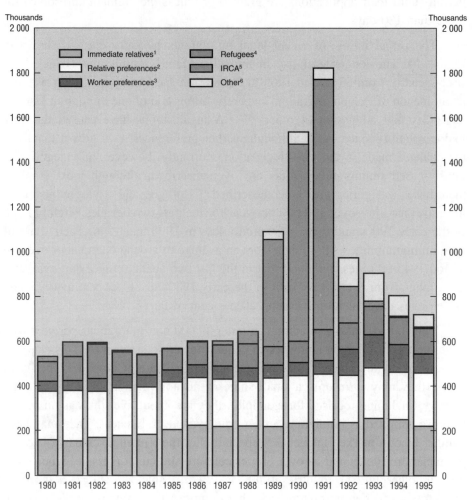

1. Numerically unrestricted immigrants comprising spouses, unmarried minor children, and orphans adopted by US citizens as well as parents of adult US citizens.
2. Numerically restricted relatives comprising: unmarried adult children of US citizens; spouses and unmarried children of permanent resident aliens; married children of US citizens; brothers and sisters of adult US citizens.
3. Prior to 1992, data include members of professions of persons of exceptional ability in the sciences and arts, skilled and unskilled workers in short supply, and special immigrant visas. Data include immigrants issued employment-based preference visas from 1992 on.
4. The Refugee Act of 1980 now governs all admissions.
5. Under the 1986 Immigration Reform and Control Act, foreigners who had been accorded temporary legal status could apply, between December 1988 and December 1990, for a permanent residence permit.
6. In recent years, these are primarily entrants under the Diversity category.
Source: OECD (1997*a*).

was passed. An estimated 54 per cent of the total stock of illegal aliens are Mexicans, and a rising share are thought to be other Latin Americans who come through Mexico; almost all of these entered without inspection. About 40 per cent reside in California. Official estimates of the net flow vary from around 250 000 to 300 000 migrants per year, around one-third of total legal immigration, but gross inflows may be as high as 2 million per year (Espenshade, 1990), implying that most enter and leave again after working for a short period (so-called ''sojourner migrants''). Indeed, in 1992, 2.3 millions Mexican adults (4 per cent of the working-age population) reported that they had migrated to the United States at least once in their lifetimes in order to work (OECD, 1996d). However, the rate of back-and-forth movement of labour seems to be slowing (Binational Study on Migration, 1997).

The magnitude and nature of recent US immigration

Critics of US immigration maintain that its scale is too large. Just how important is US immigration then in volume terms? In the last Census year (1990), 19.8 million or nearly 8 per cent of the US population was foreign born (including illegal aliens), up from a century low of 4.7 per cent in 1970, but well below the peak level of nearly 15 per cent of the total population in 1910. Estimates from the Current Population Survey point to a foreign-born share of 9.3 per cent in March 1996, the same as in both 1850 and 1940. With continued immigration at recent levels, the foreign-born population is projected to reach 10.2 per cent of the total population in 2000. It is difficult to make international comparisons of such stock figures, as it is customary in most other OECD Member countries to define the immigrant population as those of foreign nationality, rather than the foreign-born; thus naturalised citizens are not considered to be immigrants, whereas temporary workers are.[65] Where national definitions are comparable, it can be seen that despite the large increase in the US foreign-born share, it remains lower than in Australia (around 22 per cent) and Canada (near 16 per cent) (OECD, 1997a); and Borjas (1994) cites figures of 17 per cent for Switzerland, 11 per cent for France and 9 per cent for the United Kingdom, as well as United Nations data for 1989 showing a world foreign-born share of 1.2 per cent.

The flow of immigration is also difficult to compare across countries. Net immigration to the United States is composed of gross immigration (legal and illegal) of over a million per year less gross emigration for which data are scarce, but which best estimates put at about 300 000 per year[66] (Ahmed and Robinson, cited in Smith and Edmonston, 1997). US inflow data represent issuance of permanent residence permits, not physical entry into the country – in 1995, 47 per cent of all immigrants were already in the country and merely adjusted their status. Average annual net immigration into the United States has risen to over 0.3 per cent of the population since 1990. By that measure it ranks around ninth out of 26 OECD Member countries for which data are available (Table 14);

Table 14. **The net immigration rate in OECD countries**

Average annual net immigration as a share of population in per cent

	1961-70	1971-80	1981-90	1991-94
Luxembourg	0.47	0.76	0.41	1.05
Greece	−0.39	0.29	0.17	0.72
Germany	0.50	0.26	0.45	0.67
Austria	0.10	0.10	0.15	0.64
Switzerland	0.59	−0.14	0.38	0.64
Canada	0.44	0.51	0.47	0.60
Sweden	0.30	0.11	0.20	0.36
Australia	0.75	0.47	0.67	0.32
United States	0.20	0.20	0.21	0.32
Norway	0.31	0.12	−0.11	0.29[2]
New Zealand	0.00	0.11	0.13	0.24
Netherlands	0.11	0.25	0.18	0.27
Denmark	0.06	0.05	0.09	0.22
Italy	−0.22	0.00	0.13	0.22
Belgium	0.16	0.11	0.01	0.20
Finland	−0.39	−0.06	0.09	0.18
Turkey		−0.02	0.29	0.17
United Kingdom	−0.01	−0.04	0.05	0.17[2]
France	0.46	0.11	0.10	0.16[1]
Spain	−0.16	0.00	0.00	0.07
Czech Republic		−0.05	−0.03	0.02
Iceland	−0.23	−0.20	0.01	0.01
Japan	0.00	−0.01	−0.01	0.00
Portugal	−1.28	0.39	−0.30	−0.01
Poland		−0.06	−0.07	−0.04
Ireland	−0.51	0.33	−0.59	−0.14

1. 1991-92.
2. 1991-93.
Source: OECD, *Labour Force Statistics.*

most notably, it ranks behind even such traditional source countries for US immigrants as Germany, Austria and Greece. Immigration has been making a steadily increasing contribution to overall US population growth in recent decades and is now playing an even greater role than in the first decade of the century because of reduced native fertility (Table 15). The recent figure of nearly a third would, however, still place it only fifteenth out of 26 in this regard. A number of countries – Greece, Italy and Luxembourg in particular – have been virtually entirely reliant on immigration for population growth in recent years, but in

Table 15. **The contribution of net immigration to the change in total population**[1]
in OECD countries

Per cent

	1960-70	1970-80	1980-90	1990-94
Greece	−74.4	n.a.	n.a.	112.5
Italy	−31.3	n.a.	n.a.	107.7
Luxembourg	57.8	96.9	88.3	97.6
Switzerland	29.3	−85.7	61.1	73.9
Denmark	8.6	11.9	340.3	69.2
Austria	19.9	27.1	57.2	64.7
Sweden	43.6	34.8	71.2	57.2
Belgium	34.6	45.4	18.0	53.0
Canada	28.8	30.6	39.8	47.0
United Kingdom	−7.2	−38.4	27.4	46.0[4]
Spain	−15.0	−0.1	−5.9	44.3
Norway	n.a.	19.8	36.8	43.7[4]
Netherlands	9.0	30.9	34.0	37.7
Finland	−104.8	−19.2	21.0	35.0
United States	16.2	19.9	21.7	30.8
France	44.1	16.2	19.1	29.6[3]
Australia	40.7	32.1	44.6	29.0
New Zealand	15.3	7.5	n.a.	24.5
Germany	53.9	138.6	175.6	11.9
Turkey	n.a.	n.a.	12.6	9.0
Iceland	−15.7	−20.3	0.4	0.8
Japan	−0.2	−1.0	−2.7	−0.4
Portugal	250.7[2]	48.5	−621.4	−10.3
Poland	n.a.	−6.6	−9.9	−14.6
Ireland	−114.0	23.9	−225.5	−29.4
Czech Republic	n.a.	n.a.	−114.2	−29.6[2]

1. Negative figures imply net emigration unless otherwise indicated.
2. Net immigration was positive, but population declined in the Czech Republic in the 1990s; population also fell in Portugal in the 1960s, but there was net emigration as well.
3. 1990-92.
4. 1990-93.
Source: OECD, *Labour Force Statistics.*

general natural increase has been more important than net immigration in total population growth in most OECD countries (OECD, 1997a). International comparisons are also possible for the composition of immigration by type of admission: in 1991 the US share attributable to family reunification (at nearly 50 per cent) was one of the highest for 13 OECD Member countries, while the employment-related share was near the mean and the refugee/asylee share was rather low (Smith and Edmonston, Table 2.12).

Table 16. **An overview of native and foreign-born populations, March 1994**

Per cent, except as indicated

| | Native | Foreign born | | | | | |
| | | Total | of which: born in Mexico | Arrived | | | |
				before 1970	1970-79	1980-89	1990-94
Total (thousands)	237 184	22 568	6 264	4 974	4 781	8 311	4 502
Characteristic							
Demographics							
Share under 18 years old	28.4	11.0	15.2	–	1.8	14.8	26.1
Share 65 years old and over	11.9	11.7	4.6	37.5	6.1	3.9	3.4
Share female	51.2	50.7	45.7	56.5	51.5	47.3	49.6
Share non-white	15.8	31.6	7.5	13.3	36.0	37.6	36.3
Share of Hispanic origin	6.9	45.5	97.8	31.4	48.8	53.0	43.8
Educational attainment[1]							
Share without high school diploma	17.1	36.0	71.2	32.0	37.8	39.1	33.3
Share with college degree	22.1	23.1	4.5	19.7	22.1	22.8	32.4
Labour force status[2]							
Participation rate	65.8	62.7	66.3	49.9	70.8	69.5	55.3
Unemployment rate	6.8	9.1	11.1	5.6	8.4	7.0	12.2
Income in 1993[2]							
Share without income	6.0	13.6	20.4	4.2	10.6	15.6	26.9
Median per capita income[3] (dollars)	15 876	12 179	n.a.	14 473	15 121	11 580	8 393
Poverty status							
Share in poverty	14.4	23.0	36.0	10.8	16.3	26.4	37.3

1. For those 25 years old and over.
2. For those 16 years old and over.
3. For those with income.
Source: OECD calculations based on data from the Current Population Survey published in Table No. 55 of the *Statistical Abstract of the United States 1996.*

Yet, aside from volume considerations, much of the debate about immigration policy reform revolves around whether the nature of immigrant flows is appropriate. In this section several basic descriptive characteristics of immigrant "quality" will be examined to evaluate the contention that "immigration is not what it used to be". Before that, however, it is useful to provide a brief overview of the foreign-born population and, in particular, what characteristics set them apart from their native counterparts. In demographic terms the foreign born are less likely to be children under the age of 18,[67] equally likely to be senior citizens, more likely to be women[68] and much more likely to be non-white or of Hispanic origin, especially if they have arrived since 1970 (Table 16). In addition, a slightly higher proportion of recent immigrant households are married-couple families, and over 70 per cent of them have children under 18, compared with 46 per cent in the aggregate (Smith and Edmonston, 1997, Table 2-8). A much larger proportion have less than a high-school education, although a marginally greater fraction has a college degree (see below).

The changing source country distribution

Prior to 1970 the overwhelming majority of cumulative total immigration had been from other developed nations; nearly 79 per cent was from Europe. By 1990, census data show that the European share had dropped to 22 per cent (Table 17), although there has been some recent revival in migration from the former Soviet Union and Poland. Nonetheless, there has been a steady decline in the number of migrants from traditional US source countries like Germany, Italy, Canada and the United Kingdom. In their place have come migrants from Latin America, especially Mexico, and Asia, from which there may well have been some pent-up demand left over from the previous entry restrictions on Asians.[69] Indeed, the share of Mexicans in total immigration flows is still rising, and in 1996 there were an estimated 7 million Mexican-born people in the United States (Binational Study on Migration, 1997), about 2½ per cent of the US population, nearly 8 per cent of Mexico's population and more than the entire population of the seven smallest OECD Member countries. While the share of Asians in US total migratory inflows has begun to decline in the 1990s and its stock share seems to have reached a plateau, Mexico's share is still rising and may continue to do so, independent of illegal flows, given the very recent eligibility of the IRCA-legalised population to sponsor family members.[70]

Table 17. **Immigrant population by place of birth, 1970-90**[1]

Per cent of total

	1970 Stock	1971-80 Flow[2]	1980 Stock	1981-90 Flow[2]	1990 Stock	1991-95 Flow[2]
Mexico	7.9	14.2	15.6	22.6	21.7	28.5
Caribbean	5.4	16.5	8.9	11.9	9.8	10.2
Cuba	4.6	5.9	4.3	2.0	3.7	1.2
Dominican Republic	..	3.3	1.2	3.4	1.8	4.2
Jamaica	..	3.1	1.4	0.3	1.7	1.7
Canada	8.4	3.8	6.0	2.1	3.8	2.0
Central America	0.6	3.0	2.5	6.4	5.7	5.7
South America	2.7	6.6	4.0	6.3	5.2	5.4
Colombia	..	1.7	1.0	1.7	1.4	1.3
Ecuador	..	1.1	0.6	0.8	0.5	0.7
Asia	8.6	35.3	18.0	37.3	25.2	30.1
China	1.8	2.8	2.0	4.7	2.7	4.0
India	0.5	3.7	1.5	3.4	2.3	3.5
Japan	1.3	1.1	1.6	0.6	1.5	0.7
Republic of Korea	0.9	6.0	2.1	4.5	2.9	1.8
Philippines	1.9	7.9	3.6	7.5	4.6	5.7
Vietnam	..	3.8	1.6	3.8	2.7	2.8
Others	2.2	10.1	5.7	12.7	8.5	11.6
Europe	59.4	17.8	36.6	10.4	22.0	14.6
Austria	2.2	0.2	1.0	0.2	0.4	0.2
France	1.1	0.6	0.9	0.4	0.6	0.4
Former CSFR	1.7	0.1	0.8	0.1	0.4	0.1
Germany	8.7	1.7	6.0	1.3	3.6	1.0
Greece	1.8	2.1	1.5	0.5	0.9	0.2
Hungary	2.0	0.1	1.0	0.1	0.6	0.1
Ireland	2.6	0.3	1.4	0.4	0.9	1.0
Italy	10.5	2.9	5.9	0.9	2.9	1.0
Netherlands	1.1	0.2	0.7	0.2	0.5	0.1
Norway	1.0	0.1	0.5	0.1	0.2	0.1
Poland	5.7	0.8	3.0	1.1	2.0	2.1
Portugal	0.9	2.3	1.5	0.6	1.1	0.3
Romania	0.7	0.3	0.5	0.4	0.5	0.5
Sweden	1.3	0.1	0.5	0.2	0.3	0.1
United Kingdom	7.4	3.1	4.8	0.2	3.2	1.7
Former USSR	4.8	0.9	2.9	0.8	2.0	4.7
Former Yugoslavia	1.7	0.7	1.1	0.3	0.7	0.4
Others	4.1	1.3	2.6	0.6	1.2	0.4
Other and not stated	7.0	2.7	8.3	3.0	6.5	3.4
Total	100.0	100.0	100.0	100.0	100.0	100.0
In millions	9.7	4.5	14.1	7.3	19.8	5.2
% of total population	4.7		6.2		7.9	

1.   Includes legalisation under the 1986 Immigration Reform and Control Act as from 1989.
2.   Fiscal years.
Source: US Department of Justice (1997).

Although cross-country comparisons are difficult, it would seem that the United States is somewhat unique in that its migratory flows still come to such a substantial degree from countries with low per capita incomes. In 1995, the weighted average GDP per capita of all source countries of migratory inflows (where data are available; they cover about 80 per cent of the total) was only $3 732, 14 per cent of the US figure (Table 18). In 1985, the ratio had been similar. Thus, it is highly likely that world output and income rise when immigrants relocate to the United States, probably because of its favourable institutional and economic environment as well as a greater capital endowment. Not all other countries have similar data, but the unweighted average across a dozen other OECD host countries in 1995 was more than triple the US 14 per cent outcome. The other major settlement countries, Canada and Australia, both had even higher figures, and both had boosted them substantially since 1985. Their points-based systems may have played an important role in this regard.

The importance of the longer-term shift from developed to developing countries as the primary source of US immigrants lies in the different amounts of skills and human capital and other characteristics valued by the labour market they possess.[71] It has been argued (Borjas, 1987) that the United States, with its open markets and dispersed income distribution, will attract relatively high-skilled candidates from wealthy source countries with narrow income distributions and, conversely, the low-skilled from among those in poor countries with wide distributions; this is termed the Roy model. Thus, independent of average skill levels in today's mix of source countries as compared with those of generations ago, source-country averages may give a misleading reading on the evolution of skill levels.

The regional distribution of settlement of the immigrant flows is largely determined by the sources of those flows because of the existence of ethnic and national enclaves and networks of job provision and social integration. Historically, most immigrants had entered the United States by crossing the Atlantic Ocean and then settled in the industrial north-east. The ''new'' immigrants, on the other hand, have come across the Pacific and the southern border and have tended to settle in California, Texas and Florida, in addition to New York and New Jersey. By 1990, California was home to one-third of the nation's foreign-born population, nearly double its 1970 share and nearly triple its overall population share. Nearly 22 per cent of its population was foreign born, compared with

Table 18. **Per capita income in source countries, 1985 and 1995**[1]

	1985				1995				
	Per cent of immigrants counted	Weighted source country GDP per capita	Ratio to United States	Ratio source country GDP per capita to host country GDP per capita	Per cent of immigrants counted	Weighted source country GDP per capita	Weighted source country GDP per capita 1985 = 100	Ratio to United States	Ratio source country GDP per capita to host country GDP per capita
United States	77.9	2 155	1.00	0.13	79.3	3 732	173	1.00	0.14
Australia	70.6	4 392	2.04	0.41	74.2	9 630	219	2.58	0.50
Belgium	21.5	3 457	1.60	0.43	90.3	19 026	550	5.10	0.72
Canada	72.6	4 021	1.87	0.30	58.3	10 658	265	2.86	0.56
Denmark	–	–	–	–	54.6	17 959	–	4.81	0.54
France	48.4	1 278	0.59	0.13	75.4	7 480	585	2.00	0.28
Germany	31.9	3 534	1.64	0.35	59.7	6 373	180	1.71	0.22
Japan	76.7	4 997	2.32	0.45	73.4	9 098	182	2.44	0.22
Netherlands	62.8	5 594	2.60	0.63	29.5	16 054	287	4.30	0.63
Norway	64.7	8 840	4.10	0.58	56.1	18 001	204	4.82	0.54
Sweden	68.8	7 102	3.30	0.59	62.0	13 366	188	3.58	0.52
Switzerland	78.3	6 581	3.05	0.46	74.9	14 222	216	3.81	0.33
United Kingdom	88.7	4 820	2.24	0.60	83.8	7 588	157	2.03	0.40

1. Some caution is required in interpreting these data. They are based on inflows only for the two years and therefore omit variations in intervening years. They also suffer from substantial differences in definition as to what constitutes immigration; in particular, US data exclude temporary workers, especially intra-company transferees, most often included in the data for other countries. Finally, emigrants may not be typical of the residents of source countries.

Source: OECD.

around 9 per cent in 1970. And 46 per cent of the increase in the nation's foreign-born population from 1970 to 1990 was located in California. Thus far in the 1990s immigration has continued at a robust pace into California, as well as Texas and Florida, but there has been something of a return to New York and New Jersey as the destination of choice for many immigrants (Table 19). While the foreign born have comprised about three-quarters of the population increase in California, their arrival has prevented a significant depopulation in the north-east in general and in New York (especially New York City) and Massachusetts in particular. Given that 93 per cent of the foreign born resided in metropolitan areas in 1990, compared with 73 per cent of the native-born, it is not surprising that they are highly concentrated; for example, the foreign-born share of Miami's population in 1990 was 46 per cent, Los Angeles' was 33 per cent and New York's reached 33 per cent in 1995 (up from 18 per cent in 1970).

Despite the shift towards developing countries as the source of immigrants, the quality and skills of recent immigrants has almost certainly increased in recent decades but not sufficiently to prevent a decline relative to native-born Americans. Census data show clearly that male foreign-born workers have increasing numbers of years of schooling: the share of the foreign born with less than 12 years of education (the equivalent to a high-school diploma) fell from over half in 1970 to 40 per cent in 1980 and to 30 per cent in 1990,[72] and the share with a college degree doubled to around one in four (Table 20). But the lower tail of the distribution of native-born workers was increasing its education level even faster over this period in response to generally high and rising returns to human capital. The number of native-born workers without a high-school diploma fell by nearly a third in the 1980s alone, while the increase in those with some post-secondary experience was more than half. Thus, foreign-born workers comprised 20 per cent of all workers with less than 12 years of schooling in 1990, up from only about 6 per cent in 1970; the corresponding figures for California are even more striking (Schoeni et al., 1996).

But there are significant differences in the levels of and trends in educational attainment among immigrants from different source countries and therefore, given regional differences in settlement patterns, among regions as well. Indeed virtually the entire increase in the wage gap between immigrants and natives from 1970 to 1990 is attributable to changing national origin (Smith and Edmonston, 1997). While, as stated above, the average number of years of

117

Table 19. Net immigration by state in the 1990s

Annual averages, 1 April 1990 to 1 July 1995

	Contribution[1]	Rate[2]		Contribution[1]	Rate[2]
United States	**28.3**	**3.0**			
Northeast	**147.9**	**3.6**	**Midwest**	**20.3**	**1.4**
New England	**130.5**	**2.0**	**East North Central**	**24.8**	**1.6**
Maine	23.1	0.5	Ohio	11.6	0.6
New Hampshire	12.8	0.8	Indiana	5.4	0.5
Vermont	13.6	1.0	Illinois	57.9	3.8
Massachusetts	145.6	2.6	Michigan	23.6	1.2
Rhode Island[3]	−50.0	1.3	Wisconsin	7.8	0.7
Connecticut[3]	−308.3	2.1	**West North Central**	**10.8**	**0.8**
Middle Atlantic	**151.5**	**4.2**	Minnesota	10.3	1.0
New York	396.6	6.1	Iowa	12.3	0.5
New Jersey	90.2	4.7	Missouri	9.2	0.7
Pennsylvania	33.3	1.0	North Dakota	66.7	0.6
			South Dakota	6.1	0.5
South	**14.2**	**2.0**	Nebraska	10.2	0.7
South Atlantic	**14.2**	**2.0**	Kansas	13.6	0.9
Delaware	7.8	1.1			
Maryland	24.8	2.5	**West**	**34.2**	**5.7**
District of Columbia[3]	−30.2	5.2	**Mountain**	**6.9**	**1.8**
Virginia	16.6	2.1	Montana	2.8	0.5
West Virginia	5.7	0.2	Idaho	4.5	1.2
North Carolina	4.1	0.6	Wyoming	3.7	0.4
South Carolina	3.7	0.4	Colorado	6.4	1.6
Georgia	5.8	1.2	New Mexico	10.6	2.1
Florida	20.9	3.6	Arizona	9.0	2.4
East South Central	**3.6**	**0.4**	Utah	4.8	1.1
Kentucky	4.6	0.4	Nevada	5.8	2.6
Tennessee	3.7	0.5	**Pacific**	**53.4**	**7.1**
Alabama	3.3	0.3	Washington	11.3	2.4
Mississippi	2.5	0.2	Oregon	9.4	1.8
West South Central	**18.8**	**2.7**	California	75.4	8.6
Arkansas	3.0	0.3	Alaska	9.3	1.7
Louisiana	9.8	0.5	Hawaii	41.8	5.5
Oklahoma	8.3	0.7			
Texas	21.4	4.0			

1. Net migration from abroad as a percentage of the net change in population.
2. Net migration from abroad per thousand average population over the period.
3. In all cases net migration from abroad was positive but the population declined.
Source: Statistical Abstract of the United States, 1996.

schooling of the typical migrant has improved in recent decades, the improvement has not been uniform. Average attainment has moved up for those from some sources, especially Europe and Canada (Table 21), but a remarkably high

Table 20. **Educational attainment among employed immigrants and natives, 1980 and 1990**[1]

| Skill level | Employed labour force (levels in thousands and shares in %) | | | | | | | | Change 1980 to 1990 (%) | | | Immigrant share of education level (%) | |
| | 1980 | | | | 1990 | | | | Immigrant | Native | Total | 1980 | 1990 |
	Immigrant		Native		Immigrant		Native						
Men													
Dropouts	1 451	41.4	11 987	25.5	1 874	33.1	7 198	14.1	29.1	-40.0	-32.5	10.8	20.7
High school	800	22.8	17 007	36.2	1 373	24.3	18 156	35.6	71.7	6.8	9.7	4.5	7.0
Some college	486	13.9	8 633	18.4	1 033	18.2	13 306	26.1	112.7	54.1	57.2	5.3	7.2
College degree	769	21.9	9 387	20.0	1 381	24.4	12 401	24.3	79.6	32.1	35.7	7.6	10.0
Total	3 505	100.0	47 015	100.0	5 661	100.0	51 061	100.0	61.5	8.6	12.3	6.9	10.0
Women													
Dropouts	994	37.2	7 817	20.8	1 137	26.8	4 923	11.0	14.5	-37.0	-31.2	11.3	18.8
High school	835	31.3	16 549	44.0	1 250	29.5	17 429	38.8	49.7	5.3	7.4	4.8	6.7
Some college	432	16.2	7 307	19.4	936	22.1	13 094	29.2	116.7	79.2	81.3	5.6	6.7
College degree	410	15.4	5 930	15.8	912	21.5	9 442	21.0	122.4	59.2	63.3	6.5	8.8
Total	2 671	100.0	37 603	100.0	4 236	100.0	44 889	100.0	58.6	19.4	22.0	6.6	8.6
Total													
Dropouts	2 445	39.6	19 804	23.4	3 011	30.4	12 121	12.6	23.2	-38.8	-32.0	11.0	19.9
High school	1 635	26.5	33 556	39.7	2 624	26.5	35 585	37.1	60.5	6.0	8.6	4.6	6.9
Some college	918	14.9	15 941	18.8	1 969	19.9	26 401	27.5	114.6	65.6	68.3	5.4	6.9
College degree	1 179	19.1	15 317	18.1	2 293	23.2	21 843	22.8	94.5	42.6	46.3	7.1	9.5
Total	6 177	100.0	84 618	100.0	9 897	100.0	95 949	100.0	60.2	13.4	16.6	6.8	9.4

Source: Jaeger (1995) and OECD.

Table 21. **Education, English language skills and unemployment rates of US immigrants**

Per cent

	Four or more years of college[1]		Less than 5 years of elementary school[1]		Speak English poorly[2]		Unemployment rate	
	1970-80 arrivals in 1980	1980-90 arrivals in 1990	1970-80 arrivals in 1980	1980-90 arrivals in 1990	1970-80 arrivals in 1980	1980-90 arrivals in 1990	1970-80 arrivals in 1980	1980-90 arrivals in 1990
Immigrants from:								
Europe	20.4	34.0	11.7	4.3	23.7	33.8	6.7	5.8
Greece	10.6	29.1	10.0	6.5	34.5	44.2	7.6	7.1
Italy	8.3	26.7	17.7	5.7	36.8	45.8	9.1	6.6
United Kingdom	30.5	39.5	0.8	1.3	0.4	1.7	4.3	3.8
Asia	34.7	37.2	7.4	9.7	25.2	59.3	6.2	7.1
China	27.6	31.9	15.8	15.1	51.0	78.5	4.3	6.4
India	63.1	58.9	2.8	4.4	8.7	11.5	6.2	6.4
Korea	31.6	32.8	4.2	5.4	30.7	72.8	6.1	6.2
Philippines	47.9	45.6	5.8	4.6	8.8	38.0	4.7	5.7
Vietnam	11.9	10.0	10.4	16.6	41.4	75.1	8.2	10.4
North and Central America	6.9	7.6	21.7	19.9	47.7	68.2	9.7	11.8
Canada	30.0	39.6	0.9	0.6	1.4	3.9	4.4	3.9
Cuba	10.3	7.4	11.4	11.3	54.7	73.7	8.4	11.2
Dominican Republic	3.4	8.2	21.3	14.9	59.9	74.2	12.3	18.0
Haiti	9.5	6.8	10.9	14.0	29.3	63.1	13.3	15.3
Jamaica	9.7	10.1	4.0	4.2	0.6	2.0	8.8	10.4
Mexico	2.7	4.4	32.9	26.9	60.5	78.5	10.3	12.0
South America	18.3	20.0	4.5	5.3	29.9	55.5	8.0	8.8
Africa	43.3	44.1	2.7	3.2	8.6	28.2	8.0	8.1
Total	**22.7**	**23.7**	**12.8**	**12.6**	–	–	–	–
Per memorandum:								
All foreign born	15.8	20.4	11.6	11.4	21.5	47.0	6.9	7.8
Foreign born who arrived prior to 1970 or 1980	13.2	18.7	11.1	10.8	13.7	37.2	5.8	6.4
Natives	16.3	20.3	2.9	0.4	0.6	2.3	6.5	6.2

1. Refers to those 25 years old and over.
2. Per cent of persons 5 years old and over who spoke a language other than English at home who claimed to speak English "not well" or "not at all" in 1980 and 1990, respectively.

Source: Greenwood *et al.* (1997) based on data from the US Bureau of the Census.

proportion of migrants from some source countries still arrive with very little if any formal schooling. Mexico, the number one source country, stands out in this respect: more than one in four migrants from Mexico who arrived in the 1980s still had less than five years of schooling. With Mexicans overwhelmingly settling in the West and Southwest, the education gap is most apparent in these parts of the country. The labour market effects of immigration (discussed below) will therefore flow not only from varying immigrant concentrations but also from differences in immigrant characteristics which influence their ability to assimilate as well as the native and previous immigrant workers with whom they compete.

Another important skill is the ability to speak English fluently. In this respect immigrant quality clearly declined from the 1970s to the 1980s, as the proportion of those who speak another language at home and who speak English poorly jumped from 22 to 47 per cent. This deterioration was widespread across source countries and may well indicate a growing problem in transferring human capital acquired abroad to the US labour market. The problem of poor English language skills also seems particularly acute for those immigrants settling in the West (Greenwood *et al.*, 1997). In any case, there seems to be clear excess demand for courses in English as a second language: in New York City, for example, places are allocated by a lottery system.

This problem of transferability of skills, once superimposed on the education gap between the immigrant and native populations, gives rise to lower wages as well as an unemployment rate that is well above that of the native population (see below), especially for recent arrivals and especially for those from Latin America and Africa, and an occupational distribution that reflects a lower degree of skill requirements and an emerging structural gap with native workers[73] (Table 22). These differences are obviously accentuated for recent arrivals who have not yet had the time to assimilate into the US labour market. That process of integration is clearly evident in the shares of immigrants who are working in managerial and professional speciality occupations: figures in the table indicate a rise in the share of pre-1980 arrivals in this high-skill category from 1980 to 1990. A similar but opposite process of moving out of the category "operators, fabricators and labourers" is also visible. In general, immigrants dominate in a number of high- and low-skill occupations (teachers and scientists at the high end, service and crafts workers at the low end), whereas they are proportionately under-represented in intermediate-level jobs.

Table 22. **Occupational distribution of US workers, 1980 and 1990**

Per cent

	All workers		Immigrants (16 and over)			
	in 1980	in 1990	Pre-1970 arrivals in 1980	1970-80 arrivals in 1980	Pre-1980 arrivals in 1990	1980-90 arrivals in 1990
Managerial and professional specialty	22.7	26.4	23.4	17.7	25.7	17.0
Technical, sales and administrative support	30.3	31.7	26.9	21.0	27.4	22.4
Service	12.9	13.2	14.8	18.0	15.2	22.3
Farming, forestry and fishing	2.9	2.5	2.6	4.1	3.0	4.9
Precision production, craft and repair	12.9	11.3	13.7	11.8	12.1	11.8
Operators, fabricators and labourers	18.3	14.9	18.7	27.3	16.5	21.6
All occupations	100.0	100.0	100.0	100.0	100.0	100.0
Total workers (thousands)	97 639	115 681	3 991	2 541	6 290	4 375

Source: US Bureau of the Census.

Immigrants' labour market outcomes are consistent with their backgrounds. It is useful to limit analysis to prime-age males in order to abstract from different demographic structures and to focus on demand effects. For example, while immigrants have a slightly lower labour force participation rate, this is attributable to women and youths.[74] For this group labour force participation is higher than for native-born men, as there has been no secular decline (Table 23). There is little noteworthy cross-country variation, except that those from Indochina/ Vietnam have an especially low rate. Joblessness, however, is a much bigger problem, especially for recent arrivals: the unemployment rate is significantly higher among foreign-born men, and the gap widened in the 1980s. The biggest percentage point increases and the highest rates are among Hispanics. Nevertheless, employment-to-population ratios are generally higher for immigrants than natives, at least for men, but the reverse is true for recent arrivals. The deficit seems to shrink the longer an immigrant remains in the country, and the most recent immigrants have had particular difficulties in finding employment.

Aggregate immigrant earnings levels have deteriorated relative to natives since 1970. However, this worsening has been limited to immigrants from Mexico and Central America, as those from all other areas experienced improvements. It is also limited to those without any post-secondary education: the labour market penalty to those with at least 13 years of schooling has been stable in the

Table 23. **Labour market outcomes of 25 to 64 year-old immigrant men, 1970-90**

	Labour force participation (per cent)			Unemployment rate (per cent)			Relative earnings (native born = 100)		
	1970	1980	1990	1970	1980	1990	1970	1980	1990
A. By country/region of origin									
Native born	91	88	87	2.7	4.8	4.9	n.a.	n.a.	n.a.
Foreign born	89	87	90	3.2	5.3	6.1	99	93	89
of which those born in:									
United Kingdom and Canada	92	89	90	3.4	3.6	3.6	113	120	130
Continental Europe	92	91	88	3.0	4.7	5.3	110	107	115
Japan, Korea and China	86	88	87	2.4	2.7	3.1	88	99	110
Middle East, Other Asia	89	86	90	2.6	4.5	4.7	107	112	120
Philippines	92	94	93	2.7	3.2	3.9	76	94	93
Indochina, Vietnam	n.a.	75	77	n.a.	9.2	7.0	n.a.	66	73
Africa, Caribbean, South America, Oceania	93	90	89	3.5	5.3	6.6	80	85	86
Central America	93	91	92	3.6	6.5	7.1	79	72	62
Mexico	89	92	91	4.7	8.0	8.3	66	65	56
B. By years of schooling									
Foreign born							99	93	89
of which those with:									
0 to 4 years							120	92	93
5 to 8 years							112	93	89
9 years							109	98	94
10 years							106	94	100
11 years							109	99	96
12 years							102	93	95
13 to 15 years							95	94	95
16 years							89	90	90
17 years or more							91	102	91

Source: Schoeni *et al.* (1996).

123

Table 24. **The wage and earnings gap between immigrants and natives, 1970-90**

Index, native born = 100

Nativity and years since arrival	Men						Women					
	1970		1980		1990		1970		1980		1990	
	Hourly wages	Annual earnings	Hourly wages	Annual earnings	Hourly wages	Annual earnings	Hourly wages	Annual earnings	Hourly wages	Annual earnings	Hourly wages	Annual earnings
All foreign-born[1]	101.5	96.9	95.5	90.9	93.0	85.0	102.5	102.9	100.0	98.8	98.6	94.8
Recent arrivals	89.9	81.0	81.6	72.1	78.2	64.8	93.1	93.3	92.7	86.9	86.7	75.0
Europe and Canada	101.1	96.1	101.1	97.5	110.9	111.7	98.1	95.7	94.9	89.0	110.0	93.3
Asia	95.2	80.3	88.5	78.6	87.4	74.6	108.0	102.0	99.8	99.6	95.7	87.5
Africa and Oceania	100.2	73.7	91.1	78.2	102.8	67.8	78.7	86.4	109.3	94.1	95.5	83.5
Other America	78.9	70.6	74.0	61.3	67.2	52.2	85.1	94.5	87.9	78.9	76.2	65.3
Mexico	61.8	54.2	61.1	50.3	50.0	38.0	79.6	59.2	75.0	59.9	60.2	43.3
Earlier arrivals[1]	107.4	104.8	104.4	103.1	103.3	99.1	107.2	107.9	103.8	105.1	104.8	105.2
Europe and Canada	114.2	112.7	113.2	115.2	124.0	125.9	108.3	109.9	103.4	104.5	107.3	108.7
Asia	105.3	102.1	121.0	124.7	127.1	123.5	107.9	109.3	120.6	130.8	123.2	129.6
Africa and Oceania	93.5	90.0	122.3	124.6	98.1	97.9	115.9	109.1	109.3	116.5	108.3	108.1
Other America	94.1	87.4	91.7	87.8	96.8	89.4	105.7	111.0	103.5	107.5	104.1	104.9
Mexico	71.4	65.8	80.5	69.6	67.9	58.2	86.4	79.0	88.0	74.1	73.7	63.4
Per memorandum:												
Native-born												
1995 dollars	19.00	37 212	19.83	37 591	19.41	37 551	12.70	14 899	12.63	16 805	13.42	20 196

1. Recent arrivals are defined as those foreign-born who arrived in the 10 years preceding the census year, and earlier arrivals include all other foreign-born in the sample. The sample comprises civilians aged 25-64 who were not self-employed.

Source: Smith and Edmonston (1997) and OECD.

range of 5 to 10 per cent relative to similarly-educated natives, while the relative earnings situation for the low-skilled has deteriorated significantly. These immigrants find themselves disproportionately in the bottom decile of the income distribution.[75] Higher shares are totally without income and live below the official poverty line; amongst those with income, median per capita income in 1993 was nearly one quarter below that received by natives, but the gap drops to about 7 per cent for those who have been resident for 15 years or more. Using more reliable Census data the hourly wage gap between immigrants and natives aged 25-64 was 7 per cent for men and about 1½ per cent for women in 1990 (Table 24); annual earnings diverged substantially more (15 and 5 per cent, respectively), indicating fewer hours worked, probably due to greater unemployment. These differences are magnified for those who arrived in the preceding decade, illegal aliens and refugees and asylees; indeed, the remainder had about the same annual earnings and higher hourly wages. But the variation across source countries is enormous, with males from Japan earning 54 per cent more than the average native man, while those from Mexico earn 37 per cent less.[76] This variation is largely due to differences in underlying skill differentials and the inability to transfer skills from developing countries.[77]

The economic effects of immigration

From an economic point of view international migration can be characterised as a flow of potential labour across a border. It changes both productive potential and factor prices and incomes in the source and destination countries in theoretically predictable ways (see Box 7). But in practice those effects are exceedingly difficult to quantify because of migrants' varying features and because different approaches are possible. The simplest static analysis points to a very small "immigration surplus", a gain to the United States of a few billion dollars per year. But there could be additional favourable effects, due, for example, to agglomeration economies or immigrants' particular entrepreneurial skills, or costs associated with crowding, social strains or budgetary pressures.

Evidence on labour market and distributional effects

Probably the foremost empirical question is whether immigrant workers reduce the wages of native workers and displace them from their jobs. This

Box 7. **Some simple theoretical expectations on the economic effects of immigration**

For the economist international migration is, at first glance, a fairly straight-forward labour supply shock that transfers labour resources from the source to the host country. In this static, partial-equilibrium sense it has certain similarities with the international capital flows that serve to finance investment: both raise the productive potential of the recipient country at the expense of the source country and boost world output, assuming factor productivity is higher in their new home. This is supported by the assumption that the migration is motivated by a skill-adjusted wage differential.[1] Both also trigger internal redistributions in the two nations. In the simplest sense, production theory tells us that the prices and incomes of the migrating factor and of others with which it competes will rise in the source country and fall in the destination country, while the prices of complementary factors will move in the opposite direction as production adjusts to the new factor intensities. However, assessing the size and nature of these effects is complex, because they are a function of numerous features of the flows – volumes, timing, settlement patterns, remittance behaviour, among others – as well as of characteristics of the migrants themselves (sex,[2] age,[3] legal status, country of origin, skill level). Many of these socio-economic traits have already been described above. A further complexity is that the effects vary over time, as in the medium term immigrants acquire new skills and experience in the local labour market, and in the long term their progeny compete with the offspring of natives in subsequent generations. Last, the impact will be a function of the institutional and policy framework, as emphasised in the Introduction. Given all these parameters, drawing secure conclusions is difficult, especially as so much of the voluminous pertinent literature adopts a partial equilibrium approach, which risks overlooking key interdependencies. Nevertheless, partial-equilibrium analysis does point to the strong probability that immigration produces small net gains for the native-born (Smith and Edmonston, 1997), the so-called immigration surplus.

A simple supply and demand analysis helps to demonstrate this result (Figure 20). Assume only one good and two kinds of labour, skilled and unskilled, and that all immigrants are unskilled. Let CF be the demand for unskilled labour, that is its marginal product. Before immigration there are S native unskilled workers who are paid W_o and the wage bill is OBDG. The remainder of the output, BCD, is paid to other factors, skilled labour in this simple case without capital. With immigration of unskilled labour, I, supply shifts to S+I and the wage falls to W_1. Domestic unskilled labour loses ABDK, immigrant labour earns GKEH and native complementary factors gain ABDE. Thus, native factors make an overall gain equal to KDE – the famous "Harberger triangle" in other contexts.[4] A series of recent estimates put its value at $1 to $10 billion for the United States (Borjas, 1995c; Smith and Edmonston, 1997; Borjas et al., 1997). However, only if skilled labour compensates the unskilled losers will immigration be Pareto improving. It should be pointed out that, with linear demand, the native gain is one half

(continued on next page)

(continued)

Figure 20. **LABOUR MARKET EFFECTS OF IMMIGRATION**

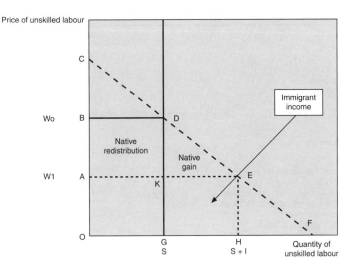

Source: Smith and Edmonston (1997).

the product of the number of immigrants and the reduction in the price of unskilled labour. Thus, as long as there is some substitution, the size of the gain is proportional to the price decline; if, on the other hand, all immigrants are complementary to domestic workers, the foregoing analysis would not be applicable and all native workers would gain. Also, unless returns to scale are not constant, immigration will only affect long-run economic growth if immigrants are and remain different from the native-born, that is if assimilation (see below) is never complete. One way immigrants may differ from natives is in their entrepreneurial abilities.[5] The media frequently mention that 12 per cent of the 500 fastest-growing companies listed by a popular business magazine in 1995 were started by immigrants and discuss the prevalence of small immigrant-run businesses in areas such as Los Angeles. But little hard evidence on the subject is available other than (Table 25) that in 1990 immigrants were only marginally more likely to be self-employed than natives, although much more likely when they are of European or Asian birth and have at least a high school education.

This simple model can be extended: to recognise that labour-market adjustment is not costless; to allow for the use of capital, in which case the owners of capital would share in the immigration-induced gains to other factors;[6] and to allow for multiple goods

(continued on next page)

(continued)

Table 25. **Self-employment rates by region of birth and education level, 1990**

Per cent of employed aged 25-64 who are self-employed

	Men	Women
Natives	13.1	7.2
All foreign born	13.1	8.3
Foreign born, by region		
Europe	18.4	10.2
Asia	15.9	9.8
Mexico	7.2	5.7
Other America	11.1	6.5
Other	11.2	7.1
Foreign born, by education level		
Eighth grade or less	9.6	6.8
Grades nine to twelve, no diploma	11.8	8.5
High-school diploma or certificate	13.4	8.8
Some post-secondary	14.1	8.4
Bachelor's degree or more	15.6	8.9

Source: Smith and Edmonston (1997).

in which case the relative price of products that are intensive in the use of immigrant labour will fall and domestic consumers of these goods and services will gain. Thus, as with opening an autarkic economy to international trade, there exist gains associated with both specialisation in consumption and production.[7] Immigration and imports are alternative ways of obtaining output that uses the relatively scarce domestic factor (unskilled labour in the US case) more intensively. Thus, immigration is likely to have smaller effects if trade is already relatively free.

There are a number of other possible mechanisms by which immigration could in theory affect the domestic economy. A key general equilibrium effect which must be accounted for is that the immigrants not only contribute to increased aggregate supply but also boost aggregate and labour demand, even if some part of their earnings are repatriated to their families in the form of remittance transfers. This demand-boosting effect would be larger the greater is immigrant wealth and non-labour income. Another effect is attributable to agglomeration economies (Ciccone and Hall, 1996): increased population density may well lower unit costs, leading to greater competitiveness and output if aggregate production is subject to scale economies. On the other hand, crowding effects may generate decreasing returns to scale because of higher congestion and pollution. In addition, theory implies that immigration will change the rates of return to skills and

(continued on next page)

(continued)

therefore bring about changes in the human capital investment decisions of the native population which, over time, will probably soften the short-run impacts on those who compete with immigrants in the labour market.

1. This is likely either because the immigrant was under- or unemployed prior to migrating or that the wage differential truly reflects relative marginal products in spite of possible distortions.

2. The economic effects of female immigration are likely to differ from those of male immigration because female immigrants have lower participation rates and wage rates; they often compete in different sectors of the labour market; they have obviously different implications for the population in the long run; and they may draw more social services because of their longer life expectancy. See Funkhouser and Trejo (1996) for an examination of some evidence.

3. Age is another characteristic which has not been much investigated but which will have important implications for entrepreneurship, duration of labour market activity and indirect demand effects as a result of non-labour income. The share of prime-age immigrants (those in the age group of around 15 to 44) in total inflows declined fairly steadily from over 80 per cent in the early years of the Twentieth Century to some 60 per cent from 1940 to 1980; since then it has again risen to around 69 per cent. On the other hand, the share of those 45 and over has also risen somewhat through this century, reaching around 16 per cent most recently, although it was even higher in the period 1931-50. The implication is that the share of young children doubled from around 13 per cent in the first couple of decades of the century to over one-quarter from 1960 to 1980 before falling back to around 15 per cent of late. See Greenwood *et al.* (1997).

4. The formula for its share of GDP is (Borjas, 1995*c*): $-\frac{1}{2}$ s e m^2, where s is labour's share of output (0.7), e is the own price elasticity of labour demand (–0.3) and m is the immigrant share of employment (0.1). Thus, in this simple model, the surplus is around 0.1 per cent of GDP.

5. See Chapter V.

6. If immigrants are identical to natives, then native workers will all lose (and, in the extended model presented below, the Harberger triangle will represent a gain to domestic owners of capital), unless those immigrants bring with them sufficient capital to maintain the previous capital/labour ratio; in that case, output will be scaled up, but there is no gain (or loss) to domestic workers. However, if capital is internationally mobile, then this part of the national gain is dissipated. Borjas *et al.* (1997) estimate that this dissipation would amount to 62 per cent of the original aggregate gain.

7. But trade and immigration are different: the latter is a semi-permanent movement in the stock of a factor (like foreign investment), whereas trade is inherently a flow which can be stopped or reversed depending on economic and policy developments. Also, natives who work in non-traded goods sectors do not compete directly with imports, but they still compete with immigrants. Nevertheless, whether trade and migration (and capital flows) are substitutes or complements is a worthy if largely unresearched question. The theoretical as well as the limited empirical evidence is ambiguous (Collins *et al.*, 1997).

"displacement hypothesis" may not be correct if US labour markets are sufficiently segmented that native workers are not substitutes for immigrant workers; this may be true for illegal immigrants who are thought to take jobs for which native workers tend not to compete (Lowell, 1995). The real wage rates of native workers will rise, in general, only if they are outright complements in production, however. Nevertheless, other factors, capital in particular, are more likely to be complements and therefore to gain as a result of immigration. The sizes of wage and employment effects of immigration are a function of the relevant elasticities of labour demand and native labour supply: in general, the lower the elasticities, the larger the wage impact of any given amount of immigration, while displacement will be greater the more elastic is domestic labour supply and the less elastic is labour demand. A consensus estimate (Hamermesh, 1993) of the elasticity of labour demand is around -0.3; thus, a 10 per cent increase in labour supply due to immigration (corresponding to the foreign-born share of the population) would be expected to lead to, at first glance, a 33 per cent reduction in the market wage. This predicted decline derives from the assumption of unchanged incomes and output which is patently false: immigrants spend most of their earnings on domestic production, thereby boosting demand for labour and offsetting the original shift in supply.

The empirical literature generally also points to only small wage and employment effects on native workers, although the consensus view is that there is some more substantial effect on other recent immigrants, especially in areas of high immigrant concentration. This does not exclude the possibility that certain specific types of native workers might not suffer measurable losses,[78] as others may gain, dulling the aggregate effects. Besides the aforementioned expansionary aggregate demand effects, regional arbitrage through internal factor mobility might also smooth the effect of locally important shocks over the much larger national labour market (see below). Finally, the contribution of immigrants to labour force growth may not have been sufficiently significant in the 1970s and 1980s to have measurable effects, even if the share has grown more recently.

It is possible to distinguish a number of separate strands of the literature to date. In the first, a narrow production-theory approach was applied, with minimal input disaggregation (immigrants and natives were considered as homogeneous populations), but a number of potentially serious technical problems were not recognised[79]; the focus was on the short run, when native workers' wage rates can be assumed to be downwardly rigid, and results were in the range of a elasticity of native employment with respect to immigrant employment of –0.08 to –0.10 (Johnson, 1980; Grossman, 1982). Eventually, however, native wages would adjust to eliminate displacement, leaving them with a wage loss of about 1.0 per cent (0.8 per cent in the second generation) for each 10 per cent increase in immigration. Previous immigrants experience a 2.3 per cent wage cut, capital-owners a gain of 4.2 per cent. Later some distinction was drawn between low- and high-skilled immigrants and natives, but the conclusions were initially simi-lar: while the segmentation hypothesis was refuted in its extreme form – immi-gration does cause a decline in the wages and employment of low-skilled natives – the effects were thought to be small. It is previous low-skilled immi-grants who suffer the greatest losses, even if there are signs of a sequential process from substitutability to complementarity.[80] Subsequent research has refined the prevailing view by demonstrating that the negative effects of low-skilled immigration are most pronounced for native youths who lack experience.

At the level of specific industries, occupations and regions or localities it may no longer be true that the aggregate supply of unskilled immigrant labour is inelastic or that aggregate demand for such labour is so elastic, and immigration effects may be larger. Of course, researchers have tended to look at the places they expected to find significant influences, and nothing is known regarding the ultimate impact on those displaced. The narrower the sector or region, the more likely it is that negative native outcomes can be uncovered. In agriculture, for instance, the effects of immigration have been shown to be large in areas of high immigrant concentration, such as the California citrus industry (Mines and Martin, 1984). In manufacturing, some research has shown that native wage reductions begin to occur only when immigrants exceed around 20 per cent of the sectoral labour force (DeFreitas and Marshall, 1984). In the footwear and apparel sectors, the continued viability of domestic manufacturing has probably been assured by the availability of low-skill immigrant labour (Waldinger, 1985), to the advantage of the owners of capital in those sectors,[81] but consumers may not be any better off than if the relevant products were manufactured abroad, in the source country in particular. Indeed, low-wage natives will have to compete with the low-wage foreign born whether or not the latter produce abroad or immigrate and produce in the United States.

The expectation that immigration effects in particular markets with heavy immigration would be larger has found very little supporting evidence. The Californian labour market effects of Mexican immigration have been much studied. Different degrees of displacement have been found (Muller and

Espenshade, 1985; McCarthy and Valdez, 1986). But perhaps the most famous studies of the impact of immigration have been of major one-off immigration shocks: the 1980 Mariel boatlift in the Miami area (Card, 1990) and the return of the *pieds noirs* from Algeria to France in 1962 (Hunt, 1992). The findings of these studies show that even major one-off migrations have had only the smallest of labour market effects, even in the short run, possibly due to changes in natives' internal migration patterns or accommodation of the influx by an expansion of the existing industrial structure. Another study looking at six metropolitan areas with high immigrant presence concludes that most of the impact of inflows is on the relative earnings of the immigrants themselves, but that even these wage-depressing effects dissipate over time as they assimilate into the US market (LaLonde and Topel, 1991).

While more recent research has gained greater sophistication, it has not succeeded in making a persuasive case for large local effects. In a structural model going beyond production relationships to include demand shifts and local export increases, localities with higher immigrant population shares are found to have lower wage rates for less-skilled natives (Altonji and Card, 1991). When still other channels of influence (such as internal migration) are included in empirical work, the negative effects on native employment and wages are substantially mitigated and possibly even overturned (Greenwood and Hunt, 1995), leading to a positive correlation between immigration and native migratory flows, as was discovered by Butcher and Card (1991). Direct empirical evidence on this question points to lower in-migration and greater out-migration by low- and middle-income whites but opposite effects for highly educated white natives (Frey, 1994) who could benefit from complementarity effects, demand stimulus or capital accumulation offsets. Thus, it could be that local effects are being arbitraged away, but only if the speed of regional adjustment is very rapid, and direct evidence on inter-regional factor dynamics indicates that adjustment lags are on the order of five to ten years (Blanchard and Katz, 1992; Treyz *et al.*, 1993). However, given the persistence of immigrant settlement patterns, local effects would have been expected to be sizeable in any case.

The major alternative view of the impact of immigration derives from a different statistical approach: using time-series rather than cross-section data, various researchers have concluded that immigration has had a much more substantial impact on low-skill native workers, high-school dropouts in particular. The justification for this type of study is that it avoids the spreading of effects on native workers across the national market via factor mobility and goods trade. The research strategy has been to examine the wages of low-skill workers relative to those of their high-skill counterparts – a good proxy for wage inequality – over time and test for the effects of immigration as well as other commonly hypothesised factors such as international trade and technical change. Unfortunately, the number of observations is limited by the availability of information on place of birth in the Current Population Survey and the decennial censuses. The results of these studies tend not to be sufficiently consistent to be certain that inter-regional factor and goods mobility is the cause of the weakness of the effects found in the cross-section literature.[82]

Immigrant assimilation

One of the key issues in analysing the progress of immigrants in the host economy is the extent to which they assimilate over time. Assimilation in this context describes the process by which immigrants acquire language and other skills and experience which are rewarded by the US labour market. Initially cross-section census earnings profiles were used to document an assimilation effect, with the result that immigrant earnings were believed to be lower upon arrival but to rise and surpass those of natives after an average lag of about 13 years (Chiswick, 1978): the explanation centred primarily on a lower market valuation of foreign work experience than domestic, at least for those from non-English-speaking source countries – proficiency in English aids in the skills transfer process. The wage penalty imposed on those with weak English language skills is also a function of location; it is smaller in areas with higher immigrant concentrations where there exists a demand for minority-language skills.

But this approach risks confusing the hypothesised assimilation (''within-cohort'') effects with changes in immigrant quality over time as manifest in vintage (''across-cohort'') effects (Borjas, 1985). One must also separate out the number of years since arrival from the immigrant's cohort in order to ensure that assimilation effects are not over-estimated. The relevant literature on declining quality is long, and statistical problems abound. Furthermore, for a long time the question was not precisely defined, as the quality of immigrants may have fallen relative to the past or relative to the native born in the aggregate or of the same race and ethnicity.[83] The debate has also shown that the issue is not independent of age at arrival: those migrating at a young age experience earnings paths which are little different from natives', as their education and work experience are obtained in the United States, but those entering at older ages face more limited economic opportunities, both initially and throughout their careers. Correcting for age at arrival weakens the case for declining immigrant quality over time (Friedberg, 1993). Return migration is another problem, as little is known about the one in three who re-emigrate, whether they are more or less successful than those who remain. Finally, a strong case has recently been made that declining initial earnings should be interpreted as a sign of a fall in the transferability of skills from source countries rather than of declining quality, because of a systematic inverse relationship between initial earnings and subsequent earnings growth (Duleep and Regets, 1996).

But overall it would seem that there has indeed been a decline in relative immigrant quality in recent decades, both in the form of observable skills (based on educational attainment) (Borjas, 1990; LaLonde and Topel, 1991) and unobservable characteristics as reflected in a growing wage differential between recent immigrants and demographically comparable natives (Borjas, 1992). While the rate of decline may have slowed (Borjas, 1995a) or even stopped (Funkhouser and Trejo, 1995) in the 1980s, the average skill level of recent immigrants in 1990 was still low by historical standards. And the overwhelming reason for the visible decline is the changing source country mix toward poorer countries (Borjas, 1992; Smith and Edmonston, 1997), at least until the mid-1980s (see Table 18 above), and the implications for educational attainment.[84] Once this quality decline is recognised, assimilation effects account for a decline of around 10 percentage points in the wage gap during the first two decades after arrival for men. But the size of the initial gap is larger for recent cohorts, implying that fewer will converge to native wages over their working lifetimes.[85] Women start with a smaller wage gap and also tend to close it slowly, but come closer to catching up than men.

Effects on prices

As explained above, the additional labour supply made available by immigrants generates changes in relative prices: those goods and services which are intensive in the use of immigrant labour fall in price and conversely. Input-output tables allow some inference about which products are in fact intensive in the use of immigrant labour: these are found to be led by household services, services to dwellings and laundry, cleaning and garment services. With this industry information in hand, examining the Consumer Expenditure Survey allows the possibility of discovering who consumes these products. The result of this exercise is that the share of consumption expenditures attributable to the cost of immigrant labour is fairly constant (at nearly five per cent) across the household distribution of income, although it does rise slightly at the top end (Smith and Edmonston, 1997). It also rises slightly with the educational attainment and age of the head of household. But in general natives benefit fairly equally from the price effects resulting from the presence of immigrants.

Effects on the public finances

Increasing attention has been paid to the impact of immigration on the public finances. In some quarters this is seen as the only worthy question for public policy towards immigration; however, even if immigrants fail to "pay their way" in budgetary terms, their overall effect on the nation can still be positive if their impact on native-born consumers and producers is favourable. Any undesired negative influence on the public purse could then be offset by taxing some of the native gains to offset the budgetary losses.

The debate has been acrimonious, partly because of its incongruence. Participants have not defined the questions precisely and make quite different assumptions about what should be considered and what excluded, what public services are pure public goods,[86] the technology of public service provision, what horizon and discount rates are appropriate, what is the optimal demographic unit of analysis, etc. Most serious early attempts to quantify immigration effects on government outlays focused on welfare spending. The foreign born have been generally found to be less likely to receive public assistance and to receive lower levels of such transfers than the native-born population with similar characteristics (Blau, 1984)[87]; similar results have been found for some other OECD host countries (OECD, 1997a). However, results are not so clear-cut if demographic controls are excluded. In that case, outcomes are a function of the sex of the head of household (with male-headed households more likely to participate in welfare programmes (Blau, 1984)), race/ethnicity (Hispanic immigrants are more frequent recipients than their native counterparts (Jensen, 1988), since many of them worked in agriculture and household services where social security rights are not earned), immigration status (refugees make many times the welfare use of any other group of natives or immigrants (Fix and Passel, 1994)) and the year of the analysis (Borjas and Trejo, 1991). In any case, even if the partial effect of being foreign born is zero, many recent immigrants are characterised by low levels of educational attainment, large families and poor English-language skills, all of which are associated with greater welfare use. The overall result is that the latest data (March 1995) show that the foreign born are some 35 per cent more likely to receive public assistance than natives.

More recently attention has focused on whether there is a distinct effect resulting from time since migration, whether propensities have changed over time and whether they are cohort-dependent. With time, assimilation should imply that immigrants improve their economic position and therefore require less public assistance; however, immigrants might conceivably "assimilate into welfare" by becoming more aware of the availability of social transfers and progressively fulfilling eligibility requirements. Borjas (1994) and Borjas and Hilton (1996) provide data which shed some light on this question (Table 26). In the aggregate, immigrant households moved from a position of near parity with native house-holds in 1970, both with respect to propensities to use welfare and amounts received, to one of greater reliance on both counts in 1980 and, even more

Table 26. **Rates of receipt and average amounts of public assistance, 1970-90**

	Per cent of households			Mean amount received [1] (1989 prices)		
	1970	1980	1990	1970	1980	1990
Native head of household	6.0	7.9	7.4	3 837	4 248	4 017
Foreign-born head of household	5.9	8.7	9.1	3 806	4 662	5 363
Cohort: arrivals						
1985-89	–	–	8.3	–	–	6 385
1980-84	–	–	10.7	–	–	6 571
1975-79	–	8.3	10.0	–	5 228	5 652
1970-74	–	8.4	9.7	–	5 220	4 884
1965-69	5.5	10.1	9.8	3 830	5 044	4 796
1960-64	6.5	9.2	8.4	4 144	5 050	4 480
1950-59	4.9	7.1	6.7	4 402	4 680	4 514
Pre-1950	6.2	9.3	8.1	3 629	4 022	4 262

1. Conditional on receiving some public assistance.
Source: Borjas (1994).

emphatically, in 1990 – by then, immigrant households received 64 per cent more than native households on a per-household basis,[88] a "welfare gap". By separating cohort and assimilation (time since arrival) effects, it is evident that probabilities of welfare receipt rose between the late 1960s arrivals and the early 1980s arrivals, with some reversal thereafter,[89] and that the proportion of immigrant households using welfare tends to rise with the duration of US residence. The mean amount received has also tended to rise more rapidly than for households headed by the native born, both overall and for most cohorts taken individually.

But welfare provides an excessively narrow focus for the examination of fiscal effects. Very recently, there has been some more rigorous and broadly-focused analysis of both static annual and dynamic long-run budgetary effects (Smith and Edmonston, 1997). Using the former, more common approach on data for New Jersey and California, the authors show immigrants benefited from higher state and local spending, especially on primary and secondary education (because of larger family size) and transfers (because of lower incomes), although some pay more tax than do native households (those from Europe, Canada and Asia) and are actually net contributors to these budgets (Europe and Canada) (Table 27, panel A). The budgetary effects on the federal government are found to be small and positive, but the overall charge on the general government budget remains an estimated $15 to $20 billion for 1996.

Yet even broad-based static analysis is of limited interest because it mixes together immigrants of different generations; it assumes that fiscal policy is unchanged; it ignores life-cycle effects on demands for public services and payment of taxes; and it may miss the effect of adult, native-born children who do not live in immigrant-headed households. Adding population to the nation will spread the cost of public goods and the burden of interest payments on the public debt, although it will also boost the need for public infrastructure and dilute the per capita value of non-reproducible public wealth. Because immigrants have different characteristics, however, they have different marginal fiscal impacts than additional natives: they may need bilingual education (see below); they make about 40 per cent less use of nursing homes for the elderly; and they have tended to congregate in states with larger public sectors.[90] Data from the Current Population Survey show that: immigrants draw less Social Security and Medicare than natives (by around $1 000 to $2 000 per year due to lower average earnings

Table 27. **Fiscal impacts of immigration: some highlights**

Dollars

	Assuming New Jersey fiscal rules	Assuming California fiscal rules
A. Static results		
1. Net annual fiscal impact per native of current immigrant-headed households		
On native households in the state	−229	−1 174
of which: Local	−144	−283
State	−88	−895
Federal	3	4
On all US native households	−166	−226
of which: Immigrants from Europe/Canada	46	167
Asia	208	111
Latin America	−579	−738
Other	314	339
2. Total net annual fiscal impact of current immigrant-headed households (billions)	−14.8	−20.2

	Immigrants	Immigrants plus their native-born children under 20	Others	Total
B. Cross-section results				
Average fiscal impact per immigrant				
Taxes	n.a.	5 650	8 300	8 170
Spending	na.	6 020	6 270	6 480
Net impact	1 800	−370	2 030	1 690
of which: State and local	490	−920	360	290
Federal	1 310	550	1 680	1 400

	Immigrants	Their descendants	Total
C. Dynamic results			
1. Net present value of average fiscal impact per immigrant			
Overall	−3 000	83 000	**80 000**
of which: State and local	n.a.	n.a.	−25 000
Federal	n.a.	n.a.	105 000
of which: Less than a high-school education	−89 000	76 000	−13 000
High school education	−31 000	82 000	51 000
More than a high-school education	105 000	93 000	198 000
2. Sensitivity analysis: the overall figure of **80 000** would become the following with the alternative assumption:			
No budgetary adjustment to ensure constant/GDP as from 2016		−15 000	
Budgetary adjustment immediately rather than in 2016		77 000	
Budgetary adjustment in 2016 entirely by tax increases		95 000	
Budgetary adjustment in 2016 entirely by spending reductions		66 000	
Enactment of 1996 welfare reform legislation		89 000	
Real interest rate of 2 rather than 3 per cent		219 000	
Real interest rate of 4 rather than 3 per cent		39 000	
All public goods spending assumed to be on congestable goods		−5 000	
All congestable goods spending assumed to be public goods		160 000	
Interest payments assumed to be private		31 000	
No population ageing and no increases in per capita health care costs		−15 000	
Immigrants have same education as natives		121 000	
Immigrants are the same age as natives		32 000	
Immigrants pay the same taxes by age as natives		152 000	
Immigrants receive the same benefits by age as natives		90 000	
Immigrants' wages continue to catch up after 10 years after arrival		124 000	

Source: Smith and Edmonston (1997) and OECD.

and shorter contribution periods), saving some $11.5 billion; they receive higher Medicaid benefits, at least until around age 80 (but the gap is much smaller); they rely more on Supplementary Security Income (SSI) after the age of about 52 (to the tune of about $700 more per year for those in their 70s and 80s when immigrants are often ineligible for Social Security and Medicare); they cost about $1 500 more per year in education outlays for those aged about 6-16; and they receive more of other income-related transfers as from the age of around 26 (an average of around $200 per year more). Aggregating over all programmes, immigrants receive more benefits from the age of 6 until around 19 and fewer from their late 40s on; on average they receive around 7 per cent less (Table 27, panel B). But the biggest difference between natives and the foreign born is in the taxes they pay during their adult lifetimes – the foreign born pay 32 per cent less. The net fiscal impact of immigrants is therefore more negative than that of natives during youth, less positive during working lifetimes and similar in retirement. On average the immigrants themselves have positive fiscal effects at all levels of government, but once their native-born dependent children are included, their net impact turns negative at the state and local level and overall.

With these cross-section figures in hand and some additional[91] assumptions and some other less important features, a baseline scenario can be developed for the net present value of the total fiscal impact per immigrant (Table 27, Panel C1). The result of the simulation is that immigrants themselves have a very small negative net fiscal impact, but once their progeny are included, immigration yields a sizeable surplus. Again, the federal government gains more than the other levels lose (because of the public goods nature of defence and interest outlays). The outcome is, however, clearly a function of education and age at arrival. Only those with at least a high-school education have a positive fiscal impact in present value terms. With the educational attainment characteristics of the current immigrant stock, all those arriving at age 40 or less have favourable fiscal effects. To maximise the positive impact immigrants should be admitted when they are 21 years old and have more than a high-school education. The worst outcome occurs when they are 70 years old at arrival and have no more than a high-school education, in which case there is a substantial net cost.

But, as mentioned above, the overall surplus is attributable to very long-run considerations: in the baseline it takes 40 years for the net present value to turn positive. Sensitivity analysis is clearly called for. A number of interesting outcomes then ensue (Table 27, Panel C2). First, if the debt-to-GDP ratio is allowed to rise indefinitely, the average impact turns negative. It also turns negative if all public goods spending is assumed to be congestible; and if there is no need for immigrants to help bear the cost of the ageing of the baby-boom generation and its attendant rise in health-care costs.[92] However, the direction of the outcome is not sensitive to any other assumptions. Interestingly, last year's welfare reform legislation, if fully implemented (see below), would have improved the baseline outcome by around 10 per cent or $8 000 per immigrant.

What are these figures worth to the average native resident? If they are accurate, they are indeed small: each extra 1 000 immigrants costs a native resident about a $0.10 per year in extra state and local taxes in present value terms which is more than offset by a $0.40 dollar decline in the federal tax burden, leaving a net gain of around $0.30. But it remains the case that immigrants are costly in the early years (for many decades at the state and local level) and will "pay their way" on a general government basis only if federal fiscal policy is eventually tightened to stabilise the federal public debt in relation to GDP. It is also obvious that the US system of government provides distorted inter-governmental incentives: the federal government has jurisdiction over immigration policy and immigrants seem to have favourable effects on its finances, whereas states and localities bear a net burden, even if high-immigration states are not in any worse financial condition than others (Funkhouser, 1995). The 1986 IRCA legislation did, in fact, authorise $1 billion per year for four years in grants to states to offset the costs of those granted amnesty, but the money was not fully appropriated. Some states have even filed suit against the federal government seeking cost reimbursement,[93] but these suits have all been dismissed by the courts.

The demographic effects of immigration

Demographers have also been important observers of immigration trends. Their models show that if there had been no immigration since 1950 the US population would have been only 225 million in 1995, rather than the actual figure of 263 million, a difference of nearly 15 per cent; that reduction would have been most keenly felt among those aged 10 to 39 and over 80 (Smith and Edmonston, 1997, Table 3.5). A smaller population would possibly have had favourable effects on the environment, but depending on one's view of scale effects, it might have generated less growth in per capita output and incomes (Ciccone and Hall, 1996). The alternative age structure would have meant a slightly higher dependency ratio,[94] implying an increased fiscal burden, but it would most likely have led to a higher household saving ratio, given life-cycle considerations.

Future immigration levels will have important effects on the population (Smith and Edmonston, 1997): if net immigration were constant at 820 000 per year,[95] population might rise by 124 million to 387 million in the year 2050, a compound rate of increase of 0.7 per cent per year, a rate not much more than half of what has been observed on average since 1950 (Table 28). Without any immigration, the population increase would be only 44 million, with growth of about a quarter of recent historical averages. Even if immigration were to double, population growth would still average only about what it has been over the past 30 years. The number of foreign born would rise unless immigration is cut back to around half current levels. There are also important effects on the ethnic composition of the population, although ethnic and racial distinctions will become increasingly blurred: under any immigration scenario, the shares of those of Asian and Hispanic ancestry will rise. Even with zero immigration, the sum of their shares would reach 22 per cent in 2050, up from 14 per cent in 1995, because of higher assumed fertility rates. Under constant immigration assumptions, it would jump to a third.

Immigration also affects the median age of the population. Higher immigration reduces average age because immigrants' median age is relatively low – 28 in 1995, for example. The youth dependency ratio (those under 15 as a share of those 20 to 64) is projected to remain fairly flat over the next half-century; different immigration assumptions would allow this to vary by around 2 percentage points, with higher immigration meaning a higher ratio. But immigration could induce important changes in the elderly dependency ratio which has been around 20 per cent of late and would finish the period at over 32 per cent with zero immigration and about 27 per cent with a doubling of immigration. Thus, overall dependency could be lowered from over 62 per cent with no immigration to below 60 per cent with a doubling.[96] Thus, the Twenty-First Century pension problem, as well as the coincident health care cost explosion, could conceivably be alleviated slightly by varying immigration levels, even if these problems

Table 28. **The prospects for US population under different immigration assumptions, 1995-2050**

	Zero	Low	Medium	High	Very high
Assumed net immigration per year (thousands)	0	410	820	1 230	1 640
Population (millions)					
1995	263	263	263	263	263
2000	272	275	277	279	281
2010	287	295	302	310	318
2020	298	313	327	341	354
2030	308	330	351	373	393
2040	310	341	370	400	429
2050	307	349	387	426	463
Average annual population growth, 1995-2050 (per cent)	0.3	0.5	0.7	0.9	1.0

Per memorandum:
Average annual population growth,
1950-95: 1.2 per cent

Source: Smith and Edmonston (1997) and OECD.

cannot by any means be avoided altogether, and this would entail substantially greater population growth (Espenshade, 1994).

Some social aspects of immigration

Besides economic, fiscal and demographic effects, immigration also has social aspects which are important to the evaluation of its full impact. Foremost among these is the success with which immigrants are integrated into US society by means of the famous so-called "melting pot". There has been much research into the fate of earlier waves of immigrants and their offspring but, of necessity, little dealing with the most recent cohorts which have the important difference of being to a much greater extent of different race than the majority of the native population. The latest readings, however, are that most are progressing satisfactorily,[97] even if convergence is seen as slow by some (Borjas, 1995d). First, other than those of Mexican origin, most Americans seem to live in neighbourhoods which are not especially segregated by ethnicity.[98] Furthermore, segregation measures decline from first- to second- generation immigrants and then fall by half again in the third generation, also with the exception of those of Mexican origin. Second, inter-marriage rates are high for those of Hispanic and Asian origins and have been growing since 1960 for all groups (Smith and Edmonston, 1997). Third, immigrants' scholastic outcomes are generally equal or superior to those of their native-born counterparts. Fourth, the language barrier ceases to play any meaningful role beyond the first generation. Fifth, immigrant contributions in a number of fields are well documented: more than a quarter of all US Nobel laureates have been foreign born (Smith and Edmonston, 1997, Table 8.5), as were 17 per cent of all members of the prestigious National Academies of Sciences and Engineering in July 1996 and 22 per cent of the cumulative recipients of Kennedy Center honours in the performing arts. However, naturalisation rates (the share of the foreign born who are citizens) – a marker for assimilation – fell sharply from 1970 until fairly recently,[99] even though much of this is attributable to the low propensity of Mexican immigrants to seek US citizenship in combination with the rising immigration share from Mexico (Jasso and Rosenzweig, 1990).

Perhaps the non-economic domain in which there has been the most recent concern has been the inter-relationship between immigration and crime. That immigrants or at least foreigners contribute disproportionately to crime has been a long-standing public perception, as witnessed by the attention paid to immigration matters in the 1996 anti-terrorism bill. The statistical problems surrounding this issue are, however, daunting. For foreign- *versus* native-born, data are available for 1990 only for those institutionalised (for whatever reason, rather than those incarcerated); otherwise available data sources identify only citizenship status. For males aged 18 to 54 (the preponderant demographic group engaging in criminal activity) overall incarceration rates for non-citizens in 1991 were about 20 per cent below those for citizens (Smith and Edmonston, 1997, Table 8.6). For some purposes it may be better to correct for socio-demographic characteristics in which case the differential widens to one-third (Butcher and Piehl, 1997). It narrows the longer the time since arrival and for 1990 as compared to 1980 – this is consistent with figures showing that non-citizens' share of the federal prison population rose significantly from 1984 to 1994. The only type of offence where non-citizens had higher incarceration rates were those related to drugs (and many of those imprisoned for such crimes may well not even be residents, much less immigrants). Moreover, non-citizens may well serve longer sentences for a given crime, in part because they are released to INS custody until a deportation decision is taken. Other evidence on the question shows that changes in local crime rates are independent of changes in immigrant shares in the community, even if there is some positive correlation in the levels (Butcher and Piehl, 1996).

The recent policy debate

As mandated by the immigration reform legislated in 1990, the Congress set up the Commission on Immigration Reform. It issued an initial report in 1995 (US Commission on Immigration Reform, 1995) which called for an immediate reduction in legal immigration of nearly one-quarter and an eventual cut of 40 per cent (once the backlog in certain categories are eliminated), including a reduction in employment-based quota of 40 000 per year, and the establishment of substantial fees (up to $10 000, used to fund private-sector initiatives to boost the competitiveness of US workers) payable by employers who wish to hire certain skilled foreign workers.[100] The result was a lengthy debate which culminated in legislation (the Illegal Immigration Reform and Immigrant Responsibility Act) signed into law on 30 September 1996 and implemented in the spring of 1997. This law did not include the Commission's recommendation to lower the level of legal immigration. Rather, the main provisions of the law in the legal immigration domain were to create an income test of 125 per cent of the official poverty level (currently around $10 600 for a childless couple and $16 000 per year for a family of four) for sponsors of legal immigrants,[101] increase the time that sponsors would be financially responsible for immigrants to five years (the so-called "deeming requirement"[102]) and make affidavits of support legally enforceable. It also threatens legal immigrants with deportation if they illegally use public benefit programmes and denies citizenship to anyone who is deportable or whose sponsor has unpaid sponsorship-related bills.

But it was in order to clamp down on illegal immigration that ultimately the most significant changes were made, despite the fact that there is no evidence that control of the borders has been lost, as some immigration critics charge.[103] The size of the Border Patrol is to be doubled over a five-year period to 10 000 agents, and 1 200 other additional INS agents will be hired.[104] The fence between California and Mexico is to be extended. Sentences for document fraud and cross-border smuggling of aliens were lengthened.[105] The deportation process has been expedited, in part by greatly reducing judges' discretion to grant waivers. Several pilot programmes to verify eligibility to work are being set up, but document verification procedures for both public benefits as well as the right to work otherwise remain largely non-existent. And asylum seekers will have to apply within one year of arrival. But several controversial provisions were dropped at the final stage, including allowing states to refuse free public education to the children of illegal immigrants (similar to a 1994 California referendum proposition which has not been implemented due to a court challenge), making the income test twice the poverty level and hiring several hundred extra inspectors to ensure that employers are not abusing their positions *vis-à-vis* immigrant labour.

Yet possibly the most significant debate and legislation concerning immigrants has been over possible restrictions on their eligibility for public transfers and benefits.[106] Such restrictions formed a substantial part of the recent welfare reform bill, the Personal Responsibility and Work Opportunity Reconciliation Act of 1996. That legislation barred most new and already admitted "qualified aliens" (lawful permanent residents, refugees and asylees, and some others) from receiving food stamps and SSI and most new qualified aliens from most means-tested federal programmes during their first five years in the United States.[107] In addition, state governments were given the right to deny them Temporary Assistance to Needy Families ("welfare"), Medicaid and various federally funded state programmes such as child care and services for the elderly. States were also required to legislate specifically if they wished to provide benefits to illegal immigrants. Immigrants were the source of 40 per cent of the overall spending cuts contained in the bill, nearly $4 billion per year. Official estimates were that half a million immigrants would have been cut from the rolls of SSI recipients and a million from the list of food stamp beneficiaries. Even though the President signed the bill, he vowed to revisit the question in 1997 before most provisions became effective in August 1997. The Administration budget for 1998 sought to restore $13 billion in spending over five years, well over half the legislated cut, by eliminating the removal of immigrants' right to Medicaid and SSI benefits. The May budget agreement with Congress and the final legislation entailed a slightly smaller restoration – about $10 billion – and grandfathered the right to SSI benefits for immigrants already in the country prior to the 1996 legislation who might eventually become disabled but did not protect elderly immigrants on SSI without disabilities. But the issue remains alive: in its final report, the US Commission on Immigration Reform (1997) urged the Congress to reconsider denying welfare benefits to legal immigrants.

Options for reform

Policies toward legal immigration

Neither polar option with respect to immigration policy – barring it altogether or allowing it to proceed largely unfettered – would seem to be economically optimal or politically viable. Thus, some sort of quota system would seem inevitable. In theory, economic efficiency would point to allocating these quotas by auction, but barring slavery would seem to rule out that possibility. Critics of the *status quo* have most often called for a shift in the focus of immigration preferences towards skills-based admission rather than family reunification, although a few years ago the Administration was proposing to reduce overall employment-based limits from 140 000 to 100 000. However, as mentioned above, it is possible that family-based immigrants overcome their initial skills disadvantage and catch up more quickly to native average outcomes than employment-based immigrants, and according to the Urban Institute, the differences between the two kinds of immigrants from a given source country seem small.[108]

Many have pointed with admiration to the points-based systems in use in Canada and Australia, similar immigrant destination countries, as an appropriate guide for US policy (for example, Papademetriou and Yale-Lohr, 1996). Such a system has allowed Canada to vary its inflow according to its needs, rather than according to an infrequently changed flexible cap; the result is that Canadian immigration rates have followed a trend decline since the 1950s, even though they remain above US rates. But the Canadian system may ultimately not have made that much difference to the kind of immigrants being admitted (Duleep and Regets, 1992):[109] in 1993 around 64 per cent of immigrants entering the United States did so based on family relationships, only 1½ points higher than those entering Canada (Greenwood *et al.*, 1997). And while Canada did attract more high-skilled workers (as proxied by the share who are either professional, technical or kindred workers or managers and proprietors) for some years in the 1980s, the reverse has been the case in the 1990s (Figure 21, Panel A). However, Canada has succeeded in attracting a different age mix of immigrants than the United States since the mid-1980s. In particular, it has avoided the shift from prime-age (those in their 20s and 30s) to older immigrants that has occurred in the United States[110] (Figure 21, Panel B). And there is some early evidence that those arriving at or after age 55 do make much heavier use of SSI benefits. The average increase in educational attainment from the early 1960s to the late 1970s was also greater in Canada, and the mix of source countries remained more firmly grounded in Europe in the 1980s (a 27 per cent share) than in the United States (10 per cent) (Borjas, 1994). Nonetheless, US immigrants have increased their relative wages more than twice as fast as their Canadian counterparts (Baker and Benjamin, 1994). Thus, to sum up, it is unclear whether moving to a points-based system would have a strong effect on US immigrants' most important characteristics.

But more modest reforms are conceivable. The Administration has become convinced that the H-1 programme for admitting foreign non-immigrant (temporary) workers and trainees (see footnote 62 above) is in need of overhaul to make it more restrictive than the 1990 reform had already done.[111] The US Commission on Immigration Reform (1997) also recommended streamlining the system of non-immigrant visa categories by consolidating them into five broad classifications. Although its existence is often justified by claiming that through it pass the "best and the brightest" candidates for entry into the US labour market, in fact half the positions in the largest (H-1B) sub-class are for physical therapists, and therefore, not surprisingly, most pay less than $50 000 per year. The Administration recently called for reducing the maximum duration of such visas from six to three years to make them truly temporary. Also, as a small number of employers have abused the programme by hiring foreigners to replace laid-off native workers, it also advocated a no-layoff provision (six months prior to and three months following an employer application), and the extension of government enforcement powers to ensure that *bona fide* attempts to recruit and retain US workers have already been made. It is clear that the temporary worker programmes serve as stepping stones toward permanent immigration. For example, in 1995 over half of employment-based skilled permanent immigrants (excluding their spouses and children) adjusted their status directly from H-1 temporary visas.

Figure 21. **COMPOSITION OF US AND CANADIAN IMMIGRATION**

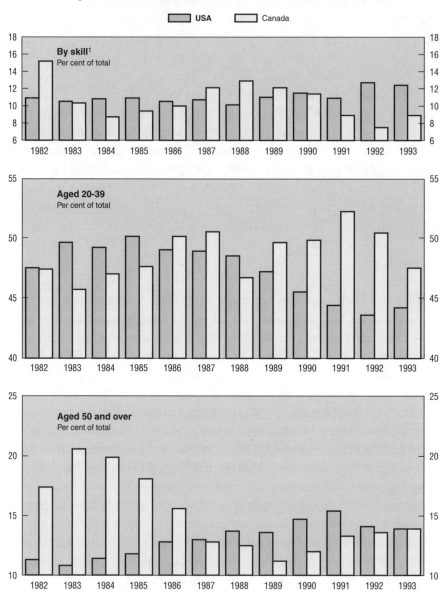

1. Refers to professional, technical, and kindred workers and managers and proprietors. US data exclude legalisations under the Immigration Reform and Control Act.
Source: Greenwood *et al.* (1997).

Policies toward illegal immigration

The dilemma facing policymakers in the domain of illegal immigration is especially daunting, given the United States' lengthy land border with Mexico, a country with a much lower level of per capita income. While policing the border is a challenge, stricter enforcement can only achieve so much. Better co-operation among the different law enforcement agencies as well as enhanced dialogue and co-operation with Mexico and other source countries might be helpful. A surprisingly high proportion of illegal immigrants have entered the United States legally, only to overstay their visas. In this situation, immigration enforcement is difficult unless society is prepared to go some way in implementing verification schemes which might invade privacy and/or infringe on individual liberties (Passel, 1996). Some argue against a national identity card system because of the potential for error and fraud. Monitoring more closely employers that might be expected to rely on illegal migrant workers and stricter enforcement of employment standards laws could have some modest restraining effect, but the process of illegal immigration is apparently so network-driven that it is difficult to overcome existing trends in the context of unregulated labour markets. The INS hopes to counter the visa-overstayer problem by automated tracking of inflows and outflows and better enforcement at the foreign embarkation point (denying repeat abusers entry immediately). Other countries have tried guestworker programmes (as has the United States with its Bracero Program from 1942 to 1964) in order to dissuade potential illegal migrants, but these have not solved the problems, merely changed the label attached to the remaining workers after the programmes are ended: they become ''permanent non-citizen residents''. The 1986 amnesty provided by IRCA does not seem to have made much long-run difference either, as the stock of illegal aliens has reached new highs, not surprising in light of moral hazard implications. The hope that barring illegal aliens from public transfers will help reduce their numbers is almost certainly forlorn as well, since what seems to attract them is more the prospect of employment – no matter how low the wage relative to US standards, it is likely to be attractive in relation to conditions in their countries of origin – rather than the magnet of welfare benefits.[112]

The most likely long-term solution must be improved economic prospects in source countries, especially Mexico. To this end the US government has been supportive of Mexican economic development through offering loans after the

Mexican crisis of 1994-95 as well as preferential access to the US market as part of the North American Free Trade Agreement (NAFTA). The Administration favours its medium-term extension to the entire hemisphere under the Free Trade Area of the Americas, broadly agreed to in 1994. But while older general equilibrium analysis pointed to slightly reduced migration from Mexico to the United States as a result of the formation of a free trade area and more so from successful Mexican growth (Hinojosa-Ojeda and Robinson, 1991), the short-run effects of increased competition from efficient US producers of some food products on the rural economy in Mexico could encourage even greater emigration (Martin, 1993; OECD, 1994b). In any case, the export-led recovery in Mexico following the 1995 crisis, fostered by NAFTA and other structural reforms, may already be influencing migration trends.

V. Pervasive entrepreneurship: a source of economic dynamism

Introduction

The OECD *Jobs Study* (OECD, 1994*c*) showed that the US labour market has performed well relative to other OECD countries. Employment growth has been very strong and unemployment has shown little tendency to rise over the long term. The *Jobs Study* also argued that entrepreneurship is one of the keys to a buoyant economy capable of adjusting to economic developments and structural change. Not only can entrepreneurship contribute to job creation, it may contribute to real income gains and greater flexibility in the job market. The US economy appears to be strongly entrepreneurial: many new firms enter the market every year, many US firms are among the most innovative in their industry, and setting up one's own business is perceived as a life-style choice. As a follow-up to the *Jobs Study*, this chapter attempts to explain why the entrepreneurial phenomenon is so pervasive in the United States. The chapter first documents various aspects of entrepreneurial activity, discusses the factors behind it and concludes with implications.

The pervasiveness of entrepreneurship

At its most general, entrepreneurship can be defined as the dynamic process of identifying economic opportunities and acting upon them by developing, producing and selling goods and services. As such, it is central to the functioning of market economies. This, however, allows many specific definitions depending on the stress put on different aspects of entrepreneurial activity. To some, it implies control of the process by the entrepreneur-owner and therefore tends to be identified with small businesses. Alternatively, entrepreneurs are seen as important risk-takers, or as essentially innovators. Thus, while there is no standard measure of entrepreneurship, it has often been connected to firms' size, their age, their growth, and the extent of their engagement in risk-taking activity or particularly innovative activity. This chapter will focus on entrepreneurship by all enterprises, as it contributes to the wider goals of developing new products, services and markets, to structural change and, finally, to job creation.

A common proxy for entrepreneurship is the small business sector. It is clear that small firms in the United States make up the bulk of enterprises: over 98 per cent of firms are Small and Medium-Sized Enterprises (SMEs, *i.e.* employ fewer than 500 workers) and employ half of the workforce. Furthermore, the claim has been made that small businesses contribute disproportionately to job creation, although this is hotly debated.[113] However, referring to the small business sector as a proxy for entrepreneurship may be misleading, since many small businesses are not particularly innovative or risk-taking.

Despite the attention focused on small firms, many larger firms behave in an entrepreneurial and dynamic manner. Furthermore, larger firms play a significant role in the economy: in the United States, firms with 500 or more employees account for 52 per cent of GDP and 46 per cent of private-sector employment (OECD, 1996*b*). Indeed, in the United States, large firms (over 500 employees) account for a high share of employment compared with most other OECD countries, suggesting either that firm size is not necessarily a good proxy for entrepreneurial activity or, instead, that it is relatively easy for US firms to start small, prosper and become large firms. This latter point suggests that indicators based on the performance of "gazelles" or fast-growing firms, may provide a better proxy for the degree of entrepreneurial activity. These firms appear to account for a disproportionate fraction of net job growth in the US economy.[114] Furthermore, and contrary to popular perception, only around one-third of these gazelles are "high-tech" companies. Fast-growing firms can be found across a wide range of activities (for example, Wal-Mart, Starbucks, Office Depot, Federal Express, Amazon Bookstore) and their success often comes from innovative approaches to marketing, organisation or distribution. Franchising has also provided a way for firms to grow quickly and good ideas to be exploited, while sharing the risks and reducing the capital the firm would otherwise require to finance expansion.

Yet another proxy measure for entrepreneurship is the pace at which firms are starting up and closing down. This notion of turbulence attempts to capture the dynamic nature of entrepreneurial activity and has the advantage of not relying on definitions of firms' size, age or growth. Unfortunately the nature of most business start-ups and close-downs make them difficult to measure accurately. The Small Business Administration (SBA), for example, uses three different proxies for new business formation for the United States: the total number of tax returns filed, the number of new employer identification numbers issued by the Department of Labor and the Dun and Bradstreet new business incorporation series. Using the measure constructed from Department of Labor data, some 900 000 firms are created each year, 16.4 per cent of the total number of firms and some 800 000 firms terminate their activities, at an average termination rate of 14.3 per cent (Figure 22.) However, relatively few of these closures – some 5 to 10 per cent – are business failures, involving losses to creditors (Dennis, 1995). Another indicator of turbulence is the firm survival rate. The United States has a lower firm survival rate than most countries, with only around 60 per cent of new firms still operating three years later, indicating a high degree of turbulence (Table 29).

It is often argued that low firm survival rates lead to lower job stability, which may, in turn, lead to firms investing less in job training. Despite low firm survival rates in the United States, overall job turnover does not seem to be markedly higher than other countries, as shown in Table 30. Job turnover, due to firm births or firm terminations, does appear to be relatively high, but this is offset by lower rates of job turnover in existing firms. And while the average and median job tenure statistics are lower for the United States than most countries, the percentage of the work-force who have held their present job for five years or less is not significantly higher in the United States than in several other OECD countries (Figure 23).

The regional dimension. Analysis across states and cities shows that those with higher job loss and lower firm survival rates are among the most prosperous economically (Birch *et al.*, 1997), suggesting that turbulence is an important feature of economic growth. Other proxies of entrepreneurship also have regional dimensions. Significant differences were found in the prevalence of nascent entrepreneurs, with higher levels in the West and North East, and lower levels in the North Central region and the South (Reynolds, forthcoming).[115] In an earlier

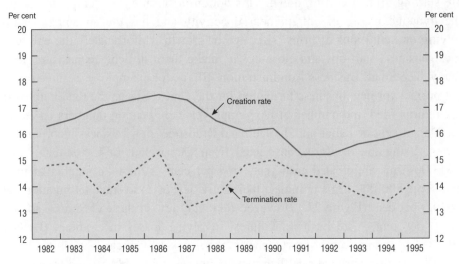

Figure 22. **FIRM CREATION AND TERMINATION RATES**

Per cent of total firm population

Source: Small Business Administration (1996).

Table 29. **Firm survival rates**

Per cent

	After 3 years	After 5 years
United States	60	50
Denmark	69	58
Finland	63	55
France	62	48
Germany	70	63
Ireland	70	57
Italy	66	54
Netherlands	74	..
Norway	68	53
Portugal	56	47
Spain	70	..
Sweden	70	59
United Kingdom	62	47

Source: European Observatory Annual Report 1995 and NFIB Small Business Primer.

154

Table 30. **Job gains and losses**
Average annual rates as a percentage of total employment

		Gross job gains from		Gross job losses from		Turnover
		openings	expansions	closures	contractions	
United States	1984-88	**8.9**	**4.3**	**7.2**	**2.9**	**23.2**
	1989-91	7.4	5.1	7.6	3.5	23.7
Canada	1983-89	3.2	11.7	2.8	7.3	25.0
	1989-91	3.4	10.0	3.7	12.8	29.9
France	1984-89	7.3	6.6	6.9	5.9	26.7
	1989-92	6.9	6.8	7.1	6.8	27.6
Germany	1983-90	2.5	6.5	1.9	5.6	16.5
Italy	1984-89	4.1	8.6	3.6	7.0	23.3
Sweden	1985-89	7.3	8.8	5.2	8.1	29.4
	1989-92	5.6	7.0	4.9	11.3	28.7
United Kingdom	1987-89	2.7	6.3	3.3	1.9	14.1
	1989-91	1.9	6.1	3.4	3.0	14.4

Source: OECD Employment Outlook 1994.

study (Reynolds and Storey, 1993), start-up rates across regions (defined as travel-to-work areas) varied between 2.4 and 114 start-ups per 10 000 persons per year.

Why is entrepreneurship more prevalent in some regions than in others? There is no clear explanation, but some variables appear particularly important. The close proximity of universities and skilled labour pools are likely to generate entrepreneurship by providing new ideas and a labour force which needs relatively little training to adapt (Birch *et al.*, 1996). This research also pointed to other determinants such as the proximity of a major, preferably international, airport and the perception that the area be ''a nice place to live''. Empirical work (Reynolds, 1995) has found that several variables are statistically relevant in explaining the variation across region of firm birth; regional economic diversity, population growth, greater personal wealth, presence of mid-career adults, low unemployment and greater flexibility of employment relationships (as proxied by the absence of unions and the presence of right-to-work laws).

Clustering. To some extent, the regionalisation of entrepreneurial activity may also reflect the phenomenon of ''clustering'' – the apparent tendency of

Figure 23. **DISTRIBUTION OF EMPLOYMENT BY EMPLOYER TENURE, 1995**

Per cent of total employment

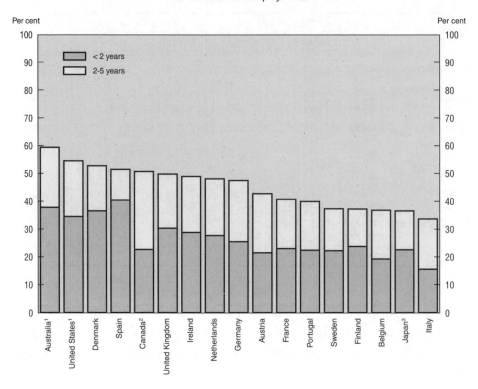

1. 1996.
2. Data shown refer to duration groups under 1 year and 1 to 5 years.
3. Data shown refer to duration groups 2 years or under and 3 to 4 years.
Source: OECD (1997*b*).

firms in the same line, or closely related lines, of business to be geographically concentrated. Silicon Valley in California is currently the most prominent cluster of computer-related entrepreneurial firms. Other clusters are found in industries as varied as financial services in New York, entertainment in Los Angeles, and carpet manufacturing in Dalton, Georgia. Clustering is thought to arise from aggregation economies, since concentrations of firms create larger markets for specialised labour and intermediate inputs and generate informational spill-overs

– the ability to stay abreast of the latest industry developments. These advantages of geographical concentration can be of particular benefit to smaller firms which, because of their size, often cannot provide specialised training or maintain in-house services such as R&D or marketing.

However, it is not clear why some regions have more enterprise clusters than others. Clusters may develop naturally because of intrinsic advantages found in a region, including natural resources such as mines or port facilities. For example, firms in the steel industry are often established close to energy supplies and good transportation networks. Or some regions may provide more fertile ground for enterprise development because of the presence of an enterprise culture or a more favourable institutional framework. Silicon Valley's origin can be traced to an enterprising individual, a Stanford University professor, who established the Palo Alto Research Center, which pioneered the development of computer technologies. The size of clusters is limited by the size of the market, which may in turn be limited to the national market if there are barriers to international trade. Thus, there is some evidence suggesting that the United States is more cluster-intensive than Europe because the US market is larger than national European markets, which are still segmented as a result of different tax regimes, regulations, and policies which favour national products ("national champions") (Krugman, 1991).

The benefits of clusters may be cumulative in that once a cluster has developed, its advantage increases with the size of the cluster: success breeds success. As a result, established clusters may be difficult to challenge and should therefore tend to be stable and long-lived. However, while a cluster can be stable over long periods of time, it would appear that these cumulative advantages are not altogether decisive, and the position of an entrenched cluster can be success-fully challenged. Examples of this abound: steel in both Europe and the United States, certain types of computer chip-making in the United States and Japan, automakers in the United States, cameras in Germany, textiles in many industrial countries. Therefore, as production becomes standardised over time, localisation within an industry can tend to fade away. There appears to be a kind of product cycle in which emergent new industries initially flourish in localised industrial districts, then disperse as they mature. Nevertheless, some clusters have proven very resilient, able to adapt to new technologies and new demands and remain at the cutting edge of their industry. Silicon Valley is one example and others can

Box 8.   Silicon Valley's regional advantage

Silicon Valley in California and Route 128 in Massachusetts, located on opposite coasts, are typically viewed as industrial counterparts and comparable centres of electronics entrepreneurship. But Silicon Valley is by far the more dynamic of the two and appears to be able to adapt better to economic change by seizing new market opportunities and developing new technologies. For example, Silicon Valley recovered rapidly from the collapse of its semiconductor business caused by cheaper foreign production by introducing a stream of high value-added semiconductors, computers, components and software-related products. By the end of the 1980s, Silicon Valley had clearly surpassed Route 128 as the national centre of computer systems innovation (see Table 31) with more firms and more employment in high-tech establishments. Silicon Valley is now home to one-third of the 100 largest technology companies created in the United States since 1965. The market value of these firms increased by $425 billion between 1986 and 1990, dwarfing the $1 billion increase of the Route 128-based counterparts. Also, Northern California attracted two to three times more venture capital than Massachusetts throughout the 1980s.

Table 31.   **High-tech establishments and their employment, Silicon Valley and Route 128**

	Establishments			Employment		
	SV	128	SV/128	SV	128	SV/128
1959	109	268	0.4	17 376	61 409	0.3
1975	831	840	1.0	116 671	98 952	1.2
1990	3 231	2 168	1.5	267 531	150 576	1.8
1992	4 063	2 513	1.6	249 259	140 643	1.8

Note: The type of high-tech establishments are: computing and office equipment, communications equipment, electronic components, guided missiles, space vehicles, instruments and software and data processing.
Source: Saxenian (1994).

The divergent performance of the Route 128 and Silicon Valley clusters cannot be attributed to regional differences in real estate costs, wages, tax levels or defence spending. A more significant consideration is the large number of smaller firms organised in a horizontal network which dominate Silicon Valley. Producers are highly specialised and compete intensely while also engaging in close, but not exclusive, relations with other specialists to produce a final product. The Route 128 region, in contrast, has been dominated by a small number of corporations that internalise a wide range of productive activities. This difference has made Silicon Valley more responsive to change because

(continued on next page)

be found in Italy (the fashion industries of Emilia-Romagna) and in Spain (the leather industries of Valencia). It has been suggested that the vitality of Silicon Valley arises from its decentralised and co-operative industrial system (Saxenian, 1994) (see Box 8).

Reasons for the prevalence of entrepreneurial activity

Culture. The United States is often described as having a strong entrepreneurial "culture". The focus on a free-market economy, a relatively small role for government and the social importance attached to self-reliance have made entrepreneurship a respectable, indeed admired, attribute. A national poll of adult Americans showed that over 90 per cent would approve of their child going into business for himself or herself (Jackson, 1986). However, there was somewhat less enthusiasm shown by owners who had started their businesses three years previously: only 54 per cent of them would approve (Cooper *et al.*, 1990). A more recent survey (Reynolds, 1996) estimates that almost a quarter of households are either starting a business, own a business or are informally investing in someone else's business. There also appears to be no stigma attached to failure, and failure is not automatically assumed to be the owner's fault. Evidence suggests that many entrepreneurs have failed in the past: in one study of bankruptcy more than one-third of the entrepreneurs had owned another business before starting the bankrupt business (Small Business Administration, 1996). The strong pro-entrepreneurial culture has helped to shape institutional characteristics of the US economy that facilitate business start-ups, reward firms based on their economic efficiency and allow rapid, low-cost exit for entrepreneurs who succeed, fail or simply want to move on to a new venture.

Ease of firm creation and closure.[116] It is relatively simple to create a firm in the United States. Compared with other countries, relatively few procedures must be carried out before and after the registration, and the registration process is not very time-consuming. Entrepreneurs can make use of private firms who undertake registration on their behalf and, in this manner, a business entity can be created by telephone or by fax and at low cost. Enterprise creation in the United States also involves fewer regulations; in some European countries craft-related activities from bakers to hairdressers to dispensing opticians require specific qualifications such as an apprenticeship or specific post-apprentice experience, which can take several years to acquire (Meager, 1993).

Just as legislation exists to regulate firm creation, bankruptcy legislation regulates firm termination, or exit. The US system offers the individual bankrupt a "clean slate" by way of discharge: the entrepreneur loses his assets to his creditors but cannot be pursued for any remaining claims which have not been met. While this approach has some disadvantages, it does allow for considerable flexibility and may help to reduce any stigma attached to business failure. In other countries, by contrast, legislation places more emphasis on creditor protection and, in some cases, the absence of discharge clauses means that failed entrepreneurs can be pursued for several years, a situation which is not conducive to risk-taking activity.

Availability of risk capital. A striking aspect of the US entrepreneurial environment is the ample availability of risk capital and generally well-functioning market mechanisms for allocating it efficiently across a wide range of size, risk and return configurations. Small-scale start-ups are typically financed through own funds and loans of various forms,[117] which are generally not difficult to obtain. It is sometimes argued that credit rationing by banks reflects a market imperfection that can be especially severe for small, innovative and risky ventures.[118] In fact, when surveyed, small businesses on average rank obtaining long-term or short-term loans as only 63rd and 64th respectively on the list of difficulties they face (Dennis, 1996). In any case, equity financing may provide a more appropriate mechanism for managing risk and return for high risk ventures.

What distinguishes the United States from the rest of the world in terms of financing entrepreneurial ventures is the availability of equity capital. The development of the private equity market which provides third-party finance to enterprises not quoted on a stock exchange and the second-tier stockmarket which provides exit opportunities for the suppliers of private equity are especially relevant for new and/or fast growing companies.

The private equity market has been the fastest growing market for corporate finance over the last 15 years or so.[119] In recent years the amount of professionally-managed private equity capital outstanding exceeded $100 billion, of which 30 per cent is venture capital. Much of the non-venture private equity managed by partnerships has been used to provide funds for the expansion of medium-sized private firms, leveraged buy-outs and investments in firms in financial distress.

Since the early 1980s venture capital gained importance as a source of funding for innovative new ventures. The stock of venture capital outstanding is currently running at about $30 billion, 80 per cent of which is managed by partnerships and the rest by subsidiaries of financial and industrial corporations.[120] In 1996, about 37 per cent of new venture investment was directed to early-stage companies (so-called seed and start-ups), compared with 12 per cent in Europe (Venture One, 1997, and European Venture Capital Association, 1997). Striking differences are also found in the sectoral distribution of venture capital investment. Technology-based firms in the United States and Canada are able to attract more funding than similar firms in other OECD countries. In 1994, 65 per cent of US venture capital disbursements went to technology-based firms, compared with only 15 per cent in Europe (OECD, 1996c). Geographically, venture capital investment is concentrated in California and Massachusetts (Table 32). Even so, it is noteworthy that about half of the new venture capital in 1996 was invested elsewhere.

An important factor in the development of venture capital was the revision of rules governing investment by pension funds under the Employment Retirement Income Security Act (ERISA) in the late 1970s, which allowed them to undertake higher-risk investment, including venture capital operations. As a result, pension funds have become the largest source of venture capital funding in the United States, accounting for close to half of the funding in 1996. In contrast, pension funds in Europe play a smaller role (contributing about a quarter of

Table 32. **Geographical distribution of venture capital, 1996**[1]

US$ million

	Amount raised	Number of deals
California	3 749.3	612
Massachusetts	1 209.0	194
Florida	472.2	32
Texas	435.6	66
Colorado	420.3	50
Illinois	394.2	39
Washington	329.1	51
Virginia	301.7	34
Connecticut	289.5	28
Pennsylvania	285.0	44
United States, total	**10 023.4**	**1 502**
United Kingdom	1 066.9	1 014
France	947.5	1 000
Germany	716.9	708
Netherlands	518.7	248
Italy	451.8	174
Sweden	300.2	158
Spain	230.0	152
Switzerland	70.0	21
Belgium	134.1	153
Europe, total	**4 755.3**	**4 081**

1. Excluding institutional buy-outs.
Source: Venture One (1997) and European Venture Capital Association Yearbook (1997).

funds) while banks and insurance companies are the primary sources of private equity.[121]

The governance structure in the venture capital industry has also contributed to its success. Venture capitalists ensure that the interests of the third-party investors (*e.g.* pension funds) are well served by the managers of the companies in which they invest. The contractual relationship between venture capitalists as general partners and the investors as limited partners is clearly defined.[122] Many of the venture capitalists have the technical expertise required in high-tech environments. They also recruit staff, explore various marketing possibilities and do not hesitate to replace the founder-CEOs if they consider it would improve the firm's performance.[123] Venture capitalists monitor closely the companies in which they invest and participate actively in their management so as to maximise the probability of their commercial success. The need for close monitoring has required venture capitalists to invest in companies located in close proximity.[124]

However, this has been changing with the development of syndication and networking. Thus, in 1996, even California-based venture capitalists directed 42 per cent of their total investments towards companies located elsewhere, even though California and Massachusetts remained major recipient states (Table 33).

The success of the venture-capital markets has also been reinforced by the easy access to exit mechanisms by which venture capitalists can "cash-in" their mature investments. These include private transactions, such as trade sales and private placements,[125] and initial public offerings (IPOs) on the securities markets. In addition to their direct role as exit vehicles, IPOs serve as benchmarks for pricing of private transactions. IPOs have been facilitated by the NASDAQ (National Association of Securities Dealers Automated Quotation system), the best known of the second-tier markets, which was created in 1971 as a nation-wide market for trades in young, innovative companies. Second-tier markets provide them easier access to public securities markets through less stringent admission requirements and lower admission and continuing costs than those for first-tier markets. The success of NASDAQ has been substantial, and it serves as a benchmark for all other second-tier markets. In 1994, there were a total of 4 902 companies quoted, compared with 2 570 on the New York Stock Exchange. Many companies which could be listed on the NYSE, such as Microsoft, Intel, MCI and Apple Computer have chosen to remain on NASDAQ rather than move to a first-tier market. A number of participants in the European venture capital market see the poor performance of the second-tier markets created in the 1980s to be a major hindrance to the full development of the European venture capital industry, and renewed attempts are being made (Euro-

Table 33. **Geographical preferences of venture capital firms, 1996**

Home state of venture capitalists	Where they invested Percentage of their total investments			
	Home state	California	Massachusetts	All other states
California	58.0	58.0	4.7	37.3
Massachusetts	30.0	17.2	30.0	52.8
New York	9.4	28.7	14.7	44.5
Connecticut	14.7	26.0	12.7	46.6
Minnesota	21.3	33.4	12.3	33.0

Source: Coopers & Lybrand, *Money Tree Report, 1996 results.*

pean-wide EASDAQ, France's *Second Marché,* Italy's METIM and the United Kingdom's AIM) to create viable second-tier markets.[126]

Small Business Investment Companies (SBICs) are SBA-licensed venture capital firms which account for 10 to 15 per cent of venture capital investment. SBICs are allowed to match their investments with SBA loans and enjoy certain tax benefits but in exchange are subject to certain limits on the size of the companies in which they invest as well as on taking controlling interests. SBICs managed to channel record amounts of equity financing to small, fast-growing companies back in the 1960s but also suffered from poor quality of managers.[127] Having been increasingly dominated by venture capital partnerships, SBICs are currently in large part subsidiaries of financial and industrial corporations. SBICs typically invest in smaller deals than do partnerships, and their presence is important in those states where there is a significant potential for promising new firms but availability of venture capital is low. SBICs therefore play a complementary role to venture capital partnerships.

Business angels are yet another source of equity finance for start-ups and their subsequent expansion. Angel capital is not an organised source of finance, and reliable statistics are scarce. But it is thought to be at least twice the size of the venture capital pool, though individual deals are much smaller. The angel capital market is fragmented and localised, and the market segmentation is exacerbated by barriers created by state securities legislation. In the absence of organised intermediaries the match-making process is difficult: potential angels hesitate to publicise their willingness to invest, and entrepreneurs are not keen on revealing what they believe to be innovative ideas (Dennis, 1996a). In these circumstances, the SBA has taken the initiative to create the Angel Capital Electronic Network (ACE-Net). This is a nation-wide Internet listing of small innovative companies with the access restricted to angels. In setting up the ACE-Net, State Securities Administrators agreed to remove restrictions on inter-state trading of unregistered stocks of those companies which are on the ACE-Net, a step which in its own right is crucial to the further development of angel capital markets.

Availability of advice. Just as the venture-backed companies benefit from the advisory role of venture capitalists, most other companies benefit from the well-developed business advisory service industry in the United States. The industry comprises management consultants, accountants, business lawyers and a whole range of government and non-profit bodies which cater to the needs of small business and start-ups. At the federal level alone there are 1 000 Small Business Development Centers in 50 states which offer training and counselling services as well as help small companies access various federal support programmes. Offices which provide similar services exist at the state, county and city levels and also in the private sector, such as chambers of commerce and industry, many of which target specific groups such as women and African Americans. Thus, one survey showed that the State of Wisconsin has at least 400 different programmes providing some 700 kinds of services (Center for the Study of Entrepreneurship, 1993). However, knowledge of these programmes among the general population was low.

Patent protection. One element of advice that entrepreneurs find particularly useful concerns patent protection. In the United States, the cost of patent application is lower than in Europe, and small businesses benefit from a 50 per cent discount on patent fees. It has been estimated that the cost of obtaining European patent protection is three times that in the United States in terms of patent office fees and representation expenses and is about ten times on the average including other related costs such as translation expenses. On the other hand, the high cost of litigation and uncertainty stemming largely from the application of the first-to-invent rule is a problem for smaller firms in the United States. A typical lawsuit on infringement costs between \$25 000 and \$200 000, and larger ones could cost \$1 million, well beyond the level with which small firms can cope effectively.

Taxation and the regulatory burden. Entrepreneurs in the United States benefit from a relatively low overall tax burden. Moreover, because of a generous carry-forward and backward of losses some 40 per cent of companies have no taxable profits. However, American entrepreneurs cite the tax burden and the complexity of the tax system among the most severe problems they face (Dennis, 1996*b*), a common complaint across OECD countries. This problem has been alleviated to some extent by tax reforms during the last decade that have generally lowered top marginal tax rates. For example, cuts in central government corporate income tax rates since the mid-eighties have averaged around 10 percentage points (OECD, 1991). Nevertheless, marginal effective corporate tax rates have increased since the 1980s from 14.4 per cent in 1980 to 24 per cent in 1990 and vary considerably across industries, asset types, financing sources and ownership (Jorgenson and Landau, 1993) (Table 34). But when combined with

Table 34. **Marginal effective corporate tax rates, 1980-90**

In per cent

	1980	1985	1990
Asset			
Machinery	−12.0	−18.6	18.5
Buildings	19.1	12.2	25.3
Inventories	28.5	28.7	26.3
Industry			
Manufacturing	33.8	27.5	34.0
Other industry	13.7	−16.7	11.0
Commerce	15.5	9.2	21.8
Source of finance			
Debt	−49.2	−55.5	−14.7
New share issues	47.1	43.0	44.1
Retained earnings	45.6	42.1	43.7
Owner			
Households	15.8	9.5	23.6
Tax-exempt institutions	9.1	2.4	19.3
Insurance companies	26.3	25.1	40.9
Overall tax rate	14.4	9.2	24.0

Source: Jorgenson and Landau (1993).

taxation on corporate earnings at the personal level, effective rates have been reduced to around 19 per cent, which is lower than in other major countries, except for the United Kingdom (Table 35).

Although the tax burden remains a concern, attention has turned to focus on the compliance burden posed by reporting requirements and the complexity of the system. Research by the Small Business Administration has concluded that, in 1992, the average annual cost of regulation, paperwork and tax compliance amounted to $5 000 per employee in firms with fewer than 500 employees and $3 400 per employee in larger firms.[128] Even though it was found that firms, when surveyed, agreed that they would have had to collect much of the required information for other purposes or found the information useful (GAO, 1996), the tax system's ambiguity, frequent changes, expiration clauses and layers of federal and state regulation remain the main sources of the high compliance burden on businesses.

The US tax code is fairly neutral with respect to the choice of legal form of a business with, in particular, the possibility of using S taxation (available to

Table 35. **Marginal effective tax rates on corporate earnings**

		Effective tax rate at the corporate level	Effective tax rate at corporate and personal level combined	*Memorandum item:* Statutory corporate tax rate
United States	1980	14.4	22.5	49.5
	1990	24.0	19.1	38.3
Japan	1980	3.1	15.6	52.6
	1990	6.1	23.0	54.7
Germany	1980	15.2	32.9	62.2
	1990	4.6	28.6	58.1
France	1980	–28.8	74.1	50.0
	1990	–34.4	65.4	37.0
Italy	1980	–91.6	58.5	36.3
	1990	–72.8	58.2	46.4
United Kingdom	1980	–31.4	30.7	52.0
	1990	28.0	13.8	34.0
Canada	1980	16.9	20.0	..
	1990	25.9	19.3	..
Australia	1980	41.8	23.4	46.0
	1990	14.6	28.1	39.0
Sweden	1980	–22.5	37.9	39.6
	1990	1.0	27.8	30.0

Note: The effective tax rate at the corporate level is defined as the ratio of the difference between pre-tax real rate of return and the post-corporate tax real rate of return to the pre-tax real rate of return. The effective tax rate at the corporate and personal level combined is the ratio between the difference of the pre-tax real rate of return and the post-tax real rate of return of the saver. The pre-tax real rate of return is assumed to be 10 per cent.
Source: Jorgenson and Landau (1993).

companies with fewer than 35 shareholders and that meet other conditions), which offers almost full elimination of double taxation (taxation of both corporate income and distributed profits) (OECD, 1994*d*). This view is supported by a survey by the NFIB in 1996, which found that choice of legal form was not related to tax issues.

The level of the capital gains tax rate (CGT) could have an important effect on the private equity market. While the large percentage of private equity capital provided by pension funds is tax-exempt (OECD, 1996*c*), the funds provided by other investors (venture capitalists, private investors, entrepreneurs) are not. The maximum CGT rate was cut from 49½ per cent to 28 per cent in 1978, to 20 per cent in 1981 and raised again to 28 per cent as part of the 1986 tax reform. The rate was cut in 1993 to 20 per cent for new investment in small companies (less than $50 million in assets) with a minimum holding period of five years. It is difficult to determine the impact of these tax changes on the supply of private equity because of structural and cyclical changes in the economy which occurred at the same time. Further changes to CGT were made in the Taxpayer Relief Act of 1997. Rates on assets held for longer than 18 months will be lowered significantly.

Flexible labour markets. Widely observed features of the US labour markets, such as high degrees of flexibility and mobility, assist the process of entrepreneurial activity. Little formal regulation of labour contracts and light-handed employment protection legislation facilitate the adjustment of labour inputs associated with high rates of turbulence. Moreover, decentralised wage formation with limited union presence (except in a few sectors) make employee compensation flexible, and this trend is reinforced by a greater use of performance-based pay, particularly in new business ventures, where employee stock options are often offered.

New and high growth ventures require skilled workers and up-skilling of existing workers. Despite the well-known weaknesses of the primary and secondary education system in the United States (OECD, 1994*e*), the diversified system of higher education does a good job in meeting these requirements. The US universities produce a large number of Ph.Ds and community colleges offer worker training that is often tailored to the needs of a particular business. And there appears to be much on-the-job training of workers occurring at the enterprise level.[129] Human capital gained at firms, however, tends to be general or industry-specific and, hence, is less likely to be lost with job changes.

The dynamic nature of the US labour markets is further enhanced by immigrant workers. Immigrants are important sources of entrepreneurs, skilled workers and unskilled ones. Notwithstanding some well-known anecdotes (*e.g.* the CEO of Intel is foreign-born), there are few official statistics on immigrant entrepreneurs. In several countries where immigration is a significant phenomenon, self-employment rates are generally higher for immigrants. Table 25 nonetheless shows that there is no significant difference in self-employment rates between natives and foreign-born in the United States. This could be an indication of the prevalence of entrepreneurship among natives or an indication of a flexible US labour market which allows immigrants to find jobs rather than create their own. A significant number of skilled immigrant workers are found in high-tech ventures. They are typically foreign graduate students who finished their advanced degrees and stay on in the United States. Finally, unskilled immigrant workers are found in many low-tech ventures.

The role of government programmes. The US government has introduced several programmes aimed at facilitating enterprise start-ups and development. These include programmes administered by the Departments of Agriculture, Commerce, Defence, Energy, Transportation and independent agencies such as Export-Import Bank, the National Institutes of Health and the Small Business Administration. The goals of these various bodies tend to differ because the target groups are different. For example, the Department of Commerce focuses on helping established enterprises become more competitive by providing assistance to raise productivity, develop new products or markets and expand R&D. The Department of Agriculture concentrates on developing businesses in rural areas and the SBA focuses on new and small businesses. The Cato Institute estimates that the federal government spends roughly $65 billion each year (close to 1 per cent of GDP) on more than 125 programmes that provide direct assistance to US firms (Moore, 1997). Little is known about the overall economic impact of these programmes. As in many OECD countries, few have been evaluated, in part because of the methodological difficulties involved. It is also difficult to establish how many existing firms or new firms would have emerged and grown anyway, in the absence of such programmes, given the overall favourable climate for entrepreneurial activity. Furthermore, it is difficult to measure the overall effectiveness of these programmes against alternative policies such as reducing corporate taxes by the same amount. (Such a reduction would be significant, since federal corporate taxes currently raise about $200 billion per year.)

Among the programmes which have been evaluated are the Advanced Technology Program (ATP) and the Manufacturing Extension Partnership (MEP). ATP provides funding to assist US businesses to apply or commercialise new scientific discoveries. Evaluating ATP was difficult because while funded projects are intended to have a commercial impact, several years can elapse between the end of technical work and commercial results. A Department of Commerce evaluation found that the ATP increased high-risk research, implying that stronger links were being forged between the research community and enterprise. However, this finding was disputed by the GAO (1995a), because the claim was not adequately supported by survey data.

MEP is a nation-wide network of locally managed manufacturing extension centres dedicated to helping smaller manufacturers improve their competitiveness by adopting modern technologies. The programme was initially designed to transfer advanced technologies developed at the government's Advanced Manufacturing Research Facility in Maryland and at other government research institutes. However, once established, the centres quickly realised that most small US firms did not need advanced technologies and that most firms would be better served by off-the-shelf technologies (Shapira *et al.*, 1995). One survey showed that 73 per cent of the manufacturers who used the service believed that MEP assistance had positively affected their overall business performance (GAO, 1995*b*). However, the survey also asked companies that could have used a MEP why they had made limited or no use of the services. About 82 per cent reported that they had not used the services because they were unaware of these programmes. A further 10 per cent said that although they knew about MEP, they had not used the services because they believed the assistance would not be necessary.

Local and regional governments in the United States also offer a wide array of enterprise development programmes with a variety of objectives and target groups. These range from developing depressed inner city areas to diversifying rural economies. Beneficiaries include large corporations receiving government subsidies to train their workforce or to relocate to a disadvantaged region. Other beneficiaries are smaller firms participating in government programmes aimed at improving exports or encouraging networking among firms. Other programmes provide start-up assistance to individuals creating their own business. Subnational programmes, much like their national counterparts, have not been rigorously evaluated and little is known of their impact (see Box 9 for an example). There is increasing concern that efforts by sub-national governments to attract existing firms from other regions may amount to a costly poaching exercise with little or no economy-wide impact. For example, the State of Alabama, caught in a bidding war with other states, offered tax breaks and other subsidies amounting to $300 million in order to win a Mercedes car plant, resulting in a cost of $200 000 per job created (Myerson, 1996). Also, New York City awarded more than $30 million each to two large financial corporations threatening to relocate to other cities. In an attempt to counter this trend, legislation is being introduced in some states to curtail the bidding war and "claw-back" public funds when companies fail to deliver on their job creation promises or move out of the state.

Box 9.   An assessment of policies supporting science parks

During the 1980s, many sub-national governments, facing decreasing revenues and increasing unemployment, looked to technological development to revive their local economies and create jobs. One of the ways they attempted to promote this high-tech strategy was through the creation of science parks. Science parks differ in size and structure across the United States but share several characteristics. Science parks are a type of business park where the primary activity of the majority of the establishments is industry-driven R&D. As such, basic research and mass production are usually not undertaken. Science parks are also expected to generate new high-tech firms through spin-off or other forms of new investments. Most science parks also feature links with a research facility (a university or institute, for example). State and local authorities support science parks through the provision of infrastructure and land, tax breaks and tax holidays, promotion – primarily through marketing campaigns and lobbying – and other fiscal and physical incentives.

The impact of policies to support science parks is difficult to ascertain because few parks have been evaluated. Failure rates appear to be high with about a half of all parks closing down. In addition, a number of science parks have been criticised because the parks' growth has occurred largely through attracting new firms from outside the region rather than through new-firm formation or spin-offs. However, when successful, science parks can generate economic development and high job creation which spill over the borders of the park. The secrets of success are not known, but it is argued that location and government assistance are critical. Successful parks have been located close to metropolitan areas which offer high-quality infrastructure such as good transportation linkages and a reputable university, suggesting that science parks are not viable in remote and sparsely populated regions. Government assistance is also required during the start-up phase and often for several years afterwards. For example, the Research Triangle Park, one of the largest science parks in the United States, took more than a decade to become viable at a significant cost to the state. Therefore, the promise offered by policies to establish or promote science parks must be viewed cautiously in view of their costs.

Source: Amirahmadi and Saff (1993).

Conclusions

This brief review of entrepreneurship in the United States has identified a range of institutional arrangements that work together to harness entrepreneurial zeal. These arrangements provide for low-cost entry to and exit from the entrepreneurial activity, multi-layered supply of risk capital to finance innovative ventures of varying size and nature at different stages in the life cycle, an abundant availability of managerial and technical advice, a flexible work force with varying skill levels, and relatively low levels of taxation of the rewards to entrepreneurial success. To be sure, there are also factors which tend to discourage entrepreneurship, such as high compliance costs of taxation and prohibitive costs of patent litigation; and the net impact of government programmes aimed at helping firms is ambiguous.

A remarkable feature of entrepreneurship in the United States is that constituents of the institutional set-ups are themselves also entrepreneurial. Venture capitalists are highly entrepreneurial, and the NASDAQ is a result of an entrepreneurial endeavour. Universities are striving to expand their research capability and their capacity to commercialise the results, while community colleges offer custom-designed courses to meet the specific training needs of companies. And examples of municipalities taking initiatives to streamline regulations affecting emerging companies are not rare. The entrepreneurial nature of the whole system has allowed it to evolve in ways that further facilitate the creation and growth of innovative ventures, for example through a greater use of networking, including syndication of venture capital, to reach promising projects in remote states and even abroad. Given these trends and the way all the elements of the institutional framework fit together, the rest of the United States may well benefit from a "virtuous circle" effect as already illustrated by the much-publicised success of the Silicon Valley as a high-tech, entrepreneurial cluster. Yet other countries striving to promote entrepreneurship should be aware that any attempt to replicate only a part of the US system is likely to be inefficient and ineffective. The key lesson from the US experience is that a recipe for success in stimulating entrepreneurial activity comprises a systemic approach to reforming the institutional set-ups in a wide range of areas.

Notes

1. Using a wealth effect that is now widely believed to be around 3 per cent, rather than the traditional 5 per cent, the increase in net financial wealth from 1995 to 1996 from Table 1 would add $57 billion in consumption. Taking disposable personal income as given, if the saving rates in 1996 and 1997 had remained equal to the 4.8 per cent rate recorded in 1995, outlays in the year and a half would have been $54.4 billion lower, suggesting the fall in the saving rate can be accounted for by the increase in net financial wealth.

2. For example, the Federal Reserve's 1995 Survey of Consumer Finances shows that one out of six families with earnings less than $25 000 had annual debt payments in excess of 40 per cent of their incomes, while the overall ratio was one in nine.

3. In particular, the Council of Economic Advisers (1997a) points to a decrease in the social stigma attached to bankruptcy, an increase in the divorce rate, which may push more individuals over the edge, and greater awareness of bankruptcy as an option through attorney advertisement as factors that help explain the overall upward trend. See also Chapter III.

4. Some of this motor vehicle inventory decline probably would have occurred in the next couple of quarters anyway, as supplies were more than adequate at that time.

5. The Bureau of Economic Analysis uses a hedonic measure for its computer deflator. When a new product like Intel's Pentium computer chip comes onto the market at prices close to those of its predecessor (in this case, the old 486 chip), the deflator falls because more computing power is available at roughly the same price declines.

6. From September 1996 to September 1997, the labour force has grown 1.6 per cent, but about $1/4$ percentage point of this growth is from a revision to population controls, mostly for immigrants (and emigrants) that added 470 000 people to the January civilian non-institutional population 16 years and over. Employment and labour force estimates were similarly adjusted. The Bureau Labor of Statistics has not revised its historical series and has no plans to do so.

7. Discretionary spending is funded by 13 different appropriations bills. If these bills are not signed into law before the fiscal year begins on 1 October, government agencies cannot legally operate unless a stopgap continuing resolution is passed, and in FY 1996 Congress and the President twice failed to pass continuing resolutions in time.

8. Final 1996 tax settlements paid in April 1997 were about $25 billion higher than expected. In addition, regular payments to the Treasury from withholding and estimated taxes ran about $10 billion higher in the first half of FY 1997. Assuming the same level increase in the second half of the year yields the $45 billion projection revision.

9. The OECD focuses its analysis on net lending, which equals receipts less current outlays, net investment and net capital transfers, while the US NIPA definition of the deficit excludes net investment. The Office of Management and Budget publishes fiscal year deficit figures, which include financial transactions and net investment – the so-called unified deficit.

10. The increase in national savings comes from the improvement in government savings less an offset to private savings. This offset was estimated using annual data from 1967 to 1995 by regressing private savings as a per cent of GDP on two lagged dependent variables, current and one lag of the cyclically-adjusted general government budget deficit as a per cent of potential GDP, the current value and two lags of the unemployment rate, a time trend, a dummy variable equal to one after 1984 and this dummy interacted with the trend term. Private saving rates appear to trend down in the data with a sharp downward break around 1985. Experiments with other lag lengths did not materially change the conclusions. The regression is run in levels because after one accounts for the break in the trend, the two savings series as a per cent of GDP appear stationary. The analysis treats the government structural budget deficit as exogenous, as well as the unemployment rate. The regression results (standard errors in parentheses) are:

$$prv_t = 15.42 + .20\ prv_{t-1} - .18\ prv_{t-2} - .48\ gvt\text{–}str_t + .24\ gvt\text{–}str_{t-1} + .10\ unmp_t$$
$$\quad\ \ (4.13)\ \ (.21)\qquad\quad (.17)\qquad\quad (.23)\qquad\qquad (.27)\qquad\qquad (.22)$$

$$- .21\ unmp_{t-1} + .27\ unmp_{t-2} + .07t + 3.25\ d85_t - .22\ t\ d85_t,\ R^2 = 0.88$$
$$\quad\ (.24)\qquad\qquad (.16)\qquad\quad (.06)\ \ (2.69)\qquad (.11)$$

The analysis also treats the state and local structural surplus, which has been moving down recently, as exogenous to federal fiscal tightening, though this may not be strictly true (see below). To calculate the effect on private savings, one takes the fitted values from the equation using actual structural government deficits less the fitted values assuming the structural federal government deficits as a per cent of potential GDP do not change from their 1992 value. Each series is solved recursively from 1993 to 1997.

11. Specifically, the child tax credit is $400 in 1998 and $500 thereafter for each child less than 17 years old, with phase-outs beginning at $75 000 income per year for single taxpayers and $110 000 for married couples. The tax credit can also be applied to payroll taxes, so those who qualify for the Earned Income Tax Credit can also benefit from the child tax credit. The total revenue loss from the child tax credit is estimated by CBO to be $73 billion over five years and $155 billion over ten years. A college tax credit for the first two years of post-secondary education of $1 500 (100 per cent of the first $1 000 and 50 per cent of the next $1 000 in tuition and fees) and a credit equal to 20 per cent of education expenses after two years is phased out starting at $40 000 annual income for singles and $80 000 for married couples. The law also sets up an educational savings account where after-tax deposits of up to $2 000 can be made; interest is tax free on withdrawal if used for post-secondary education. In addition, interest on student loans is deductible for low-income tax payers, and employer-assisted tuition programmes remain untaxed. The estimated cost of the education tax package is $39 billion over five years and $99 billion over ten years. Besides the education savings account, the law raises the income limits on those who can contribute pre-tax earnings to a regular individual retirement savings account (IRA), and it allows penalty-free withdrawal for a first-time home purchase or post-secondary education. In addition, it sets up a ''backloaded'' IRA where contributions are taxed as normal income, but the

interest accrues tax free without penalty if the funds are ultimately used for a first-time home purchase or the taxpayer is older than 59 years. The estimated revenue loss from these savings provisions is roughly $2 billion and $20 billion over the next five and ten years, respectively.

12. Estimating the revenue impact of a capital gains tax cut remains controversial in the economic literature (Zodrow, 1995). A tax cut can generate added revenue in the short run if it leads to a proportional higher increase in realisations than the cut in the rate. Investors previously ''locked in'' because of the high tax liability could feel it is now worthwhile to realise gains. The extent of this effect, however, depends on whether investors perceive these tax cuts as permanent or transitory (Auerbach, 1988). In addition, unrealised capital gains on assets are not taxed at all if the holder dies, so to the extent that tax cuts increase realisations, the base on which capital gains taxes are collected is permanently broadened. While the magnitude of these effects on revenue in the short run remains unsettled, in the long run it is likely that a capital gains tax cut reduces revenue (Zodrow), as is assumed by the Joint Tax Committee and the Department of Treasury.

13. Feenberg and Summers (1990) estimate that taxpayers in the top 0.5 percentile of average gross income over five years received 36.1 per cent of all capital gains in 1979-84; those in the top two percentiles received 49.4 per cent. Only 1.4 per cent of heirs paid estate taxes in 1995; undoubtedly most were well-to-do, as with a minimal amount of planning a household could have increased its effective exemption dramatically under the old law.

14. The 1995 average levels of tuition and required fees were: Two-year public colleges $1 194, four-year public colleges $2 982, all private institutions $11 128. (Source: US National Center for Education Statistics, *Digest of Education Statistics*).

15. Medicare is the government-sponsored health care system for senior citizens and some of the disabled. It is composed of two parts: Part A provides for hospital services, skilled nursing care and hospice care and is paid for out of a fund which collects revenues from a payroll tax. Part B covers physician care and outpatient hospital services and is paid for out of general revenues and premiums on enrolees that are supposed to cover 25 per cent of the costs. Before the shift in home health care services, the Part A trust fund was projected to be exhausted in 2001.

16. According to the annual report of the Trustees of the Social Security system, tax revenue will exceed payouts through 2011. Between 2012 and 2018, interest income will offset the gap between taxes and payouts. Afterwards, the fund begins to shrink, reaching zero in 2029. Demographics are currently helping as the number of retirees is small, but demographics will hurt later when ''the baby-boom generation'' retires.

17. This is a market-based system where rival plans compete to sign up members to a specific package of benefits at a negotiated price. The programme pays a percentage of the premium up to a dollar limit. The overhead costs for the government are very small: about $20 million for the 9 million members. For more details see Butler and Moffit (1997).

18. In the past five years, however, the Supreme Court has voided several federal laws that unlawfully compelled states to enact and enforce Federal programmes especially when no money was provided to carry out the mandate.

19. In February 1996, the range of FOMC members' predictions for the unemployment rate in the fourth quarter of 1996 was 5½ to 6 per cent, while in February 1997 it was 5¼ to 5½ per cent for the last quarter of this year. The actual rate in 1996's final quarter was 5.3 and in the second quarter of this year it was 4.9 per cent.

20. Indicative is the fact that the range of forecasts made by members of the FOMC for real GDP growth over the four quarters of 1996 and 1997 were being steadily raised from rates slightly lower than consensus views of potential growth to rates well above that crucial figure.

21. One indicator pointing in that direction is the spread between yields on 10-year conventional Treasury notes and those on new "Treasury Inflation-Protection Securities" (see Chapter III): it averaged about 3¼ percentage points in the first three months of the latter's trading following its late-January 1997 introduction before starting on a steady decline to around 2½ points by September. Factors other than changed expectations might, however, have played some role in this decline. In the United Kingdom this proxy for expected inflation has recently been around 3.6 points, while in Canada it has been only 2.3 points of late. The Livingston Survey of professional economists also shows that ten-year inflation expectations are about a half percentage point lower than in 1994 (2.9 per cent, down from 3.4 per cent).

22. But the Federal Reserve takes the stock market into account in its interest-rate-setting deliberations only to the extent that it affects spending decisions.

23. However, despite increased gross equity issuance both in the form of initial public and "seasoned" offerings, equity continues to be retired on net because of withdrawals related to the ongoing boom in mergers and acquisitions and business repurchases of their own outstanding shares. Thus, the much discussed market inflows from mutual funds are merely replacing shares previously held by private pension funds, as households are switching their retirement pension saving from defined benefit plans to self-directed defined contribution plans, such as 401ks.

24. Regressing the spread on the current and twice lagged unemployment rate, the once- and twice-lagged dependent variables and a time trend over the period January 1980 to May 1997 using monthly observations shows a significant positive impact effect of unemployment on the spread but with a slow approach to the smaller long-term effect of 0.14. The residual pattern looks "clean", implying that the slight negative trend (possibly attributable to improvements in risk management techniques) and the lower unemployment rate are sufficient to explain the fall in the spread without alluding to any unusual increase in the market's appetite for risk.

25. For example, comparable growth rates averaged several percentage points more in the 1980s expansion.

26. For example, the gap between what banks have been paying on small time deposits and savings deposits relative to what can be earned on Treasury bills has been unusually wide at some 95 basis points. If this margin had been only the 1992 figure of 7 basis points, 85 per cent of the rise in the ratio of pre-tax income to assets would have been eliminated.

27. But the number of bank branches actually rose by some 2 per cent in 1996 to 62 786.

28. A regression of the monthly long-term interest-rate differential against the change in the unemployment rate gap and a lagged dependent variable explains 86 per cent of the variance

from 1980 to the present and shows small but persistent residuals in this direction since March 1996.

29. The inclusion of estimated currency flows as a capital import is a new feature of the US balance of payments. Estimates are that the stock of such currency abroad is between $200 and $250 billion out of a total of $375 billion in circulation (Porter and Judson, 1996). This represents 5 to 7 per cent of foreign assets in the United States. The flow was estimated at $14 billion in 1995, about 3 per cent of recorded capital inflows, well down from an 11 per cent share in previous years.

30. Mexico repaid its final medium-term swap arrangement of $3.5 billion with the Treasury's Exchange Stabilisation Fund on 16 January 1997.

31. In 1995, the last year for which data are currently available, there were only 18 petitions for such duties, down from an average of 76 in the period 1980-94 (Leidy, 1996).

32. Similar talks have got underway once again in the area of financial services. These negotiations have a year-end deadline.

33. A particularly sensitive point among opponents is the supposed loss of US jobs to lower-cost producers in Mexico. While studies generally show about as much employment created in incremental exports as lost in imports, what matters is that the United States has been at near full employment for some time in any case, so those whose jobs have been lost have probably not had a great deal of difficulty in becoming re-employed. Also, the propensity for plants to close and relocate in Mexico has probably not changed as a result of the agreement itself. NAFTA is also criticised for its lack of any mechanism to adjust for currency fluctuations, but it is not a monetary union; indeed, in the presence of such a mechanism, the necessary adjustment in Mexico's external balance would have been much more painful.

34. The Congress recently decided to renew China's most favoured nation (MFN) status. While the economic case for renewal was strong, opponents claimed that the bilateral trade imbalance, which reached about $40 billion in China's favour in 1996, reflects unfair trading practices. In February 1997 the two nations agreed to extend until end-2000 a 1994 treaty in the area of textiles and clothing which boosts some US import quotas in exchange for Chinese measures to improve market access for the purpose of raising the limited amount of US exports.

35. In a related matter, the EU and the United States came to a partial deal in April over meat inspection standards (except for poultry).

36. Under section 20 of the Glass-Steagall Act, banks are prohibited from engaging principally in securities underwriting, such as commercial paper, mortgage-related securities and securitised commercial loans. In 1987, the Board allowed some subsidiaries of bank holding companies to underwrite these securities, but it limited the total revenue share to 5 per cent. In 1989 it raised the limit to 10 per cent, and it approved applications to underwrite corporate debt and equity securities subject to restrictive firewalls between the subsidiary and the holding company.

37. Some states, such as Illinois and Georgia, did begin to pass their own telecoms legislation in 1997.

38. White (1997) finds that the states who are implementing reforms are precisely those who would be expected to gain the most from deregulation. These are also the states where cost

overruns and bad investment decisions have been most prevalent and where therefore state regulators have the strongest incentives to shift such risks in the future away from consumers and towards financial markets.

39. The ability of certain large firms to participate in this consolidation and to be full-fledged competitors is reduced by the terms of the 1935 Public Utilities Holding Companies Act. It was designed to prevent large utilities from merging, raising capital or diversifying across regions or industries. It now applies to only 15 firms (of which 12 electric utilities with a combined market share of 17 per cent) and is clearly discriminatory. In June a Senate Committee voted its repeal, but prospects for passage of that bill are poor. Another holdover piece of legislation from the regulation era under scrutiny is the Public Utility Regulatory Policies Act of 1978, which requires utilities to buy power from producers of alternative energy forms, such as renewable energy.

40. However, that error derives from the unpredictable effects of rail deregulation on the price of coal transportation and of technological change, both of which cannot be counted on in the ozone case.

41. OECD (1996b, Chapter 3) showed that in 1995 earnings dispersion narrowed for the first time in many years for women and for both sexes in the bottom half of the distribution. Census Bureau data for the shares of income received by families show that 1993 marked the turning point, with the shares for the bottom quintile, two quintiles and three quintiles rising from 4.1, 14.0 and 29.7 per cent, respectively, in 1993 to 4.4, 14.5 and 30.3 per cent in 1995. Correspondingly, the share received by the top quintile fell from 47.0 per cent to 46.5 per cent. Nonetheless, inequality remains probably greater than in any post-war year other than 1993 and 1994.

42. The minimum wage was boosted from $4.25 per hour to $4.75 on 1 October 1996 and was further increased to $5.15 on 1 September 1997. The labour market reactions to the first rise accord with orthodox predictions to this point: while overall employment grew at a 2.2 per cent annualised rate from the three months ending in September 1996 to the three months ending in August 1997, the corresponding figure was 0.9 per cent for those aged 16-19; whereas the overall unemployment rate fell by 0.4 points, the teenage rate was essentially flat, as teenage participation rate has fallen significantly, while the overall rate has risen.

43. Bartel (1995) shows that firms that increase their training outlays receive a productivity bonus.

44. About 13 per cent of all US workers benefit from profit sharing, similar to the share in Japan, the United Kingdom, Canada and the Netherlands and ahead of Germany, Italy and Australia but well behind levels in France.

45. For example, Hoxby (1996) claims that the presence of a teachers' union raises the dropout rate, despite boosting costs per child by around 12 per cent.

46. A 1996 study of a voucher system in Milwaukee showed a significant improvement in performance for the participants – overwhelmingly poor and minority children – relative to children in public schools.

47. In January 1997, however, a state judge struck down a Milwaukee plan to allow publicly-funded vouchers to pay for religious schools and blocked an overall expansion of the programme.

48. Krueger and Levy (1997) show that coverage declined most sharply in the 1980s, rather than in the 1990s when the employment cost index slowed most abruptly. But it does appear to be true that the differences in costs between plans are rather small. Lower coverage may well ultimately translate into higher wages rather than lower labour costs.

49. An advisory commission appointed by the President to look at the managed care industry is expected to report on the appropriate degree of government involvement in the sector by the end of the year.

50. The problem of the uninsured more generally was tackled, in part, by last year's Kennedy-Kassebaum health care reform bill. The implementing regulations for this legislation were issued in April 1997. They prevent employers from denying coverage to new employees because of pre-existing conditions (although they do allow a waiting period of up to a year); they require insurers to offer individual coverage to those losing their jobs; and they institute a four-year pilot programme of "medical savings accounts" whereby individuals with catastrophic health insurance alone would accrue tax-deductible savings to pay for regular medical expenses.

51. Some experts believe that expanded Medicaid coverage since 1986 has crowded out private coverage. In 2002 Medicaid is scheduled to be extended to children aged 13 to 18 with family incomes under the poverty line.

52. For example, the three-month limit in any three-year period for receipt of Food Stamps applicable to able-bodied adults without children began to bite on 22 February 1997. Most of the rest of the changes took effect on 1 July. A key political issue this year was whether those moving from welfare to work should be guaranteed the federal minimum wage and whether they should benefit from other labour regulations applied to other workers. Ultimately, the decision was to grant them these guarantees.

53. In this case tobacco companies' profits probably would not be affected very much; some have suggested that the small fall in operating profits from a reduction in volumes would be offset by declines in marketing and legal expenses. The latter amount to $600 million per year.

54. Along the same lines, and consistent with the thrust of welfare reform, a proposal has been made to reduce dependence on this form of non-cash transfer by putting a time limit, say of two years, on public housing (Husock, 1997). One quarter of all households in public housing have been there more than 10 years, nearly half more than five. Time limits might provide an additional work incentive in order to be able to confront the need to return to the private market in a reasonable time; they might also allocate these scarce places more equitably among the needy.

55. Like conventional bonds, the current coupon (real component) is taxable interest income, but the inflation-compensating adjustment in the face value is as well, even if it is not realised. The effective tax rate is therefore boosted by a factor which varies with the inflation rate relative to the coupon rate – about 70 per cent at current rates. The result is that savers are unable to protect themselves completely from inflation, reducing their risk-sharing benefits and therefore the attractiveness of the instruments (Campbell and Shiller, 1996).

56. This chapter has benefited in no small way from a background consultants' report (Greenwood et al., 1997).

57. Simon (1995) cites, for example, an article by (later Senator) Paul A. Douglas of Cobb-Douglas production function fame in the June 1919 issue of the *Journal of the American Statistical Association* entitled "Is the New Immigration More Unskilled Than the Old?" (pp. 393-403).

58. But these penalties have not reduced the flow of illegal immigration (see below) because of increased use of fraudulent documents and lax enforcement associated with limited albeit increased Border Patrol resources (Bean *et al.*, 1990; Fix, 1991). A February 1996 Executive order preventing firms with IRCA convictions from obtaining government contracts has apparently still not been implemented (Passel, 1996).

59. These visas are allocated to natives of countries which have sent fewer than 50 000 legal immigrants to the United States over the latest five years. Applicants must have at least a high-school education and at least two years of training and experience during the last five years. Allocation is *via* a lottery, for which there were 6.5 million eligible applications and a further 1.1 million disqualifications for the FY 1997 draw in September 1996. Lotteries have also been used since the late-1980s to allocate "green cards" (work permits). Such lottery winners from 1988 to 1990 were more skilled than the average family-based immigrant (Barrett, 1996).

60. But the flexibility of the cap is limited, as family-based preferences other than immediate relatives are determined by 480 000 less the number of immediate relatives who entered in the previous year, with a floor of 226 000.

61. The waiting list in January 1995 was 3.7 million long, most of which were siblings of adult US citizens (4th preference), with a projected 25-year queue, and spouses and unmarried adult children of legal immigrants (2nd preference), with nearly a 10-year wait. Most employment-base queues have been eliminated, except for least-skilled workers. Quotas are sometimes surpassed because of carry-over provisions from previous years or from other categories (when unused).

62. For 1995, these included: 197 000 temporary workers and trainees, along with 47 000 members of their families, mostly under the so-called "H-1" admission class; 112 000 intra-company transferees, together with 62 000 of their families; 31 000 NAFTA workers (including their families); and a variety of smaller categories; see US Department of Justice (1997, Table 39). It does not include students and their spouses, some of whom may also work.

63. The specific economic effects of temporary workers and trainees have never been assessed.

64. For the Immigration and Naturalization Service immigrants are aliens admitted as lawful permanent residents. Thus, illegal or "undocumented" aliens in the country, as well as non-immigrants (those not intending to become permanent residents) are generally included only in the broader Census definition which is most often used for immigration research.

65. An unweighted average of the foreign population share in 16 OECD Member countries in the early 1990s was nearly 7 per cent. For a full discussion of the issues involved in comparing international migration data across countries see the introduction to the statistical annex in OECD (1997*a*).

66. Official Census Bureau projections are made using the assumption that 30 per cent of immigrants re-emigrate, but there have been no statistics available on emigration of either

the foreign- or native-born since 1957. It is believed that 35 to 45 per cent of immigrants eventually re-emigrate, especially those from Europe (Jasso and Rosenzweig, 1990). Many illegal Mexican immigrants return to their home villages after one or more sojourns in the United States (Massey *et al.,* 1990). The US Social Security Administration assumes that one-third of all immigrants re-emigrate and that they all do so before they have enough work experience to have the right to a pension (Duleep, 1994).

67. Recent inflows have been overweighted in the 15-34 age group (relative to the native-born population) and underweighted elsewhere (Smith and Edmonston, 1997, Figure 2.10). But compared with the age distribution in 1907-10, the recent inflow is comprised to a greater degree of children and those over 40 and to a much lesser extent of those 15 to 29 (Smith and Edmonston, 1997, Figure 2.11).

68. Data for 1990 show that females comprised 54 per cent of the non-legalised inflows, about the average since World War I; prior to that point women were outnumbered by men by about two to one. Women are also the primary migrants in many other migration streams around the world. The gender split may have implications for re-emigration probabilities and for labour market, demographic and fiscal impacts.

69. Many observers claim that the 1965 policy reform stimulated this ongoing evolution. Indeed, it would appear that an acceleration in the shift among source countries took place in the 1960s; however, part of that may well have had to do with economic conditions in traditional source countries, Europe in particular, which were rapidly improving at the time.

70. But Mexicans have had a low propensity to naturalise in the United States, and recent legislation has placed important constraints on sponsor income and support affidavits (see below).

71. Once source-country characteristics are added to a cross-sectional wage equation the coefficients on the set of country dummy variables tend to be insignificant, implying that only observable characteristics are influencing migrant earnings (Jasso and Rosenzweig, 1990).

72. This share is believed to be up to 75 per cent for illegal aliens and 46 per cent for refugees and asylees (Lowell, 1995).

73. The data in the table show that the gain from 1980 to 1990 in the share of immigrants who had arrived more than 10 years previously and are classified as managerial and professional speciality workers was more than a third less than the corresponding gain for all workers. Similarly, the relative movements into low-pay occupations in services, farming, forestry and fishing, and operators, fabricators and labourers all reflect a declining skill orientation. While these Census-based data include illegal immigrants, INS data for 1977, 1982 and 1994 admissions of legal immigrants show similar tendencies (Smith and Edmonston, 1997).

74. Supporting evidence comes from Funkhouser and Trejo (1996) who point out that female employment rates are fully 10 points lower than those of native women, especially among those with less than five years since arrival.

75. For example, immigrants comprised 23 per cent of those in the bottom decile in California; in Los Angeles the figure was nearly 30 per cent.

76. It should be remembered that the figures cited here are based on Census data, which include foreign workers who reside in the United States as a result of intra-firm transfers, but who have no intention of seeking immigrant status. For example, the 1990 Census counted

153 000 people born in Japan who entered the United States in the 1980s, but INS data indicate that only about one-third that number received immigrant status.

77. See the regression results reported in footnote 84 below.

78. The case of farm workers is perhaps the most obvious: in that sector average wages have been falling in real terms for some 20 years, with the cumulative loss up to 20 per cent by some estimates. With weak union representation there has been a significant risk of labour laws and regulations not being respected. The Labor Department was hoping to add several hundred extra inspectors in 1997 to ensure that labour laws are properly enforced, especially in garment manufacturing, janitorial services and agriculture in high-immigration states, but the Congress dropped the necessary funding (see below).

79. Greenwood et al. (1997) point out that the regularity conditions were rarely verified with the underlying non-flexible functional forms and that the authors confused Allen-Uzawa with Hicksian elasticities.

80. DeFreitas (1988) argues that some newcomers move out of competition with other immigrants and disperse from job enclaves to positions in competition with low-skilled natives. Gang and Rivera-Batiz (1994) maintain that the process goes further, with immigrants initially substitutes for native unskilled labour but complements eventually. See also OECD (1994a).

81. One of the recurrent themes in this literature is that immigrant hiring networks are cost-reducing for employers.

82. Borjas et al. (1992) focus on the supply of high-school dropouts in the 1980s and find that it was some 13 per cent higher in 1980 than it would otherwise have been because of immigration, but that the figure had risen to 25 per cent by 1987-88; both figures were much higher than what was attributable to international trade. The authors conclude that immigration was responsible for around 20 to 50 per cent of the nearly 10 percentage point change in the wage gap between high-school graduates and dropouts over this period, depending on the price elasticity of labour demand assumed. Very recently the same authors (Borjas et al., 1997) attribute nearly half of the 11 point decline in the relative wage of high-school dropouts from 1980 to 1994 to the increased supply of less-skilled immigrants. In a similar vein, Topel (1994) explored the wage gap between the wage of a worker at the 50th percentile and one at the 16th percentile of the wage distribution from 1972 to 1990 across nine Census regions. He finds that the wage gap widened far more in the Pacific region than elsewhere and that this was primarily due to less favourable supply effects, especially due to unskilled Asians and Hispanics, whether native or foreign born. Last, Borjas and Ramey (1994) conduct co-integration tests for the period 1963-88 on various hypothesised explanatory factors for the college-high school dropout wage gap and the college-high school graduate wage gap and find an insignificant result in both cases for the immigrant share. Separately, it might be added that there is some evidence for Australia that immigration there has had favourable (i.e. negative) unemployment effects, especially in the short run (Pope and Withers, 1993). Finally, Williamson (1996) argues that both the late Nineteenth Century and more recent patterns of inequality developments around the world are consistent with the effects emanating from globalisation (mainly migratory flows) and unskilled-labour-saving technical change.

83. There is some evidence of a decline in quality for immigrants from Europe and non-Mexican Hispanics but none for other groups (Friedberg, 1993). Other research (LaLonde and Topel, 1992) finds no decline in within-group quality even if the mix of source countries has shifted toward those providing immigrants, on average, with less human capital.

84. The wage differential between immigrants and natives in the United States in 1990 across 42 source countries is a function of the average educational attainment of those immigrants plus an additional amount for those from developed countries. The regression results (using data from Borjas (1994, Table 8) are as follows (t-ratios in parentheses):

Per cent wage gap = –11.6 + 6.3*education gap in years + 32.1*developed country dummy
        (6.0)   (9.3)   (10.4)

RBSQ = 0.86 SEE = 9.53

For pre-1980 arrivals the education gap coefficient rises to 7.7 and that on the dummy falls to 23.3. Thus, being from a developed country is equivalent to having five years of extra education for the all-immigrant sample and about three for those who have been in the United States for over 10 years.

85. In fact, male Mexican immigrants have tended to fall further behind in relative wage terms over time (Smith and Edmonston, 1997).

86. The Smith and Edmonston (1997) study assumes that public goods accounted for 23.7 per cent of total federal spending in 1995, other (congestible) goods 7.0 per cent, interest payments 13.9 per cent and age-related outlays 55.4 per cent.

87. A relevant but largely unanswered question is whether immigration status plays any role: in particular, are illegal immigrants different in their pattern of welfare use, perhaps because of a fear of being discovered and deported? If this is the case, then it is possible that conferring legal status on illegal aliens, such as was done by IRCA, would boost such social spending. Little empirical evidence is available, but there is some that shows that they make less use of income-transfer programmes, if for no other reason than that they are generally young, healthy males who have been in the United States only a short time (North and Houstoun, 1976; Massey *et al.*, 1990);

88. This is merely the product of the rate of receipt and the average amount of receipt per household for households with foreign-born heads compared with those with native-born heads. Mean spell duration is also longer for immigrant recipients (Borjas and Hilton, 1996).

89. The structural increase in welfare use is generally attributed to the changing source-country mix of immigrants (Borjas, 1995*b*).

90. Borjas (1997) claims that welfare is a magnet, with immigrants clustering in generous states due to an elasticity with respect to welfare generosity three times that of natives. But his results are largely attributable to California, and Zavodny (1997) argues that the correlation is not causal and disappears once the presence of earlier immigrants is accounted for in the location decision.

91. These assumptions are: a 300-year horizon, a 3 per cent real interest rate, budgetary adjustment to stabilise the federal debt-to-GDP ratio in 2016, half that adjustment to take place by tax increases and half by spending cuts; and immigrants' wages not to continue to catch up to natives' beyond 10 years after arrival. This last assumption is an unresolved

point in the literature. Duleep and Regets (1996) have controversially argued that the bigger wage gaps found in recent cohorts of immigrants have been associated with faster wage growth.

92. Other possible assumptions which would help turn this figure around would be: less assimilation in the future than in the past; decreasing returns to scale in public service provision; and displacement effects of natives by immigrant workers.

93. Some reimbursement for the costs of incarceration of undocumented aliens has been made since 1994 – $300 million in FY 1996, a fraction of the costs claimed by states.

94. Using data provided in Smith and Edmonston (1997, Table 3.5), it is possible to show that if the overall dependency ratio is defined as under 20 plus those over 64 divided by those 20-64, it would have been 45.9 per cent, as opposed to the actual share of 45.4 per cent.

95. When this work was undertaken, official estimates for illegal immigration were 225 000 per year; they have since been boosted by 50 000 per year. Thus, the 820 000 figure for net immigration (815 000 gross legal immigration plus 225 000 net illegal immigration less 220 000 gross emigration) is somewhat below the average recorded in the first half of the 1990s.

96. The gap between the ratios of these two extreme scenarios would be even larger in 2035 at around 4 percentage points. Also, it should be noted that the fiscal burden of supporting an elderly dependent is about 2.5 times that of a child dependent (Espenshade, 1994).

97. However, some unpublished work by Jorge Chapa at the University of Texas at Austin shows that for Hispanic immigrants convergence stops after the second generation. In other words, the situation stagnates for the grandchildren of immigrants.

98. Possibly the best data in this domain are now rather dated: Borjas (1995d) shows that those aged 14-22 in 1979 shared zip (postal) codes with 30.4 per cent of others from the same ethnic group, indicating much more residential segregation than portrayed by Census data which take larger geographic areas. The figure ranged from 63 per cent for blacks and 50 per cent for Mexicans down to 4 per cent for Chinese.

99. About half of all those classified as legal permanent resident aliens eventually become US citizens (US Department of Justice, 1997, Chapter V). Total naturalisations were not much more than 100 000 per year in the years immediately following the 1965 reform but then began to climb, doubling by the late 1980s and then again by 1995. In FY 1996 there was a naturalisation boom, with some 1.2 million people receiving US citizenship. Explanatory factors include the threat that they would otherwise become ineligible for some forms of public transfers (see below), an increase in the size of the eligible population (especially resulting from IRCA), a switch to a costly new "green card" and greater efforts in this direction by community-based organisations. However, the naturalisation rate fell from over 70 per cent in 1970 to around 40 per cent in 1990, the lowest level in a century (Smith and Edmonston, 1997).

100. Specifically, it would have eliminated the diversity programme, cut refugee numbers and limited family-based immigration to immediate relatives who themselves would be subject to a fixed quota. It would also have eliminated all unskilled employment-based immigration and subjected most others to a labour-market test. Its final report (US Commission on Immigration Reform, 1997) contained broadly similar recommendations.

101. This could be quite inhibiting for potential sponsors: about half of all Mexicans and Salvadorans who did in fact sponsor immigrants in 1994 had incomes below that figure,

102. Sponsors' incomes are "deemed" to be part of immigrants' resources. This was first instituted for some SSI applicants in 1987 and applied to other programmes in the 1990s.

103. Passel (1996) points out that net inflows of undocumented migrants of 300 000 per year represents only 0.1 per cent of total alien entries of 300 million per year, and visa over-stayers represent some 0.7 per cent of total non-immigrant admissions.

104. However, the Administration requested only 500 additional agents in its FY 1998 Budget.

105. The growing importance of cross-border smuggling can be gauged indirectly by the fact that the number of aliens located by the Border Patrol who were smuggled into the United States more than doubled from 1989 to 1995, reaching 103 000. Document fraud is rife, especially in certain visa categories.

106. The number of aged immigrant recipients of SSI rose by 580 per cent from 1982 to 1994. Fear of such restrictions helped drive the number of immigrants eligible for naturalisation who sought it to over 1 million in fiscal years 1995 and 1996. This was controversial in an election year, as it was revealed that many were granted citizenship without any check on their criminal records. A further 1.8 million applications are expected in FY 1997.

107. The 1996 reforms did not change the waiting period for SSI for those willing to naturalise, as it had already been extended from three to five years in 1994.

108. It is possible, however, that shifting away from family-based quotas would break into the circle of immigrant networks and chain migration and would shift the source-country mix away from its current structure.

109. While Canadian immigrants tend to be younger and more language-proficient than their US counterparts from the same source countries, there is no difference in education nor in earnings profiles (Duleep and Regets, 1992).

110. The share of US immigrants in their 20s and 30s fell from 50.1 per cent in 1985 to 42.3 per cent in 1995, while the share 50 and over climbed from 11.8 to 14.4 per cent.

111. The Family Unity and Employment Opportunity Immigration Act of 1990 revised and established new non-immigrant admission categories, instituted a publicly-funded training requirement and transformed the Labor Department's responsibility from merely processing applications to investigating and adjudicating labour attestations (Leibowitz, 1994). It has probably had a restrictive effect on non-immigrant unskilled labour.

112. Evidence suggests (Greenwood and Hunt, 1995) that immigrant labour supply is not sensi-tive to real wages, whereas natives' supply is positively, even if only modestly, associated with remuneration.

113. Measuring the effects of new and small firms on job creation is difficult. A number of statistical biases tend to overstate the contribution of small firms in generating jobs. And in any case, the interpretation of differences in net job growth by firm or establishment size is questionable (see OECD, 1994c).

114. The average gazelle is neither young nor small; more than half are over 15 years of age, compared with 12 years for US companies as a whole, and most gazelles have over 100 employees. According to one study (Birch et al., 1997), fast-growing firms account for

only 3 per cent of all firms but are responsible for nearly 80 per cent of gross job growth. A similar picture holds true in the United Kingdom and Australia, where it is estimated that about 5 to 20 per cent of firms are responsible for as much as 70 to 80 per cent of gross job creation (Hall, 1995).

115. The Reynolds study surveyed households to estimate the number of nascent entrepreneurs, defined as individuals who were identified as taking steps to found a new business but who had not yet succeeded in making the transition to new business ownership.

116. Legislation exists in all OECD countries to regulate business start-ups. The laws detail the necessary information and documents required by a firm before it can register, the various authorities with whom it must register, and can also define the internal structure of an enterprise, how it is taxed and, in some cases, special qualifications needed to enter certain activities.

117. These include commercial loans from banks and financing companies (both with and without collateral), trade credit and leasing, home equity loans and credit card loans.

118. For example Stiglitz and Weiss (1981).

119. The private equity market comprises professionally managed private equity, angel capital, the informal market and the Rule 144A market. The informal and Rule 144A markets operate more like the public equities market where investors do not generally have controlling interests in the issuing firms. See Fenn et al. (1995) for a comprehensive study of the private equity market.

120. Venture capital firms average about $90 million in size, compared with $25-30 million in the early 1980s. Venture capital firms that specialise in early-stage investments tend to be smaller than those that are mainly involved in later-stage investments which carry lower risks.

121. This comparison is approximate due to definitional differences, particularly the inclusion of buy-outs in the European Venture Capital statistics. See EVCA (1997) and Fenn et al. (1995).

122. Venture capitalists typically receive an initiation fee of 1 per cent of investment, a 2 per cent annual management fee and 15 to 20 per cent of realised capital gains upon liquidation of a given project.

123. A survey carried out within the purview of Stanford University's project on emerging companies shows that 45 per cent of the companies are headed by a CEO who did not found the company.

124. The often-cited rule of thumb is that they do not invest in companies which are further than two hours drive or one hour plane ride.

125. A trade sale is the sale of a venture capital-backed company to another company. Private placement is the purchase of a venture capitalist's interest by another investor also acting as a venture capitalist.

126. IPOs of venture-backed companies amounted to $11.8 billion in 1996, more than ten times the size in Europe. See Venture One (1997) and European Venture Capital Association (1997).

127. Tighter supervision followed the shocking revelation in June 1966 by the deputy administrator of the SBA that 232 of the nation's 700 SBICs were problem companies because of dubious practices and self-dealing and that the SBA was likely to lose $18 million as the result. By 1977 the number of SBICs declined to 276 (Fenn *et al.*, 1995).

128. These figures are estimates for 1992 based on many assumptions, including those about the business share of total regulatory costs, the industry sector shares of the business costs and employee wages. These assumptions were needed in the absence of hard information, and the resulting estimates are subject to considerable uncertainty.

129. Even so, employers may underinvest in on-the-job training because of a high job turnover, which is in turn partly due to inefficiency in the recruitment process (Bishop, 1996).

Bibliography

Altonji, Joseph G. and David Card (1991), "The Effects of Immigration on the Labor Market Outcomes of Less-Skilled Natives" in John M. Abowd and Richard B. Freeman (eds.), *Immigration, Trade and the Labor Market*, University of Chicago Press, Chicago.

Amirahmadi, Hooshang and Grant Saff (1993), "Science Parks: A Critical Assessment", *Journal of Planning Literature*, 8, 2, November.

Auerbach, Alan J. (1988), "Capital Gains Taxation in the United States: Realisations, Revenue and Rhetoric," *Brookings Papers on Economic Activity,* 2.

Baker, Michael and Dwayne Benjamin (1994), "The Performance of Immigrants in the Canadian Labor Market", *Journal of Labor Economics*, 12, 3, July.

Barrett, Alan (1996), "The Greencard Lottery Winners: Are They More or Less Skilled Than Other Immigrants?", *Economic Letters*, 52, 3, September.

Bartel, Ann P. (1995), "Training, Wage Growth and Job Performance: Evidence From a Company Database", *Journal of Labor Economics*, 13, 3, July.

Bean, Frank D., Barry Edmonston and Jeffrey S. Passel (eds.) (1990), *Undocumented Migration to the United States: IRCA and the Experience of the 1980s*, Urban Institute Press, Washington, D.C.

Bennett, Paul and Spence Hilton (1997), "Falling Reserve Balances and the Federal Funds Rate", *Current Issues in Economics and Finance*, Federal Reserve Bank of New York, 3, 5, April.

Binational Study on Migration (1997), *Migration Between Mexico and the United States.*

Birch, David, Anne Haggerry and William Parsons (1996), *Entrepreneurial Hot Spots: The Best Places in America to Start and Grow a Company*, Cognetics Inc., Massachusetts.

Birch, David, Anne Haggerry and William Parsons (1997), *Corporate Almanac 1994,* Cognetics Inc., Massachusetts.

Bishop, John H. (1996), "What Do We Know About Employer-Provided Training: A Review of the Literature", Center for Advanced Human Resource Studies, Working Paper 96-09, Cornell University, New York.

Bishop, John (1997), research cited in *Business Week*, 30 June, p. 11.

Blanchard, Olivier and Lawrence Katz (1992), "Regional Evolutions", *Brookings Papers on Economic Activity*, 1.

Blank, Rebecca M. and David Card (1995), "Poverty, Income Distribution and Growth: Are They Still Connected?", *Brookings Papers on Economic Activity*, 2.

Blau, Francine D. (1984), "The Use of Transfer Payments by Immigrants", *Industrial and Labor Relations Review*, 37, 2, January.

Borjas, George J. (1985), "Assimilation, Changes in Cohort Quality, and the Earnings of Immigrants", *Journal of Labor Economics*, 3, 4, October.

Borjas, George J. (1987), "Self-Selection and the Earnings of Immigrants", *American Economic Review*, 77, 4, September.

Borjas, George J. (1990), *Friends or Strangers: The Impact of Immigrants on the U.S. Economy*, Basic Books, New York.

Borjas, George J. (1992), "National Origin and the Skills of Immigrants in the Postwar Period" in George J. Borjas and Richard B. Freeman (eds.), *Immigration and the Workforce: Economic Consequences for the United States and Source Areas*, University of Chicago Press, Chicago.

Borjas, George J. (1994), "The Economics of Immigration", *Journal of Economic Literature*, 32, 4, December.

Borjas, George J. (1995*a*), "Assimilation and Changes in Cohort Quality Revisited: What Happened to Immigrant Earnings in the 1980s", *Journal of Labor Economics*, 13, 2, April.

Borjas, George J. (1995*b*), "Immigration and Welfare, 1970-1990", *Research in Labor Economics*, 14.

Borjas, George J. (1995c), "The Economic Benefits from Immigration", *Journal of Economic Perspectives*, 9, Spring.

Borjas, George J. (1995d), "Ethnicity, Neighbourhoods, and Human Capital Externalities", *American Economic Review*, 85, 3, June.

Borjas, George J. (1997), "Immigration and Welfare Magnets", unpublished, March.

Borjas, George J., Richard B. Freeman and Lawrence F. Katz (1992), "On the Labor Market Effects of Immigration and Trade" in George J. Borjas and Richard B. Freeman (eds), *Immigration and the Work Force*, University of Chicago Press, Chicago.

Borjas, George J., Richard B. Freeman and Lawrence F. Katz (1997), "How Much Have Immigration and Trade Affected the U.S. Job Market?", *Brookings Papers on Economic Activity*, 1.

Borjas, George J. and Lynette Hilton (1996), "Immigration and the Welfare State: Immigrant Participation in Means-Tested Entitlement Programs", *Quarterly Journal of Economics*, 111, 2, May.

Borjas, George J. and Valerie A. Ramey (1994), "Time Series Evidence on the Source and Trends in Wage Inequality", *Papers and Proceedings,* American Economic Association, 84, 2, May.

Borjas, George J. and Steven J. Trejo (1991), "Immigrant Participation in the Welfare System", *Industrial and Labor Relations Review*, 44, 2, January.

Boskin, Michael J., Ellen R. Dulberger, Robert J. Gordon, Zvi Griliches, and Dale W. Jorgenson (1996), *Toward a More Accurate Measure of the Cost of Living*, Final Report to the Senate Finance Committee from the Advisory Commission to Study the Consumer Price Index, Senate Finance Committee, Washington, D.C.

Bureau of Labor Statistics (1997), "Measurement Issues in the Consumer Price Index", mimeo, June.

Butcher, Kristin F. and David Card (1991), "Immigration and Wages: Evidence from the 1980s", *Papers and Proceedings*, American Economic Association, 81, 2, May.

Butcher, Kristin F. and Anne Morrison Piehl (1996), "Cross-City Evidence on the Relationship Between Immigration and Crime", unpublished paper, September.

Butcher, Kristin F. and Anne Morrison Piehl (1997), "Recent Immigrants: Unexpected Implications for Crime and Incarceration", National Bureau of Economic Research Working Paper No. 6067, June.

Butler, Stuart M. and Robert E. Moffit (1997), "Congress's Own Health Plan as a Model for Medicare Reform", The Heritage Foundation, Roe Backgrounder No. 1123, 12 June.

Campbell, John Y. and Robert J. Shiller (1996), "A Scorecard for Indexed Government Debt" in Ben S. Bernanke and Julio J. Rotemberg (eds.), *NBER Macroeconomics Annual 1996,* MIT Press, Cambridge (USA) and London.

Card, David (1990), "The Impact of the Mariel Boatlift on the Miami Labor Market", *Industrial and Labor Relations Review*, 43, 2, January.

Center for the Study of Entrepreneurship (1993), 'Wisconsin's Entrepreneurial Climate Study', Marquette University, mimeo.

Chiswick, Barry R. (1978), "The Effect of Americanization on the Earnings of Foreign-Born Men", *Journal of Political Economy*, 85, 5, October.

Ciccone, Antonio and Robert E. Hall (1996), "Productivity and the Density of Economic Activity", *American Economic Review*, 86, 1, March.

Collins, William J., Kevin H. O'Rourke and Jeffrey G. Williamson (1997), "Were Trade and Factor Mobility Substitutes in History?", National Bureau of Economic Research Working Paper No. 6059, June.

Congressional Budget Office (1996), *Reducing the Deficit: Spending and Revenue Options,* Washington, D.C., August.

Congressional Budget Office (1997), *Long-Term Budgetary Pressures and Policy Options*, Washington, D.C., March.

Cooper, Arnold C., William C. Dunkelberg, Carolyn Y. Woo and William J. Dennis, Jr. (1990), *New Business in America: The Firms and their Owners*, NFIB Foundation, Washington, D.C.

Corrado, Carol and Larry Slifman (1996), "Decomposition of Productivity and Unit Costs", Board of Governors of the Federal Reserve System, Occasional Staff Studies.

Council of Economic Advisers (1997a), *Economic Report of the President, 1997*, US Government Printing Office, Washington, D.C.

Council of Economic Advisers (1997b), "Explaining the Decline in Welfare Receipt, 1993-1996", 9 May.

DeFreitas, Gregory (1988), "Hispanic Immigration and Labor Market Segmentation", *Industrial Relations*, 27, 2, Spring.

DeFreitas, Gregory and Adriana Marshall (1984), "Immigration and Wage Growth in U.S. Manufacturing in the 1970s", *Proceedings of the Thirty-Sixth Annual Meeting*, Industrial Relations Research Association, 28-30 December 1983, San Francisco.

Dennis, William J., Jr. (1995), *A Small Business Primer*, NFIB Foundation, Washington, D.C.

Dennis, William J., Jr. (1996*a*), ''Small Business Access to Capital: Impediments and Options'', Testimony before the Committee on Small Business, House of Representatives, 28 February, Serial No. 104-62, US Government Printing Office, Washington, D.C.

Dennis, William J., Jr. (1996*b*), *Small Business Problems and Priorities*, NFIB Education Foundation, Washington, D.C.

Dornbusch, Rudiger (1987), ''Exchange Rates and Prices'', *American Economic Review, 77*, 1, March.

Duleep, Harriet Orcutt (1994), ''Social Security and the Emigration of Immigrants'' in International Social Security Association, *Migration: A Worldwide Challenge for Social Security*, International Social Security Association, Geneva.

Duleep, Harriet Orcutt and Mark C. Regets (1992), ''Some Evidence on the Effect of Admission Criteria on Immigrant Assimilation'' in Barry R. Chiswick (ed.), *Immigration, Language and Ethnic Issues: Canada and the United States*, American Enterprise Institute, Washington, D.C.

Duleep, Harriet Orcutt and Mark C. Regets (1996), ''The Elusive Concept of Immigrant Quality: Evidence from 1970-1990'', unpublished paper, December.

Espenshade, Thomas J. (1990), ''Undocumented Migration to the United States: Evidence from a Repeated Trials Model'' in Frank D. Bean, Barry Edmonston and Jeffrey S. Passel (eds.), *Undocumented Migration to the United States: IRCA and the Experience of the 1980s*, Urban Institute Press, Washington, D.C.

Espenshade, Thomas J. (1994), ''Can Immigration Slow U.S. Population Aging?'', *Journal of Policy Analysis and Management*, 13, 4, Fall.

European Venture Capital Association (1997), *A Survey of Venture Capital and Private Equity in Europe, 1997 Yearbook*, Zaventen, Belgium.

Farber, Henry S. (1997*a*), ''The Changing Face of Job Loss in the United States, 1981-1995'', *Brookings Papers on Microeconomics 1997*, forthcoming.

Farber, Henry S. (1997*b*), ''Trends in Long-Term Employment in the United States, 1979-96'', Working Paper No. 384, Industrial Relations Section, Princeton University, 17 July.

Federation for American Immigration Reform (1992), *Immigration 2000: The Century of the New American Sweatshop*, Washington, D.C.

Feenberg, Daniel and Lawrence Summers (1990), ''Who Benefits from Capital Gains Tax Reductions'' in Lawrence Summers (ed.), *Tax Policy and the Economy*, 4, MIT Press, Cambridge, USA.

Feinberg, Robert M. (1989), ''The Effects of Foreign Exchange Movements in U.S. Domestic Prices,'' *Review of Economics and Statistics*, 71, 3, August.

Fenn, George W., Nellie Liang and Stephen Prowse (1995), *The Economics of the Private Equity Market*, Board of Governors of the Federal Revenue System, Washington, D.C.

Fix, Michael (ed.) (1991), *The Paper Curtain: Employer Sanctions' Implementation, Impact and Reform*, Urban Institute Press, Washington, D.C.

Fix, Michael and Jeffrey S. Passel (1994), *Immigration and Immigrants: Setting the Record Straight*, Urban Institute Press, Washington, D.C.

Frey, William H. (1994), "The New White Flight", *American Demographics*, 16, 4, April.

Friedberg, Rachel M. (1993), "The Labor Market Assimilation of Immigrants in the United States: The Role of Age at Arrival", unpublished manuscript, March.

Froot, Kenneth A. and Paul D. Klemperer (1989), "Exchange Rate Pass-Through when Market Share Matters", *American Economic Review,* 79, 4, September.

Funkhouser, Edward (1995), "The Impact of Immigration on the States: What Have We Learned?", unpublished, August.

Funkhouser, Edward and Steven J. Trejo (1995), "The Labor Market Skills of Recent Male Immigrants: Evidence from the Current Population Survey", *Industrial and Labor Relations Review*, 48, 4, July.

Funkhouser, Edward and Steven J. Trejo (1996), "Female Immigrants in the United States", unpublished paper, February.

Gang, Ira N. and Francisco L. Rivera-Batiz (1994), "Labor Market Effects of Immigration in the United States and Europe: Substitution vs. Complementarity", *Journal of Population Economics*, 7, 2, June.

General Accounting Office (1995*a*), *Efforts to Evaluate the Advanced Technology Program,* Report GAO/RCED-95-68, Washington, D.C.

General Accounting Office (1995*b*), *Manufacturing Extension Programs: Manufacturers Views of Services,* Report GAO/GGD-95-216BR, Washington, D.C.

General Accounting Office (1996), *Regulatory Burden: Measurement Challenges and Concerns Raised by Selected Companies*, GAO/GGD-97-2, Washington, D.C.

General Accounting Office (1997*a*), "Employment-Based Health Insurance: Costs Increase and Family Coverage Decreases", Letter Report, GAO/HEHS-97-35, February.

General Accounting Office (1997*b*), "Medicare", High Risk Series Report, GAO/HR-97-10, February.

Goldberg, Pinelopi Koujianou (1995), "Product Differentiation and Oligopoly in International Markets: The Case of the U.S. Automobile Industry", *Econometrica,* 63, 4, July.

Goldberg, Pinelopi K. and Michael M. Knetter (1996), "Goods Prices and Exchange Rates: What Have We Learned?", National Bureau of Economic Research Working Paper No. 5862, December.

Gordon, Robert J. and Zvi Griliches (1997), "Quality Change and New Products", *American Economic Review*, 87, 2, May.

Greenlees, John S. and Charles C. Mason (1996), "Overview of the 1998 Revision of the Consumer Price Index", *Monthly Labor Review*, 119, 2, December.

Greenwood, Michael J. and Gary L. Hunt (1995), "Economic Effects of Immigrants on Native and Foreign-Born Workers: Complementarity, Substitutability, and Other Channels of Influence", *Southern Economic Journal*, 61, 4, April.

Greenwood, Michael J., John M. McDowell and Gary L. Hunt (1997), "The Economic Consequences of U.S. Immigration", background consultants' report prepared for the OECD, February.

Grossman, Jean Baldwin (1982), ''The Substitutability of Natives and Immigrants in Production'', *Review of Economics and Statistics*, 64, 4, November.

Hall, Christopher (1995), ''The Entrepreneurial Engine'', paper presented at the OECD *High-Level Workshop on SMEs: Employment, Innovation and Growth,* held in Washington, D.C., 16-17 June, mimeo.

Hamermesh, Daniel S. (1993), *Labor Demand*, Princeton University Press, Princeton, New Jersey.

Helkie, William L. and Peter Hooper (1988), ''An Empirical Analysis of the External Deficit, 1980-86'' in Ralph C. Bryant, Gerald Holtham and Peter Hooper (eds.), *External Deficits and the Dollar: The Pit and the Pendulum*, Brookings Institution, Washington, D.C.

Hensley, David and Deborah Burnham (1997), ''Pleasant GDP Arithmetic'', Economic and Market Analysis, Salomon Brothers, June.

Hinojosa-Ojeda, Raul and Sherman Robinson (1991), ''Alternative Scenarios of U.S.-Mexico Integration: A Computable General Equilibrium Approach'', Working Paper No. 609, Department of Agricultural and Resource Economics, University of California, April.

Hooper, Peter and Catherine L. Mann (1989), ''Exchange Rate Pass-Through in the 1980s: The Case of U.S. Imports of Manufactures'', *Brookings Papers on Economic Activity,* 1.

Hoxby, Carolyn Minter (1996), ''How Teachers' Unions Affect Education Production'', *Quarterly Journal of Economics*, 111, 3, August.

Hunt, Jennifer (1992), ''The Impact of the 1962 Repatriates from Algeria on the French Labor Market'', *Industrial and Labor Relations Review*, 45, 3, April.

Husock, Howard (1997), ''We Did It for Welfare ... Now Let's Put Time Limits on Public Housing'', *The American Enterprise*, January/February.

Jackson, John E. (1986), *The American Entrepreneurial and Small Business Culture*, Institute for Enterprise Advancement, Washington, D.C.

Jacobs, Jill (1997), ''Now You See It ... The Pattern of CPI Inflation in 1996'', U.S. Economic Research, Goldman Sachs, April.

Jaeger, David (1995), ''Skill Differences and the Effect of Immigrants on the Wages of Natives'', US Department of Labor, Bureau of Labor Statistics Working Paper 273, December.

Jasso, Guillermina and Mark Rosenzweig (1990), *The New Chosen People: Immigrants in the United States*, Russell Sage Foundation, New York.

Jensen, Leif (1988), ''Patterns of Immigration and Public Assistance Utilization, 1970-80'', *International Migration Review*, 22, 1, Spring.

Johnson, George E. (1980), ''The Labor Market Effects of Immigration'', *Industrial and Labor Relations Review*, 33, 3, April.

Jorgenson, Dale W. and Ralph Landau (eds.) (1993), *Tax Reform and the Cost of Capital: An International Comparison*, The Brookings Institution, Washington, D.C.

Krueger, Alan B. and Helen Levy (1997), ''Accounting for the Slowdown in Employer Health Care Costs'', National Bureau of Economic Research Working Paper No. 5891, January.

Krugman, Paul (1986), ''Pricing to Market When the Exchange Rate Changes'', National Bureau of Economic Research Working Paper No. 1926, May.

Krugman, Paul (1991), *Geography and Trade*, MIT Press, Cambridge, USA.

LaLonde, Robert J. and Robert H. Topel (1991), "Labor Market Adjustments to Increased Migration" in John M. Abowd and Richard B. Freeman (eds.), *Immigration, Trade and the Labor Market*, University of Chicago Press, Chicago.

LaLonde, Robert J. and Robert H. Topel (1992), "The Assimilation of Immigrants in the U.S. Labor Market" in George J. Borjas and Richard B. Freeman (eds.), *Immigration and the Work Force: Economic Consequences for the United States and Source Areas*, University of Chicago Press, Chicago.

Lebow, David E., John M. Roberts and David J. Stockton (1994), "Monetary policy and 'the price level'", mimeo, Board of Governors of the Federal Reserve System.

Leibowitz, Arnold H. (1994), "Temporary Migration to the United States in Relation to the Labour Market", unpubished.

Leidy, Michael (1996), "Macroeconomic Conditions and Pressures for Protection Under Antidumping and Countervailing Duty Laws – Empirical Evidence From the United States", IMF Working Paper WP/96/88, August.

Lowell, B. Lindsay (1995), "The Effects of Immigration on the U.S. Economy and Labor Market", unpublished.

Martin, Philip L. (1993), *Trade and Migration: NAFTA and Agriculture*, Institute for International Economics, Washington, D.C.

Massey, Douglas S., Katherine M. Donato and Zai Liang (1990), "Effects of the Immigration Reform and Control Act of 1986: Preliminary Data from Mexico" in Frank D. Bean, Barry Edmonston and Jeffrey S. Passel (eds.), *Undocumented Migration to the United States: IRCA and the Experience of the 1980s*, Urban Institute Press, Washington, D.C.

McCarthy, Jonathan (1997), "Debt, Delinquencies, and Consumer Spending", *Current Issues in Economics and Finance,* Federal Reserve Bank of New York, 3, 3, February.

McCarthy, Kevin F. and R. Burciaga Valdez (1986), *Mexican Immigration in California: Dispelling the Myths About Migrants*, Rand, Santa Monica, California.

Meade, Ellen E. (1991), "Computers and the Trade Deficit: The Case of the Falling Prices", in Peter Hooper and J. David Richardson (eds.), *International Economic Transactions: Issues in Measurement and Empirical Research*, University of Chicago Press, Chicago.

Meager, Nigel (1993), *Self-Employment and Labour Market Policy in the European Community*, WZB Discussion Paper FS I 93-201, Berlin.

Mines, Richard and Philip L. Martin (184), "Immigrant Workers and the California Citrus Industry", *Industrial Relations*, 23, 1, Winter.

Moon, Marilyn and Stephen Zuckerman (1995), "Are Private Insurers Really Controlling Spending Better than Medicare?", Henry J. Kaiser Family Foundation Discussion Paper, July.

Moore, Stephen (1997), "The Advanced Technology Program and Other Corporate Subsidies", Testimony before the Senate Committee on Governmental Affairs, Subcommittee on Government Management, Restructuring and the District of Columbia, Washington, D.C., 3 June.

Muller, Thomas and Thomas J. Espenshade (1985), *The Fourth Wave: California's Newest Immigrants*, Urban Institute, Washington.

Myerson, Allen R. (1996), "O Governor, Won't You Buy Me a Mercedes Benz?", *New York Times* 1 September.

Neal, Derek (1997), "The Effects of Catholic Secondary Schooling on Educational Achievement", *Journal of Labor Economics*, 15, 1, Part 1.

North, David S. and Marion F. Houstoun (1976), *The Characteristics and Role of Illegal Aliens in the US Labor Market: An Exploratory Study*, New TransCentury Foundation, Washington, D.C.

OECD (1991), *Taxing Profits in a Global Economy*, Paris.

OECD (1994*a*), *Trends in International Migration Annual Report 1993*, Paris.

OECD (1994*b*), *Migration and Development: New Partnerships for Co-operation*, Paris.

OECD (1994*c*), *Jobs Study: Facts, Analysis, and Strategies*, Paris.

OECD (1994*d*), *Taxation and Small Businesses*, Paris.

OECD (1994*e*), *Economic Survey of the United States 1994*, Paris, November.

OECD (1995), *Economic Survey of the United States 1995*, Paris, November.

OECD (1996*a*), *Economic Survey of the United States 1996*, Paris, November.

OECD (1996*b*), *Employment Outlook*, Paris, July.

OECD (1996*c*), "Venture Capital in OECD Countries", *Financial Market Trends,* No. 63, February.

OECD (1996*d*), *Economic Survey of Mexico*, Paris, December.

OECD (1996*e*), "SMES: Employment, Innovation and Growth, The Washington Workshop", Paris.

OECD (1997*a*), *Trends in International Migration Annual Report 1996*, Paris.

OECD (1997*b*), *Employment Outlook*, Paris, July.

Papademetriou, Demetrios G. and Stephen Yale-Lohr (1996), *Balancing Interests: Rethinking U.S. Selection of Skilled Immigrants*, Carnegie Endowment for International Peace, Washington, D.C.

Parker, Robert P. and Eugene P. Seskin (1997), "Annual Revision of the National Income and Product Accounts", *Survey of Current Business*, 77, 8, August.

Passel, Jeffrey S. (1996), "Recent Efforts to Control Illegal Immigration to the United States", unpublished.

Pigott, Charles and Vincent Reinhart (1985), "The Strong Dollar and U.S. Inflation", *Federal Reserve Bank of New York Quarterly Review*, 10, 3, Autumn

Polivka, Anne E. (1996), "Into Contingent and Alternative Employment: By Chance?", *Monthly Labor Review*, 119, 10, October.

Pope, David and Glenn Withers (1993), "Do Migrants Rob Jobs? Lessons of Australian History, 1861-1991", *Journal of Economic History*, 53.

Porter, Richard D. and Ruth A. Judson (1996), "The Location of US. Currency: How Much is Abroad?", *Federal Reserve Bulletin*, 82, 10, October.

Reynolds, Paul (1995), "Explaining Regional Variation in Business Births and Deaths: US 1976-88" in *Small Business Economics*, 7, 5, October.

Reynolds, Paul (forthcoming), "Who Starts New Firms? – Preliminary Explorations of Firms-in-Gestation", *Small Business Economics.*

Reynolds, Paul and David Storey (1993), "Regional Characteristics Affecting Small Business Formation", ILE Notebooks No. 18, OECD, Paris.

Saxenian, Annalee (1994), *Regional Advantage: Culture and Competition in Silicon Valley and Route 128,* Harvard University Press, Cambridge, USA.

Schoeni, Robert F., Kevin F. McCarthy and Georges Vernez (1996), *The Mixed Economic Progress of Immigrants*, Center for Research on Immigration Policy, Rand, Santa Monica, California.

Shapira, Philip, David Roessner and Richard Barke (1995), "New Public Infrastructures for Small Firm Industrial Modernization in the USA", *Entrepreneurship and Regional Development, 7,* 4, October-December.

Shapiro, Matthew D. and David W. Wilcox (1996), "Mismeasurement in the Consumer Price Index: An Evaluation" in Ben S. Bernanke and Julio J. Rotemberg (eds.), *NBER Macroeconomics Annual 1996*, MIT Press, Cambridge (USA) and London.

Simon, Julian (1995), *Immigration: The Demographic and Economic Facts*, Cato Institute and National Immigration Forum, Washington, D.C.

Small Business Administration (1996), *The State of Small Business 1995*, Washington, D.C.

Smith, James P. and Barry Edmonston (eds.) (1997), *The New Americans: Economic, Demographic, and Fiscal Effects of Immigration*, National Research Council, National Academy Press, Washington, D.C.

Stiglitz, Joseph E. and Andrew Weiss (1981), "Credit Rationing in Markets with Imperfect Information", *American Economic Review*, 71, 3, June.

Swagel, Phillip (1995), "Import Prices and the Competing Good Effect", Board of Governors of the Federal Reserve System, International Finance Discussion Papers No. 508, April.

Timmer, Ashley S. and Jeffrey G. Williamson (1996), "Racism, Xenophobia or Markets? The Political Economy of Immigration Policy Prior to the Thirties", National Bureau of Economic Research Working Paper No. 5867, December.

Topel, Robert H. (1994), "Regional Labor Markets and the Determinants of Wage Inequality", *Papers and Proceedings*, American Economic Association, 84, 2, May.

Treyz, George I., Dan S. Rickman, Gary L. Hunt and Michael J. Greenwood (1993), "The Dynamics of U.S. Internal Migration", *Review of Economics and Statistics*, 75, 2, May.

Twentieth Century Fund (1995), *Medicare Reform: A Twentieth Century Guide to the Issues*, Twentieth Century Press, New York.

US Commission on Immigration Reform (1995), *Legal Immigration: Setting Priorities; A Report to Congress,* Washington, D.C., June.

US Commission on Immigration Reform (1997), *Becoming an American: Immigration and Immigrant Policy,* Washington, D.C., September.

US Department of Justice, Immigration and Naturalization Service (1997), *1995 Statistical Yearbook of the Immigration and Naturalization Service*, US GPO, March.

Venture One (1997), *National Venture Capital Association: 1996 Annual Report*, San Francisco.

Waldinger, Roger (1985), "Immigration and Industrial Change in the New York City Apparel Industry" in George J. Borjas and Marta Tienda (eds.), *Hispanics in the U.S. Economy*, Academic Press, Orlando.

Warren, Robert (1997), "Estimates of the Unauthorized Immigrant Population Residing in the United States: October 1996", Immigration and Naturalization Service, Office of Policy and Planning.

Wei, Shang-Jin (1997), "How Taxing is Corruption on International Investors?", National Bureau of Economic Research Working Paper No. 6030, May.

White, Matthew W. (1997), "Power Struggles: Explaining Deregulatory Reforms in Electricity Markets", *Brookings Papers on Economic Activity, Microeconomics, 1996*.

Williamson, Jeffrey G. (1996), "Globalization and Inequality Then and Now: The Late 19th and Late 20th Centuries Compared", National Bureau of Economic Research Working Paper No. 5491, March.

Wolak, Frank A. (1997), "The Welfare Impacts of Competitive Telecommunications Supply: A Household-Level Analysis", *Brookings Papers on Economic Activity, Microeconomics, 1996*.

Zavodny, Madeline (1997), "Welfare and the Locational Choices of New Immigrants", *Economic Review*, Federal Reserve Bank of Dallas, Second Quarter.

Zodrow, George R. (1995), "Economic Issues in the Taxation of Capital Gains", *Canadian Public Policy*, 21, Supplement, November.

Specific Medicare savings proposals

The following is a list of proposals contained in the Balanced Budget Act of 1997 to reduce Medicare costs.

Reduce/delay updates of reimbursement rates: Periodically the Health Care Financing Administration revises Medicare's reimbursement rates based on inflation and cost estimates, and the Act lowers some of the specific fees-for-service and delays their increases.

Modify payment system: The Act extends the prospective payer system used for inpatient hospital services to home health providers, skilled nursing facilities, outpatient hospital services departments, rehabilitation facilities and ambulance services. This system pays a fixed amount for all services during a single "episode of care", thereby encouraging health providers to reduce their costs.

Increase enrolee payments: Currently, senior citizens pay about $44 per month, and payments were expected to rise by about 3 per cent per year to over $60 per month at the end of ten years. Premiums are supposed to cover 25 per cent of Part B costs, and partly because of the shift of home health care to Part B, premiums will rise substantially, 9 per cent per year, to $105 in 2007. The Senate considered including a $5 co-payment for home health care visits and means-testing Medicare by raising premiums for high-income households, but both provisions were dropped.

Encourage more risk-based plans: About 12 per cent of Medicare beneficiaries are enrolled in HMOs, and the Act adjusts capitated payments to HMOs to encourage the development of more managed care plans in areas of the country that currently have none. Other reforms include developing preferred-provider plans, allowing hospitals to set up their own managed care plans and creating a pilot programme for 390 000 seniors that combines medical savings accounts with a high-deductible catastrophic insurance plan.

Alter/lower disproportionate share payments: Currently, Medicare (and Medicaid) provides added money to help support teaching hospitals and medical providers that specialise in delivering government-sponsored care. These payments are implicitly included in the formula that compensates HMOs. The new law strips out these payments from the formula and makes them directly to hopsitals, thereby lowering the base on which compensation to HMOs is calculated. In addition, these payments are reduced by 5 per cent over five years.

Reduce fraud and abuse: The General Accounting Office (1997b) estimates that 3 to 10 per cent of health expenditures are wasteful and fraudulent, implying Medicare losses in 1996 were $6 to $20 billion. The law includes new provisions to combat fraud, such as denying Medicare payments to frequent violators, a version of ''Three Strikes, You're Out''.

Other reforms: The law reduces payments to hospitals for capital expenditures, while a proposal to raise the eligibility age to 67 was deleted.

Annex II

Calendar of main economic events

1996

October

Minimum wage rises from $4.25 to $4.75 an hour as stipulated in a law passed in August.

November

The Environmental Protection Agency proposes new rules limiting the emissions of fine particles and revised limits on ozone emissions, which the President approves in June 1997.

Voters re-elect President Clinton for a second term and return a Republican majority in both houses of Congress.

The Federal Open Market Committee (FOMC) announces no change to interest rates, keeping the federal funds rate at 5¼ per cent and the discount rate at 5 per cent but with a bias towards firming.

The Office of the Comptroller of the Currency announces a new policy to allow banks to set up subsidiaries to engage in other financial activities. The following month the Federal Reserve Board raises the revenue limit banking subsidiaries can receive from securities underwriting, chipping away another piece of the Depression-era law restricting banking activities.

December

The Advisory Commission to Study the Consumer Price Index issues its final report stating that the CPI overstates inflation by 1.1 percentage points a year.

Chairman Greenspan asks in a speech how one would know if there was "irrational exuberance" in the markets. The stock market subsequently drops, and analysts speculate that the speech means the Federal Reserve will take specific actions to lower equity prices.

The 1994-96 Advisory Council on Social Security issues its recommendations, presenting three plans to bring the system into long-term balance.

Boeing and McDonnell Douglas propose to merge, creating the world's largest aerospace company. In July 1997, the Federal Trade Commission approves the merger without changes, while EU officials threaten to impose sanctions if the deal goes through.

The FOMC announces no change to interest rates.

1997

January

The Securities and Exchange Commission (SEC) announces new rules requiring companies to present estimates of losses they could suffer from derivative instruments.

The President orders a new six-month moratorium on lawsuits under the Libertad (Helms-Burton) Act.

The Treasury issues ten-year notes indexed to inflation.

February

The FOMC announces no change in policy. In testimony to Congress, the Chairman reports M2 and M3 growth targets for the year of 1-5 per cent and 2-6 per cent, respectively, and a monitoring range of non-financial debt growth of 3-7 per cent. Members of the Board and bank presidents project that GDP growth over the four quarters of 1997 will be 2-2¼ per cent; CPI inflation will be 2¾-3 per cent; and the unemployment rate will remain in the 5¼-5½ per cent range.

The Administration announces its five-year budget plan calling for small tax changes, some important cuts to expenditures and sales of rights to the electromagnetic spectrum, which generate a $17 billion surplus in 2002. Under the baseline projection and economic assumptions of the Congressional Budget Office, the budget would be $69 billion in deficit in 2002.

Sixty-nine countries sign a wide-ranging telecommunications agreement.

March

The Senate fails to pass a balanced-budget amendment by one vote.

Citing increased aggregate demand at high resource utilisation levels, the FOMC raises the federal funds rate 25 basis points to 5½ per cent but keeps the discount rate at 5 per cent. It also changes its future stance towards neutral.

Forty countries sign an agreement to reduce tariffs on information technology products.

April

A US district court judge voids the line-item veto as a violation of the constitutional separation of powers, but in June the US Supreme Court overturns the district court ruling on the grounds that the plaintiffs do not have proper standing to bring the suit because the veto power has not been exercised. The dispute is not settled, however, as once the veto is used, a "harmed" party can then bring suit.

May

The President and Republican congressional leaders announce an agreement to balance the budget by 2002. The plan calls for $85 billion in net tax cuts over five years but more significant outlay cuts than were included in the President's budget.

The FOMC announces no change to interest rates, but it changes its bias for future action to firming.

The Treasury Department announces its plan for major banking reform, including two options for Congress, one of which removes the prohibition on banks engaging in non-financial activities.

June

The United States, Canada and the EU sign a Mutual Recognition Agreement for the inspection and certification of various goods.

The SEC votes to begin quoting stock prices by the penny (rather than fractions of dollars) as soon as systems are in place. In the interim prices will be priced in 1/16th increments.

The Treasury announces it will auction five-year inflation-indexed securities in July and October. It will also issue new ten-year notes and a thirty-year bond in 1998.

Congress passes an $8½ billion emergency appropriations bill, which makes funds available for flood victims in the Midwest as well as additional expenditures, after the President vetoed a previous bill that included riders to which the Administration objected.

States' attorneys-general and representatives of US tobacco firms reach an agreement to end various lawsuits brought against the firms in exchange for a $368 billion cash settlement over 25 years and restrictions on advertising and distribution. Congress and the President still need to pass implementing legislation.

The House renews most-favoured nation status for China.

The House and Senate pass reconciliation bills that govern tax and mandatory spending programmes. The bills are then sent to a committee to negotiate differences.

July

The July deadline for states to implement their welfare reform plans passes with seven states still debating reform, including the two largest, California and New York.

The FOMC announces no change to interest rates or its bias for future action. In his July Humphrey-Hawkins testimony, Chairman Greenspan reaffirms the monetary targets set in his February testimony and announces that they will carry over into 1998.

The Administration releases its report on NAFTA arguing that it has had a small, positive, effect on employment and incomes.

The Financial Accounting Standards Board announces its revised proposal governing marking to market derivatives holdings, to which business leaders and the Federal Reserve Board object.

A US appeals court voids FCC rules governing how local phone companies must open their networks as specified in the 1996 Telecommunications Act.

The EU approves the Boeing-McDonnell Douglas merger after Boeing agrees to drop its exclusive-supplier provisions in contracts with three US airlines.

August

President Clinton signs the Taxpayer Relief Act of 1997 and the Balanced Budget Act of 1997 that implement the tax and mandatory spending provisions of the May balanced budget agreement. The OMB and CBO subsequently announce that they project a budget deficit for FY 1997 of only about $35 billion and that they expect a surplus for 2002.

President Clinton exercises his line-item veto authority for the first time, striking three narrow provisions from the budget legislation.

Employees of United Parcel Service strike for two weeks, eventually agreeing to a settlement that boosts full-time workers' wages by about 3 per cent, protects the union-sponsored pension plan and converts some part-time jobs to full-time jobs.

The FOMC announces no change to monetary policy.

September

The minimum wage is raised 35 cents to $5.15 an hour as stipulated in a law passed last year.

The Administration makes a formal request to Congress to grant it fast-track authority on negotiating trade agreements.

The United States imposes sanctions on three Japanese shipping companies as a result of a dispute over Japanese harbour practices.

A series of financial services mergers are announced over the summer, culminating with Travelers intention to purchase Salomon Brothers.

The US Commission on Immigration Reform issues its final report, recommending that the Immigration and Naturalization Service be abolished and its duties assigned to other agencies.

The Census Bureau announces that the US poverty rate in 1996, at 13.7 per cent, was essentially unchanged from the 1995 rate.

The FOMC announces no change to monetary policy.

The United States reaffirms its position that China has not made sufficient progress in opening its markets to allow it to join the WTO.

The International Trade Commission votes to impose anti-dumping duties on supercomputers from Japan.

STATISTICAL ANNEX AND STRUCTURAL INDICATORS

Table A. Selected background statistics

	Average 1987-96	1987	1988	1989	1990	1991	1992	1993	1994	1995	1996
A. Percentage change from previous year at constant 1992 prices											
Private consumption	2.4	3.1	3.9	2.3	1.7	-0.6	2.8	2.9	3.3	2.4	2.6
Public consumption	1.0	2.2	2.0	2.7	2.3	1.0	-0.1	-0.3	0.4	-0.1	0.0
Gross fixed capital formation	2.5	0.4	1.5	2.0	-1.4	-6.6	5.2	5.1	6.5	4.4	7.5
Private residential	0.9	0.2	-2.0	-3.7	-9.3	-12.3	16.6	7.6	10.1	-3.8	5.9
Private non-residential	3.6	-1.1	4.4	4.0	-0.6	-6.4	1.9	7.6	8.0	9.0	9.2
Public	1.2	5.2	-2.0	3.4	6.3	-1.1	3.4	-4.2	-2.1	0.5	3.2
GDP	2.4	2.9	3.8	3.4	1.2	-0.9	2.7	2.3	3.5	2.0	2.8
GDP price deflator	3.2	3.1	3.7	4.2	4.3	4.0	2.8	2.6	2.4	2.5	2.3
Industrial production	2.6	4.6	4.4	1.8	-0.2	-2.0	3.2	3.4	5.0	3.3	2.8
Employment	1.5	2.6	2.3	2.0	1.3	-0.9	0.7	1.5	2.3	1.5	1.4
Compensation of employees (current prices)	5.6	7.2	7.8	6.0	6.4	3.1	5.4	4.7	5.2	5.1	5.0
Productivity (GDP/employment)[1]	0.6	0.2	0.7	1.0	-0.1	-0.2	3.1	0.3	0.5	-0.4	1.0
Unit labour costs (compensation/GDP)	3.2	4.1	3.9	2.5	5.1	4.1	2.6	2.3	1.6	3.0	2.2
B. Percentage ratios											
Gross fixed capital formation as per cent of GDP at constant prices	16.8	18.0	17.5	17.1	16.9	16.5	15.5	15.9	16.3	16.8	17.2
Stockbuilding as per cent of GDP at constant prices	0.3	0.2	0.5	0.2	0.5	0.2	0.0	0.1	0.3	0.9	0.4
Foreign balance as per cent of GDP at constant prices	-1.5	-3.0	-2.8	-2.0	-1.4	-1.0	-0.4	-0.5	-1.1	-1.6	-1.5
Compensation of employees as per cent of GDP at current prices	58.3	58.2	58.8	58.9	57.9	58.4	58.4	58.4	58.2	57.8	58.0
Direct taxes as per cent of household income	14.6	14.3	15.2	14.7	15.1	14.7	14.0	13.9	14.2	14.6	15.1
Household saving as per cent of disposable income	5.6	6.7	5.5	5.7	5.3	5.5	6.1	6.0	5.4	4.5	5.1
Unemployment as per cent of total labour force	6.2	7.0	6.2	5.5	5.3	5.6	6.8	7.5	6.9	6.1	5.6
C. Other indicator											
Current balance (billion dollars)	-109.0	-150.9	-166.3	-127.1	-103.8	-92.7	-7.4	-61.5	-99.9	-151.2	-129.1

1. Ratio of business sector GDP to business sector employment.
Source: US Department of Commerce, Survey of Current Business, and OECD.

Table B. National product and expenditure

Seasonally adjusted, percentage changes from previous period, annual rates, 1992 prices

	Average 1986-96	1986	1987	1988	1989	1990	1991	1992	1993	1994	1995	1996
Private consumption	2.6	4.0	3.1	3.9	2.3	1.7	-0.6	2.8	2.9	3.3	2.4	2.6
Public consumption	1.3	4.6	2.2	2.0	2.7	2.3	1.0	-0.1	-0.3	0.4	-0.1	0.0
Gross fixed investment	2.4	2.1	0.4	1.5	2.0	-1.4	-6.6	5.2	5.1	6.5	4.4	7.5
Private residential	1.9	12.0	0.2	-2.0	-3.7	-9.3	-12.3	16.6	7.6	10.1	-3.8	5.9
Private non-residential	2.9	-3.5	-1.1	4.4	4.0	-0.6	-6.4	1.9	7.6	8.0	9.0	9.2
Public	1.8	7.6	5.2	-2.0	3.4	6.3	-1.1	3.4	-4.2	-2.1	0.5	3.2
Final domestic demand	2.3	3.7	2.4	3.2	2.3	1.3	-1.3	2.7	2.7	3.3	2.4	3.0
Stockbuilding[1]	2.4	3.8	2.5	3.3	2.4	1.3	-1.4	2.7	2.7	3.4	2.4	3.0
Total domestic demand	2.3	3.4	2.7	2.9	2.7	0.9	-1.6	2.8	3.0	3.9	1.8	3.0
Exports of goods and services	8.9	7.4	11.0	15.9	11.7	8.5	6.3	6.6	2.9	8.2	11.1	8.3
Imports of goods and services	6.6	8.4	6.1	4.0	3.9	3.9	-0.7	7.5	8.9	12.2	8.9	9.1
Foreign balance[1]	0.7	0.8	0.6	0.4	0.4	0.4	-0.1	0.8	1.0	1.4	1.1	1.2
GDP	2.4	3.1	2.9	3.8	3.4	1.2	-0.9	2.7	2.3	3.5	2.0	2.8

	1996 levels (Current $ billions)	1994 Q4	1995 Q1	Q2	Q3	Q4	1996 Q1	Q2	Q3	Q4	1997 Q1	Q2
Private consumption	5 207.6	3.2	1.5	2.9	2.6	1.8	3.1	3.7	0.5	3.3	5.3	0.9
Public consumption	1 182.4	-3.4	0.9	-0.6	1.3	-6.8	0.3	6.4	-0.3	-0.4	0.7	2.9
Gross fixed investment	1 315.0	4.6	6.5	-0.1	0.7	5.4	10.7	13.9	7.8	3.1	2.2	11.5
Private residential	309.2	-5.1	-6.9	-15.5	8.4	8.6	8.4	17.8	-4.4	-4.3	3.3	7.4
Private non-residential	781.5	12.6	14.3	5.7	1.6	4.9	11.7	13.0	16.5	6.0	4.1	14.6
Public	224.3	-6.5	-0.2	1.6	-11.1	2.9	10.0	12.1	-5.3	2.4	-6.5	4.7
Final domestic demand	7 705.0	2.4	2.2	1.8	2.1	1.0	4.0	5.8	1.7	2.7	4.0	3.1
Stockbuilding[1]	25.8	0.8	-0.9	-1.6	-0.3	0.3	-0.8	0.8	1.0	-0.3	1.8	0.8
Total domestic demand	7 730.8	3.2	1.3	0.2	1.8	1.3	3.1	6.6	2.6	2.4	5.8	3.8
Exports of goods and services	870.9	14.7	7.2	9.2	13.5	11.5	1.8	9.6	1.9	25.5	9.9	18.4
Imports of goods and services	965.7	10.0	10.1	7.7	2.3	2.4	13.2	14.0	13.2	6.8	17.9	20.6
Foreign balance[1]	-94.8	0.3	-0.5	0.0	1.2	1.0	-1.4	-0.7	-1.5	1.9	-1.2	-0.6
GDP	7 636.0	3.6	0.9	0.3	3.0	2.2	1.8	6.0	1.0	4.3	4.9	3.3

1. Changes as a percentage of previous period GDP.
Source: US Department of Commerce, Survey of Current Business.

Table C. Labour market

Seasonally adjusted

	1988	1989	1990	1991	1992	1993	1994	1995	1996	1996 Q2	1996 Q3	1996 Q4	1997 Q1	1997 Q2
1. Number of persons, millions														
Population of working age[1,2]	184.6	186.4	188.1	189.8	192.0	194.8	196.8	198.6	200.6	200.3	200.8	201.5	202.4	202.8
Civilian labour force[1]	121.7	123.9	125.9	126.4	128.1	129.2	131.0	132.3	133.9	133.6	134.1	134.8	135.9	136.2
Unemployment[1]	6.7	6.5	7.1	8.6	9.6	8.9	8.0	7.4	7.2	7.3	7.1	7.1	7.2	6.7
Employment[1]	115.0	117.3	118.8	117.7	118.5	120.3	123.1	124.9	126.7	126.4	127.0	127.7	128.7	129.5
Employment[3]	105.2	107.9	109.4	108.3	108.6	110.7	114.2	117.2	119.5	119.2	119.9	120.5	121.1	121.9
Federal government	3.0	3.1	3.1	3.0	3.0	2.9	2.9	2.8	2.8	2.8	2.7	2.7	2.7	2.7
State and local	14.4	14.8	15.2	15.4	15.7	15.9	16.3	16.5	16.7	16.7	16.8	16.8	16.8	16.9
Manufacturing	19.3	19.4	19.1	18.4	18.1	18.1	18.3	18.5	18.5	18.5	18.4	18.4	18.5	18.5
Construction	5.1	5.2	5.1	4.7	4.5	4.7	5.0	5.2	5.4	5.4	5.4	5.5	5.6	5.6
Other	63.4	65.6	66.9	66.8	67.4	69.1	71.7	74.2	76.2	76.0	76.5	77.0	77.5	78.1
2. Percentage change from previous period (s.a.a.r.)														
Population of working age[1,2]	1.0	1.0	0.9	0.9	1.2	1.5	1.0	0.9	1.0	1.0	1.1	1.2	1.9	0.9
Civilian labour force	1.5	1.8	1.6	0.4	1.4	0.8	1.4	1.0	1.2	1.5	1.5	2.1	3.3	0.7
Employment[1]	2.3	2.0	1.3	-0.9	0.7	1.5	2.3	1.5	1.4	2.2	0.0	2.1	3.2	2.3
Employment[3]	3.2	2.6	1.4	-1.1	0.3	2.0	3.1	2.7	2.0	2.7	2.2	1.9	2.3	2.4
Federal government	1.0	0.6	3.3	-3.9	0.0	-1.8	-1.5	-1.7	-2.3	-2.0	-3.1	-2.1	-2.1	-2.1
State and local government	2.5	2.6	2.9	1.4	1.5	1.6	2.1	1.4	1.3	1.8	2.7	0.2	1.3	1.6
Manufacturing	1.7	0.4	-1.6	-3.5	-1.6	-0.2	1.4	1.1	-0.4	-0.1	-0.5	0.0	0.7	0.6
Construction	2.8	1.5	-0.9	-9.2	-3.5	3.9	6.8	3.7	4.5	7.4	3.6	4.8	6.7	2.3
Other	4.0	3.4	2.0	-0.2	0.8	2.6	3.8	3.5	2.7	3.4	2.9	2.6	2.7	3.1
3. Unemployment rates														
Total	5.5	5.3	5.6	6.8	7.5	6.9	6.1	5.6	5.4	5.4	5.3	5.3	5.3	4.9
Married men	3.2	3.1	3.4	4.4	5.1	4.4	3.7	3.3	3.0	3.0	3.0	3.0	2.8	2.7
Females	5.5	5.4	5.5	6.4	7.0	6.6	6.0	5.6	5.4	5.4	5.3	5.4	5.4	5.0
Youths	15.3	15.0	15.6	18.8	20.1	19.0	17.6	17.3	16.7	16.5	16.6	16.5	16.9	15.9
4. Activity rate[4]	62.3	62.9	63.2	62.0	61.7	61.7	62.5	62.9	63.2	63.1	63.3	63.4	63.6	63.8

1. Household survey. Data from the household survey for 1994 are not directly comparable to data for 1993 and earlier years because of the implementation in January 1994 of a major redesign of the survey and the introduction of 1990 Census-based population controls, adjusted for the estimated undercount.
2. Non-institutional population aged 16 and over.
3. Non-agricultural payroll.
4. Employment as percentage of population aged from 16 to 64.
Source: US Department of Labor, *Monthly Labor Review.*

Table D. Costs and prices

Percentage changes from previous period, s.a.a.r.

	1988	1989	1990	1991	1992	1993	1994	1995	1996	1996			1997	
										Q2	Q3	Q4	Q1	Q2
Rates of pay														
Major wage settlements[1]	2.6	3.2	3.5	3.5	3.0	2.9	2.7	2.4	n.a.					
Hourly earnings index[2]	2.8	3.9	4.2	3.9	3.0	2.7	2.7	3.1	3.5	3.4	4.3	3.7	5.6	2.8
Wages and salaries per person	5.6	3.8	4.8	3.5	4.9	1.9	2.5	4.3	4.4	6.0	3.7	3.9	4.9	3.0
Compensation per person	5.5	3.9	5.1	4.1	4.7	3.1	2.8	3.5	3.5	5.5	3.1	3.3	4.4	2.7
Productivity, non-farm business														
Hourly	0.7	0.5	0.5	0.7	3.2	0.1	0.4	0.2	1.3	2.0	-0.8	1.6	1.6	2.8
Per employee	0.9	0.7	-0.6	-0.4	2.7	0.8	0.7	-0.2	1.3	3.6	-0.9	3.3	3.0	1.2
Unit labour cost, non-farm business	3.7	2.2	4.9	4.3	1.9	2.2	1.4	2.3	1.8	1.9	4.2	1.5	3.0	0.4
Prices														
GDP deflator	3.7	4.2	4.3	4.0	2.8	2.6	2.4	2.5	2.3	1.7	2.6	1.8	2.4	1.8
Private consumption deflator	4.2	4.9	5.1	4.2	3.3	2.7	2.4	2.6	2.4	2.9	2.5	2.9	2.2	1.0
Consumer price index	4.1	4.8	5.4	4.2	3.0	3.0	2.6	2.8	2.9	4.0	2.1	2.9	2.7	1.6
Food	4.1	5.8	5.8	2.9	1.2	2.1	2.5	2.9	3.3	3.7	5.6	4.7	0.3	0.9
Wholesale prices	4.0	5.0	3.6	0.2	0.6	1.5	1.3	3.6	2.3	4.9	1.0	0.8	0.2	-3.9
Crude products	2.5	7.4	5.7	-7.0	-0.8	2.0	-0.7	1.0	10.8	17.7	1.1	3.8	2.7	-24.1
Intermediate products	5.5	4.6	2.2	0.0	0.2	1.4	2.0	5.4	0.7	3.2	1.0	-1.1	0.3	-1.8
Finished products	2.5	5.1	4.9	2.1	1.2	1.2	0.6	1.9	2.6	4.7	1.8	2.9	-1.1	-2.2

1. Total effective wage adjustment in all industries under collective agreements in non-farm industry covering at least 1 000 workers, not seasonally adjusted.
2. Production or non-supervisory workers on private non-agricultural payrolls.
Source: US Department of Labor, Bureau of Labor Statistics, Monthly Labor Review; US Department of Commerce, Survey of Current Business.

Table E. **Monetary indicators**

	1988	1989	1990	1991	1992	1993	1994	1995	1996	1996 Q2	1996 Q3	1996 Q4	1997 Q1	1997 Q2
Monetary aggregates (percentage changes from previous period s.a.a.r)														
M1	4.2	1.0	3.6	6.0	12.4	11.7	6.1	-0.2	-3.2	-1.5	-6.3	-7.2	-0.7	-5.4
M2	5.4	4.2	5.5	3.7	1.9	1.1	1.4	2.1	4.9	4.5	3.5	5.2	6.2	4.3
M3	6.4	4.6	2.7	1.7	0.6	0.2	1.7	4.5	6.6	6.6	5.6	8.5	8.4	7.2
Velocity of circulation														
GDP/M1	6.5	7.0	7.1	6.9	6.5	6.1	6.1	6.4	6.9	6.8	7.0	7.2	7.4	7.6
GDP/M2	1.7	1.8	1.8	1.8	1.8	1.9	2.0	2.0	2.0	2.0	2.0	2.0	2.1	2.1
GDP/M3	1.3	1.4	1.4	1.4	1.5	1.6	1.6	1.6	1.6	1.6	1.6	1.6	1.6	1.6
Federal Reserve Bank reserves ($ billion)														
Non-borrowed	37.8	38.7	39.9	42.7	50.0	57.2	59.8	57.4	52.8	54.2	51.9	49.8	48.9	46.9
Borrowed	2.4	1.1	0.9	0.4	0.2	0.2	0.3	0.2	0.2	0.2	0.4	0.2	0.1	0.3
Total	40.1	39.8	40.9	43.1	50.2	57.4	60.0	57.6	53.0	54.5	52.2	50.0	48.9	47.2
Required	39.1	38.9	39.9	41.9	49.2	56.3	59.0	56.6	51.9	53.4	51.2	48.8	47.8	46.0
Excess	1.0	1.0	1.0	1.2	1.0	1.1	1.1	1.0	1.1	1.0	1.0	1.2	1.1	1.2
Free (excess – borrowed)	-1.3	-0.2	0.0	0.8	0.9	0.9	0.8	0.8	0.9	0.8	0.7	0.9	1.1	0.9
Interest rates (%)														
Federal funds rate	7.6	9.2	8.1	5.7	3.5	3.0	4.2	5.8	5.3	5.2	5.3	5.3	5.3	5.5
Discount rate[1]	6.2	7.0	7.0	5.4	3.2	3.0	3.6	5.2	5.0	5.0	5.0	5.0	5.0	5.0
Prime rate[2]	9.3	10.9	10.0	8.5	6.3	6.0	7.1	8.8	8.3	8.3	8.3	8.3	8.3	8.5
3-month Treasury bills	6.7	8.1	7.5	5.4	3.4	3.0	4.3	5.5	5.0	5.0	5.1	5.0	5.1	5.0
AAA rate[3]	9.7	9.3	9.3	8.8	8.1	7.2	8.0	7.6	7.4	7.6	7.6	7.2	7.4	7.6
10-year Treasury notes	8.8	8.5	8.5	7.9	7.0	5.9	7.1	6.6	6.4	6.7	6.8	6.3	6.6	6.7

1. Rate for Federal Reserve Bank of New York.
2. Prime rate on short-term business loans.
3. Corporate Bonds, AAA rating group, quoted by Moody's Investors Services.
Source: Board of the Governors of the Federal Reserve System, Federal Reserve Bulletin.

Table F. Balance of payments, OECD basis

Millions of dollars

	1985	1986	1987	1988	1989	1990	1991	1992	1993	1994	1995	1996
Exports, fob[1]	215 915	223 344	250 208	320 230	362 120	389 307	416 913	440 352	456 823	502 485	575 871	612 069
Imports, fob[1]	338 088	368 425	409 765	447 189	477 365	498 337	490 981	536 458	589 441	668 584	749 431	803 239
Trade balance	-122 173	-145 081	-159 557	-126 959	-115 245	-109 030	-74 068	-96 106	-132 618	-166 099	-173 560	-191 170
Services, net[2]	20 884	18 413	16 326	24 900	37 511	49 763	59 776	66 705	66 776	50 615	71 703	80 130
Balance on goods and services	-101 290	-126 671	-143 232	-102 060	-77 734	-59 269	-14 293	-29 402	-65 842	-115 484	-101 857	-111 040
Private transfers, net	-9 548	-10 126	-10 600	-12 010	-12 698	-13 043	-13 865	-13 330	-13 988	-15 700	-19 530	-20 704
Official transfers, net	-13 406	-14 063	-12 507	-13 024	-13 409	-20 352	20 703	-18 817	-20 095	-20 061	-14 516	-19 264
Current balance	-124 243	-150 860	-166 339	-127 083	-103 840	-92 662	-7 425	-61 551	-99 926	-151 245	-129 095	-148 184
US assets abroad other than official reserves	-35 368	-105 131	-80 591	-95 447	-143 451	-68 205	-57 275	-65 411	-146 519	-131 197	-297 465	-359 112
US private assets, net[3]	-32 547	-103 109	-81 597	-98 414	-144 710	-70 512	-60 175	-63 759	-146 213	-130 875	-296 916	-358 422
Reported by US banks	-1 323	-59 975	-42 119	-53 927	-58 160	12 379	-610	20 895	29 947	915	-75 108	-98 186
US government assets[4]	-2 821	-2 022	1 006	-2 967	1 259	2 307	2 900	-1 652	-306	-322	-549	-690
Foreign assets in the United States												
Liabilities to foreign official monetary agencies[5]	-1 119	35 648	45 387	39 758	8 503	33 910	17 199	40 858	71 681	39 409	110 729	122 354
Other liabilities to foreign monetary agencies[6]	142 301	190 463	197 596	200 507	209 987	88 282	80 935	105 646	159 017	251 956	340 505	425 201
Reported by US banks	41 045	76 737	86 537	63 744	51 780	-3 824	3 994	15 461	20 859	114 396	30 176	9 784
Allocation of SDR's												
Errors and omissions	22 950	31 501	-4 029	-13 096	54 094	44 480	-28 936	-26 398	35 985	-14 269	-14 931	-46 927
Change in reserves (+ = increase)												
a) Gold												
b) Currency assets	3 869	942	-7 589	5 065	25 229	2 697	-6 307	-4 276	798	-5 293	6 468	-7 578
c) Reserve position in IMF	-909	-1 501	-2 070	-1 024	-471	-731	366	2 691	43	-494	2 466	1 280
d) Special drawing rights	897	246	510	-127	535	193	176	-2 316	537	441	808	-370

1. Excluding military goods.
2. Services include reinvested earnings of incorporated affiliates.
3. Including: Direct investment financed by reinvested earnings of incorporated affiliates; foreign securities; US claims on unaffiliated foreigners reported by US non-banking concerns; and US claims reported by US banks, not included elsewhere.
4. Including: US credits and other long-term assets; repayments on US credits and other long-term assets, US foreign currency holdings and US short-term assets, net.
5. Including: US Government securities and other US Government liabilities; US liabilities reported by US banks not included elsewhere and other foreign official assets.
6. Including direct investment; US Treasury securities; other US securities; US liabilities to unaffiliated foreigners reported by US non-banking concerns; US liabilities reported by US banks not included elsewhere.

Source: US Department of Commerce, Survey of Current Business.

Table G. **Public sector**

Per cent of GDP

	1960	1970	1980	1990	1994	1995	1996
A. General government accounts							
Receipts							
Total direct taxes	13.6	13.8	14.3	13.3	13.3	13.9	14.6
Social security contributions	4.2	6.0	8.1	9.0	9.1	9.1	9.1
Indirect taxes	8.6	9.1	7.6	7.7	8.2	8.0	7.9
Total current receipts	26.4	28.9	30.0	30.1	30.6	31.0	31.6
Disbursements							
Government consumption	16.2	18.5	17.1	17.0	15.9	15.7	15.5
Property income payable	1.3	1.2	1.1	2.1	1.9	2.1	2.0
Susbsidies	0.1	0.5	0.5	0.4	0.4	0.3	0.3
Transfers	5.6	8.1	11.4	11.8	13.6	13.8	13.9
Total current disbursements	23.1	28.3	30.2	31.4	31.9	32.0	31.7
Saving	3.3	0.6	-0.2	-1.3	-1.3	-1.0	-0.1
Gross investment	5.4	4.2	3.5	3.5	3.0	2.9	2.9
Consumption of fixed capital	2.8	2.5	2.3	2.0	2.0	2.0	1.9
Total expenditure	25.7	30.0	31.4	32.8	32.8	32.9	32.7
Net lending	0.7	-1.1	-1.4	-2.7	-2.3	-1.9	-1.1
B. Central government accounts							
Current receipts	18.4	18.8	20.2	19.7	19.8	20.1	20.8
Total non-interest expenditure	16.5	18.8	20.4	19.5	19.6	19.4	19.2
Primary deficit	2.0	0.1	-0.3	0.2	0.2	0.8	1.6
Interest expenditure	1.3	1.4	1.9	3.1	2.9	3.1	3.0
Net lending	0.7	-1.3	-2.2	-3.0	-2.7	-2.3	-1.4
Net lending excluding Social Security	0.6	-1.7	-2.0	-3.9	-3.5	-3.1	-2.1
C. State and local government accounts							
Current receipts	9.2	12.5	13.0	12.7	13.7	13.7	13.7
Total non-interest expenditure	9.2	12.5	13.0	13.5	14.2	14.3	14.3
Primary deficit	0.0	0.0	0.0	-0.8	-0.6	-0.6	-0.6
Interest expenditure	0.0	-0.2	-0.8	-1.1	-1.0	-1.0	-1.0
Net lending	0.0	0.2	0.7	0.2	0.4	0.4	0.3
D. Government debt (% GDP)							
General government gross debt	56.9	41.5	37.0	55.5	62.5	63.1	63.1
Net debt	45.1	29.5	21.8	38.6	46.9	47.9	48.4

Source: Bureau of Economic Analysis; OECD.

Table H. **Financial markets**

	1970	1975	1980	1990	1993	1994	1995	1996
A. Financial and corporate flows								
Share of private financial institutions' financial assets in total credit market debt (%)[1]	89.9	88.9	87.9	80.9	85.9	84.7	88.9	92.1
Market value of equities including corporate farm equities (billions of dollars)[1]	677.0	699.1	1 214.7	2 529.7	4 126.0	4 141.8	5 481.1	6 367.4
Debt-to-equity ratio in non-financial corporate business excluding farms (%)[1]	54.2	82.1	74.9	98.5	61.3	64.4	52.5	47.9
Ratio of market value to net worth[1]	69.8	40.4	38.3	49.7	87.2	80.8	100.3	108.0
B. Foreign sector (billions of dollars)								
Net foreign assets outstanding[1, 3]	61.0	38.7	212.6	−573.2	−1 301.0	−1 420.3	−1 715.7	−2 210.1
Changes in net foreign investment[2]	3.6	23.4	10.8	−68.0	−100.3	−141.7	−88.0	−132.8
Foreign purchases of US corporate equities[2]	2.0	3.3	7.6	−24.2	48.1	−11.5	39.3	12.8
US purchases of foreign equities[2]	1.3	−0.7	1.4	2.8	83.1	37.4	55.9	42.3
C. Debt to financial asset ratio (%)[1, 4]								
Household	17.4	19.5	21.0	24.1	22.7	23.8	22.7	22.0
Non-financial business	122.9	102.7	92.5	90.6	77.9	75.8	74.0	72.3
of which:								
Corporate business	86.0	73.8	62.5	68.6	59.0	58.4	57.8	56.7
Non-farm non-corporate business	345.7	331.2	298.0	236.3	217.6	201.0	193.7	192.2
Farm business	441.9	555.8	668.1	285.6	243.6	234.3	228.0	223.7
D. Debt to net worth ratios, private sector (%)[4]								
Household	12.9	13.8	14.5	17.5	17.5	18.4	18.0	17.6
Non-financial corporate business excluding farms	37.8	33.2	28.6	49.0	53.4	52.0	52.6	51.8

1. Data are year-end outstandings.
2. Data are annual flows.
3. Net foreign assets exclude US holdings of foreign equities and foreign holdings of US equities.
4. Debt is credit market debt.
Source: Board of Governors of the Federal Reserve System, *Balance Sheets for the US Economy.*

Table I. Labour market indicators

A. Evolution

	Peak	Trough	1992	1993	1994	1995	1996
Standardised unemployment rate	1982: 9.6	1969: 3.4	7.4	6.8	6.0	5.5	5.4
Unemployment rate							
Total	1982: 9.5	1969: 3.4	7.5	6.9	6.0	5.5	5.4
Male	1983: 9.7	1969: 2.7	7.8	7.1	6.1	5.5	5.3
Female	1982: 9.4	1969: 4.7	7.1	6.6	6.0	5.6	5.4
Youth[1]	1982: 17.0	1969: 7.4	14.2	13.4	12.5	12.1	12.0
Share of long-term unemployment[2]	1983: 13.4	1969: 1.9	11.2	11.7	12.2	9.7	9.6
Productivity index, 1992 = 100[3]			100.0	100.8	101.9	102.4	103.4

B. Structural or institutional characteristics

	1970	1980	1992	1993	1994	1995	1996
Participation rate[4]							
Global	60.4	63.8	66.4	66.3	66.6	66.6	66.8
Male	79.7	76.0	75.8	75.4	75.0	75.0	74.9
Female	43.3	51.4	57.8	57.9	58.8	58.9	59.3
Employment/population between 16 and 64 years	57.4	59.2	61.7	61.7	62.5	62.9	63.2
Employment by sector							
Agriculture – per cent of total	4.5	3.6	2.9	2.7	2.9	2.9	2.8
– per cent change	-3.6	0.6	-0.2	-3.4	8.6	0.3	-0.7
Industry – per cent of total	34.3	30.5	24.6	24.0	24.0	24.0	23.9
– per cent change	-1.8	-1.9	-2.0	-0.8	2.2	1.5	0.8
Services – per cent of total	61.1	65.9	72.5	73.2	73.1	73.1	73.3
– per cent change	3.0	1.7	1.6	2.5	2.1	1.5	1.7
of which: Government – per cent of total	0.2	0.2	0.2	0.2	0.2	0.2	0.2
– per cent change	3.0	1.8	1.3	1.1	1.5	1.0	0.7
Part-time work for non-economic reasons[5]	13.5	14.2	13.6	13.7	15.4	15.2	15.0
Social insurance as a per cent of compensation	10.8	16.7	18.1	18.9	19.2	18.8	18.4
Government unemployment insurance benefits[6]	12.3	12.6	13.1	12.0	9.1	8.7	
Minimum wage: as a percentage of average wage[7]	49.6	46.6	40.2	39.3	38.3	37.2	37.1

1. People between 16 and 24 years as a percentage of the labour force of the same age group.
2. People looking for a job since one year or more as a percentage of total unemployment.
3. Production as a percentage of employment.
4. Labour force as a percentage of the corresponding population aged between 16 and 64 years.
5. As a percentage of salary workers, non-agricultural industries.
6. Value of the unemployment benefits per unemployed divided by the compensation per employee.
7. Private non-agricultural sector.

Source: US Department of Labor, Bureau of Labor Statistics, Data Resources Incorporated, and OECD.

BASIC STATISTICS

BASIC STATISTICS:

INTERNATIONAL COMPARISONS

	Units	Reference period [1]	Australia	Austria
Population				
Total	Thousands	1995	18 054	8 047
Inhabitants per sq. km	Number	1995	2	96
Net average annual increase over previous 10 years	%	1995	1.4	0.6
Employment				
Total civilian employment (TCE)[2]	Thousands	1994	7 943	3 737
of which: Agriculture	% of TCE	1994	5.1	7.2
Industry	% of TCE	1994	23.5	33.2
Services	% of TCE	1994	71.4	59.6
Gross domestic product (GDP)				
At current prices and current exchange rates	Bill. US$	1995	360.3	233.3
Per capita	US$	1995	19 957	28 997
At current prices using current PPPs[3]	Bill. US$	1995	349.4	167.2
Per capita	US$	1995	19 354	20 773
Average annual volume growth over previous 5 years	%	1995	3.3	2
Gross fixed capital formation (GFCF)	% of GDP	1995	20.1	24.7
of which: Machinery and equipment	% of GDP	1995	10.5 (94)	9 (9)
Residential construction	% of GDP	1995	5.6 (94)	6.4 (9)
Average annual volume growth over previous 5 years	%	1995	3	3
Gross saving ratio[4]	% of GDP	1995	16.9	24.9
General government				
Current expenditure on goods and services	% of GDP	1995	17.2	18.9
Current disbursements[5]	% of GDP	1994	36.2	47.8
Current receipts	% of GDP	1994	34.2	47.3
Net official development assistance	% of GNP	1994	0.33	0.33
Indicators of living standards				
Private consumption per capita using current PPPs[3]	US$	1995	12 090	11 477
Passenger cars, per 1 000 inhabitants	Number	1993	438	418
Telephones, per 1 000 inhabitants	Number	1993	482	451
Television sets, per 1 000 inhabitants	Number	1992	482	480
Doctors, per 1 000 inhabitants	Number	1994	2.2 (91)	2.4
Infant mortality per 1 000 live births	Number	1994	5.9	6.3
Wages and prices (average annual increase over previous 5 years)				
Wages (earnings or rates according to availability)	%	1995	2	5
Consumer prices	%	1995	2.5	3.2
Foreign trade				
Exports of goods, fob*	Mill. US$	1995	53 092	57 200
As % of GDP	%	1995	14.7	24.5
Average annual increase over previous 5 years	%	1995	6	6.9
Imports of goods, cif*	Mill. US$	1995	57 406	65 293
As % of GDP	%	1995	15.9	28
Average annual increase over previous 5 years	%	1995	8.1	5.9
Total official reserves[6]	Mill. SDRs	1995	8 003	12 600
As ratio of average monthly imports of goods	Ratio	1995	1.7	2.3

* At current prices and exchange rates.
1. Unless otherwise stated.
2. According to the definitions used in OECD *Labour Force Statistics.*
3. PPPs = Purchasing Power Parities.
4. Gross saving = Gross national disposable income minus private and government consumption.
5. Current disbursements = Current expenditure on goods and services plus current transfers and payments of property income.
6. Gold included in reserves is valued at 35 SDRs per ounce. End of year.

EMPLOYMENT OPPORTUNITIES

Economics Department, OECD

The Economics Department of the OECD offers challenging and rewarding opportunities to economists interested in applied policy analysis in an international environment. The Department's concerns extend across the entire field of economic policy analysis, both macro-economic and microeconomic. Its main task is to provide, for discussion by committees of senior officials from Member countries, documents and papers dealing with current policy concerns. Within this programme of work, three major responsibilities are:

– to prepare regular surveys of the economies of individual Member countries;
– to issue full twice-yearly reviews of the economic situation and prospects of the OECD countries in the context of world economic trends;
– to analyse specific policy issues in a medium-term context for the OECD as a whole, and to a lesser extent for the non-OECD countries.

The documents prepared for these purposes, together with much of the Department's other economic work, appear in published form in the *OECD Economic Outlook, OECD Economic Surveys, OECD Economic Studies* and the Department's *Working Papers* series.

The Department maintains a world econometric model, INTERLINK, which plays an important role in the preparation of the policy analyses and twice-yearly projections. The availability of extensive cross-country data bases and good computer resources facilitates comparative empirical analysis, much of which is incorporated into the model.

The Department is made up of about 80 professional economists from a variety of backgrounds and Member countries. Most projects are carried out by small teams and last from four to eighteen months. Within the Department, ideas and points of view are widely discussed; there is a lively professional interchange, and all professional staff have the opportunity to contribute actively to the programme of work.

Skills the Economics Department is looking for:

a) Solid competence in using the tools of both microeconomic and macroeconomic theory to answer policy questions. Experience indicates that this normally requires the equivalent of a Ph.D. in economics or substantial relevant professional experience to compensate for a lower degree.

b) Solid knowledge of economic statistics and quantitative methods; this includes how to identify data, estimate structural relationships, apply basic techniques of time series analysis, and test hypotheses. It is essential to be able to interpret results sensibly in an economic policy context.

c) A keen interest in and extensive knowledge of policy issues, economic developments and their political/social contexts.

d) Interest and experience in analysing questions posed by policy-makers and presenting the results to them effectively and judiciously. Thus, work experience in government agencies or policy research institutions is an advantage.

e) The ability to write clearly, effectively, and to the point. The OECD is a bilingual organisation with French and English as the official languages. Candidates must have excellent knowledge of one of these languages, and some knowledge of the other. Knowledge of other languages might also be an advantage for certain posts.

f) For some posts, expertise in a particular area may be important, but a successful candidate is expected to be able to work on a broader range of topics relevant to the work of the Department. Thus, except in rare cases, the Department does not recruit narrow specialists.

g) The Department works on a tight time schedule with strict deadlines. Moreover, much of the work in the Department is carried out in small groups. Thus, the ability to work with other economists from a variety of cultural and professional backgrounds, to supervise junior staff, and to produce work on time is important.

General information

The salary for recruits depends on educational and professional background. Positions carry a basic salary from FF 305 700 or FF 377 208 for Administrators (economists) and from FF 438 348 for Principal Administrators (senior economists). This may be supplemented by expatriation and/or family allowances, depending on nationality, residence and family situation. Initial appointments are for a fixed term of two to three years.

Vacancies are open to candidates from OECD Member countries. The Organisation seeks to maintain an appropriate balance between female and male staff and among nationals from Member countries.

For further information on employment opportunities in the Economics Department, contact:

Administrative Unit
Economics Department
OECD
2, rue André-Pascal
75775 PARIS CEDEX 16
FRANCE

E-Mail: compte.esadmin@oecd.org

Applications citing "ECSUR", together with a detailed *curriculum vitae* in English or French, should be sent to the Head of Personnel at the above address.

MAIN SALES OUTLETS OF OECD PUBLICATIONS
PRINCIPAUX POINTS DE VENTE DES PUBLICATIONS DE L'OCDE

AUSTRALIA – AUSTRALIE
D.A. Information Services
648 Whitehorse Road, P.O.B 163
Mitcham, Victoria 3132   Tel. (03) 9210.7777
Fax: (03) 9210.7788

AUSTRIA – AUTRICHE
Gerold & Co.
Graben 31
Wien I   Tel. (0222) 533.50.14
Fax: (0222) 512.47.31.29

BELGIUM – BELGIQUE
Jean De Lannoy
Avenue du Roi, Koningslaan 202
B-1060 Bruxelles Tel. (02) 538.51.69/538.08.41
Fax: (02) 538.08.41

CANADA
Renouf Publishing Company Ltd.
5369 Canotek Road
Unit 1
Ottawa, Ont. K1J 9J3   Tel. (613) 745.2665
Fax: (613) 745.7660

Stores:
71 1/2 Sparks Street
Ottawa, Ont. K1P 5R1   Tel. (613) 238.8985
Fax: (613) 238.6041

12 Adelaide Street West
Toronto, QN M5H 1L6   Tel. (416) 363.3171
Fax: (416) 363.5963

Les Éditions La Liberté Inc.
3020 Chemin Sainte-Foy
Sainte-Foy, PQ G1X 3V6 Tel. (418) 658.3763
Fax: (418) 658.3763

Federal Publications Inc.
165 University Avenue, Suite 701
Toronto, ON M5H 3B8   Tel. (416) 860.1611
Fax: (416) 860.1608

Les Publications Fédérales
1185 Université
Montréal, QC H3B 3A7 Tel. (514) 954.1633
Fax: (514) 954.1635

CHINA – CHINE
Book Dept., China National Publications
Import and Export Corporation (CNPIEC)
16 Gongti E. Road, Chaoyang District
Beijing 100020 Tel. (10) 6506-6688 Ext. 8402
(10) 6506-3101

CHINESE TAIPEI – TAIPEI CHINOIS
Good Faith Worldwide Int'l. Co. Ltd.
9th Floor, No. 118, Sec. 2
Chung Hsiao E. Road
Taipei   Tel. (02) 391.7396/391.7397
Fax: (02) 394.9176

**CZECH REPUBLIC –
RÉPUBLIQUE TCHÈQUE**
National Information Centre
NIS – prodejna
Konviktská 5
Praha 1 – 113 57   Tel. (02) 24.23.09.07
Fax: (02) 24.22.94.33
E-mail: nkposp@dec.niz.cz
Internet: http://www.nis.cz

DENMARK – DANEMARK
Munksgaard Book and Subscription Service
35, Nørre Søgade, P.O. Box 2148
DK-1016 København K   Tel. (33) 12.85.70
Fax: (33) 12.93.87

J. H. Schultz Information A/S,
Herstedvang 12,
DK – 2620 Albertslung   Tel. 43 63 23 00
Fax: 43 63 19 69
Internet: s-info@inet.uni-c.dk

EGYPT – ÉGYPTE
The Middle East Observer
41 Sherif Street
Cairo   Tel. (2) 392.6919
Fax: (2) 360.6804

FINLAND – FINLANDE
Akateeminen Kirjakauppa
Keskuskatu 1, P.O. Box 128
00100 Helsinki

Subscription Services/Agence d'abonnements :
P.O. Box 23
00100 Helsinki   Tel. (358) 9.121.4403
Fax: (358) 9.121.4450

***FRANCE**
OECD/OCDE
Mail Orders/Commandes par correspondance :
2, rue André-Pascal
75775 Paris Cedex 16 Tel. 33 (0)1.45.24.82.00
Fax: 33 (0)1.49.10.42.76
Telex: 640048 OCDE
Internet: Compte.PUBSINQ@oecd.org

Orders via Minitel, France only/
Commandes par Minitel, France
exclusivement : 36 15 OCDE

OECD Bookshop/Librairie de l'OCDE :
33, rue Octave-Feuillet
75016 Paris   Tel. 33 (0)1.45.24.81.81
33 (0)1.45.24.81.67

Dawson
B.P. 40
91121 Palaiseau Cedex   Tel. 01.89.10.47.00
Fax: 01.64.54.83.26

Documentation Française
29, quai Voltaire
75007 Paris   Tel. 01.40.15.70.00

Economica
49, rue Héricart
75015 Paris   Tel. 01.45.78.12.92
Fax: 01.45.75.05.67

Gibert Jeune (Droit-Économie)
6, place Saint-Michel
75006 Paris   Tel. 01.43.25.91.19

Librairie du Commerce International
10, avenue d'Iéna
75016 Paris   Tel. 01.40.73.34.60

Librairie Dunod
Université Paris-Dauphine
Place du Maréchal-de-Lattre-de-Tassigny
75016 Paris   Tel. 01.44.05.40.13

Librairie Lavoisier
11, rue Lavoisier
75008 Paris   Tel. 01.42.65.39.95

Librairie des Sciences Politiques
30, rue Saint-Guillaume
75007 Paris   Tel. 01.45.48.36.02

P.U.F.
49, boulevard Saint-Michel
75005 Paris   Tel. 01.43.25.83.40

Librairie de l'Université
12a, rue Nazareth
13100 Aix-en-Provence   Tel. 04.42.26.18.08

Documentation Française
165, rue Garibaldi
69003 Lyon   Tel. 04.78.63.32.23

Librairie Decitre
29, place Bellecour
69002 Lyon   Tel. 04.72.40.54.54

Librairie Sauramps
Le Triangle
34967 Montpellier Cedex 2 Tel. 04.67.58.85.15
Fax: 04.67.58.27.36

A la Sorbonne Actual
23, rue de l'Hôtel-des-Postes
06000 Nice   Tel. 04.93.13.77.75
Fax: 04.93.80.75.69

GERMANY – ALLEMAGNE
OECD Bonn Centre
August-Bebel-Allee 6
D-53175 Bonn   Tel. (0228) 959.120
Fax: (0228) 959.12.17

GREECE – GRÈCE
Librairie Kauffmann
Stadiou 28
10564 Athens   Tel. (01) 32.55.321
Fax: (01) 32.30.320

HONG-KONG
Swindon Book Co. Ltd.
Astoria Bldg. 3F
34 Ashley Road, Tsimshatsui
Kowloon, Hong Kong   Tel. 2376.2062
Fax: 2376.0685

HUNGARY – HONGRIE
Euro Info Service
Margitsziget, Európa Ház
1138 Budapest   Tel. (1) 111.60.61
Fax: (1) 302.50.35
E-mail: euroinfo@mail.matav.hu
Internet: http://www.euroinfo.hu//index.html

ICELAND – ISLANDE
Mál og Menning
Laugavegi 18, Pósthólf 392
121 Reykjavik   Tel. (1) 552.4240
Fax: (1) 562.3523

INDIA – INDE
Oxford Book and Stationery Co.
Scindia House
New Delhi 110001   Tel. (11) 331.5896/5308
Fax: (11) 332.2639
E-mail: oxford.publ@axcess.net.in

17 Park Street
Calcutta 700016   Tel. 240832

INDONESIA – INDONÉSIE
Pdii-Lipi
P.O. Box 4298
Jakarta 12042   Tel. (21) 573.34.67
Fax: (21) 573.34.67

IRELAND – IRLANDE
Government Supplies Agency
Publications Section
4/5 Harcourt Road
Dublin 2   Tel. 661.31.11
Fax: 475.27.60

ISRAEL – ISRAËL
Praedicta
5 Shatner Street
P.O. Box 34030
Jerusalem 91430   Tel. (2) 652.84.90/1/2
Fax: (2) 652.84.93

R.O.Y. International
P.O. Box 13056
Tel Aviv 61130   Tel. (3) 546 1423
Fax: (3) 546 1442
E-mail: royil@netvision.net.il

Palestinian Authority/Middle East:
INDEX Information Services
P.O.B. 19502
Jerusalem   Tel. (2) 627.16.34
Fax: (2) 627.12.19

ITALY – ITALIE
Libreria Commissionaria Sansoni
Via Duca di Calabria, 1/1
50125 Firenze   Tel. (055) 64.54.15
Fax: (055) 64.12.57
E-mail: licosa@ftbcc.it

Via Bartolini 29
20155 Milano   Tel. (02) 36.50.83

Editrice e Libreria Herder
Piazza Montecitorio 120
00186 Roma   Tel. 679.46.28
Fax: 678.47.51

Libreria Hoepli
Via Hoepli 5
20121 Milano   Tel. (02) 86.54.46
                             Fax: (02) 805.28.86
Libreria Scientifica
Dott. Lucio de Biasio 'Aeiou'
Via Coronelli, 6
20146 Milano   Tel. (02) 48.95.45.52
                             Fax: (02) 48.95.45.48
JAPAN – JAPON
OECD Tokyo Centre
Landic Akasaka Building
2-3-4 Akasaka, Minato-ku
Tokyo 107   Tel. (81.3) 3586.2016
                             Fax: (81.3) 3584.7929
KOREA – CORÉE
Kyobo Book Centre Co. Ltd.
P.O. Box 1658, Kwang Hwa Moon
Seoul   Tel. 730.78.91
                             Fax: 735.00.30
MALAYSIA – MALAISIE
University of Malaya Bookshop
University of Malaya
P.O. Box 1127, Jalan Pantai Baru
59700 Kuala Lumpur
Malaysia   Tel. 756.5000/756.5425
                             Fax: 756.3246
MEXICO – MEXIQUE
OECD Mexico Centre
Edificio INFOTEC
Av. San Fernando no. 37
Col. Toriello Guerra
Tlalpan C.P. 14050
Mexico D.F.   Tel. (525) 528.10.38
                             Fax: (525) 606.13.07
E-mail: ocde@rtn.net.mx
NETHERLANDS – PAYS-BAS
SDU Uitgeverij Plantijnstraat
Externe Fondsen
Postbus 20014
2500 EA's-Gravenhage   Tel. (070) 37.89.880
Voor bestellingen: Fax: (070) 34.75.778
Subscription Agency/Agence d'abonnements :
SWETS & ZEITLINGER BV
Heereweg 347B
P.O. Box 830
2160 SZ Lisse   Tel. 252.435.111
                             Fax: 252.415.888
NEW ZEALAND –
NOUVELLE-ZÉLANDE
GPLegislation Services
P.O. Box 12418
Thorndon, Wellington   Tel. (04) 496.5655
                       Fax: (04) 496.5698
NORWAY – NORVÈGE
NIC INFO A/S
Ostensjoveien 18
P.O. Box 6512 Etterstad
0606 Oslo   Tel. (22) 97.45.00
                             Fax: (22) 97.45.45
PAKISTAN
Mirza Book Agency
65 Shahrah Quaid-E-Azam
Lahore 54000   Tel. (42) 735.36.01
                             Fax: (42) 576.37.14
PHILIPPINE – PHILIPPINES
International Booksource Center Inc.
Rm 179/920 Cityland 10 Condo Tower 2
HV dela Costa Ext cor Valero St.
Makati Metro Manila   Tel. (632) 817 9676
                       Fax: (632) 817 1741
POLAND – POLOGNE
Ars Polona
00-950 Warszawa
Krakowskie Prezdmiescie 7 Tel. (22) 264760
                           Fax: (22) 265334

PORTUGAL
Livraria Portugal
Rua do Carmo 70-74
Apart. 2681
1200 Lisboa   Tel. (01) 347.49.82/5
                             Fax: (01) 347.02.64
SINGAPORE – SINGAPOUR
Ashgate Publishing
Asia Pacific Pte. Ltd
Golden Wheel Building, 04-03
41, Kallang Pudding Road
Singapore 349316   Tel. 741.5166
                             Fax: 742.9356
SPAIN – ESPAGNE
Mundi-Prensa Libros S.A.
Castelló 37, Apartado 1223
Madrid 28001   Tel. (91) 431.33.99
                             Fax: (91) 575.39.98
E-mail: mundiprensa@tsai.es
Internet: http://www.mundiprensa.es
Mundi-Prensa Barcelona
Consell de Cent No. 391
08009 – Barcelona   Tel. (93) 488.34.92
                             Fax: (93) 487.76.59
Libreria de la Generalitat
Palau Moja
Rambla dels Estudis, 118
08002 – Barcelona
                (Suscripciones) Tel. (93) 318.80.12
                (Publicaciones) Tel. (93) 302.67.23
                             Fax: (93) 412.18.54
SRI LANKA
Centre for Policy Research
c/o Colombo Agencies Ltd.
No. 300-304, Galle Road
Colombo 3   Tel. (1) 574240, 573551-2
                   Fax: (1) 575394, 510711
SWEDEN – SUÈDE
CE Fritzes AB
S–106 47 Stockholm   Tel. (08) 690.90.90
                             Fax: (08) 20.50.21
For electronic publications only/
Publications électroniques seulement
STATISTICS SWEDEN
Informationsservice
S-115 81 Stockholm   Tel. 8 783 5066
                             Fax: 8 783 4045
Subscription Agency/Agence d'abonnements :
Wennergren-Williams Info AB
P.O. Box 1305
171 25 Solna   Tel. (08) 705.97.50
                             Fax: (08) 27.00.71
Liber distribution
International organizations
Fagerstagatan 21
S-163 52 Spanga
SWITZERLAND – SUISSE
Maditec S.A. (Books and Periodicals/Livres
et périodiques)
Chemin des Palettes 4
Case postale 266
1020 Renens VD 1   Tel. (021) 635.08.65
                            Fax: (021) 635.07.80
Librairie Payot S.A.
4, place Pépinet
CP 3212
1002 Lausanne   Tel. (021) 320.25.11
                            Fax: (021) 320.25.14
Librairie Unilivres
6, rue de Candolle
1205 Genève   Tel. (022) 320.26.23
                            Fax: (022) 329.73.18

Subscription Agency/Agence d'abonnements :
Dynapresse Marketing S.A.
38, avenue Vibert
1227 Carouge   Tel. (022) 308.08.70
                             Fax: (022) 308.07.99
See also – Voir aussi :
OECD Bonn Centre
August-Bebel-Allee 6
D-53175 Bonn (Germany) Tel. (0228) 959.120
                       Fax: (0228) 959.12.17
THAILAND – THAÏLANDE
Suksit Siam Co. Ltd.
113, 115 Fuang Nakhon Rd.
Opp. Wat Rajbopith
Bangkok 10200   Tel. (662) 225.9531/2
                             Fax: (662) 222.5188
TRINIDAD & TOBAGO, CARIBBEAN
TRINITÉ-ET-TOBAGO, CARAÏBES
Systematics Studies Limited
9 Watts Street
Curepe
Trinidad & Tobago, W.I. Tel. (1809) 645.3475
                        Fax: (1809) 662.5654
E-mail: tobe@trinidad.net
TUNISIA – TUNISIE
Grande Librairie Spécialisée
Fendri Ali
Avenue Haffouz Imm El-Intilaka
Bloc B 1 Sfax 3000   Tel. (216-4) 296 855
                       Fax: (216-4) 298.270
TURKEY – TURQUIE
Kültür Yayinlari Is-Türk Ltd.
Atatürk Bulvari No. 191/Kat 13
06684 Kavaklidere/Ankara
                       Tel. (312) 428.11.40 Ext. 2458
                       Fax : (312) 417.24.90
Dolmabahce Cad. No. 29
Besiktas/Istanbul   Tel. (212) 260 7188
UNITED KINGDOM – ROYAUME-UNI
The Stationery Office Ltd.
Postal orders only:
P.O. Box 276, London SW8 5DT
Gen. enquiries   Tel. (171) 873 0011
                             Fax: (171) 873 8463
The Stationery Office Ltd.
Postal orders only:
49 High Holborn, London WC1V 6HB
Branches at: Belfast, Birmingham, Bristol,
Edinburgh, Manchester
UNITED STATES – ÉTATS-UNIS
OECD Washington Center
2001 L Street N.W., Suite 650
Washington, D.C. 20036-4922
                             Tel. (202) 785.6323
                             Fax: (202) 785.0350
Internet: washcont@oecd.org

Subscriptions to OECD periodicals may also
be placed through main subscription agencies.
Les abonnements aux publications périodiques
de l'OCDE peuvent être souscrits auprès des
principales agences d'abonnement.
Orders and inquiries from countries where Dis-
tributors have not yet been appointed should be
sent to: OECD Publications, 2, rue André-Pascal, 75775 Paris Cedex 16, France.
Les commandes provenant de pays où l'OCDE
n'a pas encore désigné de distributeur peuvent
être adressées aux Éditions de l'OCDE, 2, rue
André-Pascal, 75775 Paris Cedex 16, France.

12-1996

OECD PUBLICATIONS, 2, rue André-Pascal, 75775 PARIS CEDEX 16
PRINTED IN FRANCE
(10 97 02 1 P) ISBN 92-64-15428-0 – No. 49811 1997
ISSN 0376-6438